Chinese Policy Priorities and Their Implications for the United States

Chinese Policy Priorities and Their Implications for the United States

ROBERT G. SUTTER

ROWMAN & LITTLEFIELD PUBLISHERS, INC.
Lanham • Boulder • New York • Oxford

144878

ROWMAN & LITTLEFIELD PUBLISHERS, INC.

Published in the United States of America
by Rowman & Littlefield Publishers, Inc.
4720 Boston Way, Lanham, Maryland 20706
http://www.rowmanlittlefield.com

12 Hid's Copse Road
Cumnor Hill, Oxford OX2 9JJ, England

British Library Cataloguing in Publication Information Available

Library of Congress Cataloging-in-Publication Data

Sutter, Robert G.
    Chinese policy priorities and their implications for the United States /
Robert G. Sutter.
      p.   cm.
    Includes bibliographical references and index.
    ISBN 0-8476-9852-1 (cloth : alk. paper) —ISBN 0-8476-9853-X (pbk. : alk. paper)
    1. United States—Relations—China. 2. China—Relations—United States. 3. United
States—Foreign relations—1993– . 4. China—Foreign relations—1976– . 5. China—
Relations—Foreign countries.   I. Title.
E183.8.C5 S89   2000
327.73051—dc21   99–046082
                                                    CIP

Printed in the United States of America

♾™ The paper used in this publication meets the minimum requirements of American
National Standard for Information Sciences—Permanence of Paper for Printed Library
Materials, ANSI/NISO Z39.48–1992.

Contents

Introduction

The rise of China is widely seen as the most important international development in the 1990s. Ironically, it comes during a decade when American officials and opinion leaders are paying notably less attention to foreign affairs than at any time since the start of World War II.

This study attempts to provide a framework and relevant details for Americans and other interested readers to assess what are the key elements and implications of China's rise to power. The assessment here is presented against the background of past analyses of Maoist China and its role in the world.[1] Before his death in 1976, Mao led his colleagues and the Chinese nation in a multifaceted quest for national development, power, and prestige, and Asian and world revolution. Combined with the Maoist leadership's often impatient and poorly thought-out development policies, and influenced by changes in the cold war and U.S.-Soviet competition, the People's Republic of China (PRC) switched foreign policy orientation dramatically. It moved from a pro-Soviet alignment against the United States, to opposition to both the United States and the USSR, then to a defacto alignment with the United States against the USSR. It concurrently moved from a policy of dependency on outside (mainly Soviet) technology and aid to increasing isolation striving for economic self-reliance to a grudging opening to the developed countries.

After a period of some leadership uncertainty following Mao's death, senior leader Deng Xiaoping and his supporters established a series of basic policy priorities that still provide the outline of Chinese policies of concern to the United States today. Since that time, Chinese leaders have given top priority to promoting economic development that in turn will benefit the people of China and thereby support the legitimacy of the continued monopoly of political power exerted by the Chinese Communist Party and its leaders. Foreign policy, like other major policy areas, needs to serve this economic development priority. In general, this has meant that Chinese foreign policy needs to work to preserve peace and avoid entangling and economically disruptive conflict, especially around China's periphery. And it means that foreign policy should open China more to contacts with other world actors that can assist China's economic modernization.

This does not mean that China has followed a passive or pacifist policy. During the latter days of the cold war, Deng and other leaders stressed the need for China to work with others opposed to the Soviet Union's perceived expansionism, as part of a broad "united front" to preserve world peace. In this context, China took military actions to confront Soviet forces along the disputed Sino-Soviet border, and to invade Vietnam after the Soviet ally invaded China's surrogate, Cambodia, in late 1978.

The decline and eventual demise of the USSR in 1991 ended the strategic danger that had dominated Chinese foreign policy actions for three decades. It did not lead to any fundamental shift in direction in Chinese foreign policy, however.[2] By this time, the consensus in the Chinese leadership focused on economic development and nation building was stronger than ever. The challenges to that effort presented by conditions inside China remained formidable. The regime therefore remained preoccupied with domestic issues of development, making life better materially for the people of China, and thereby solidifying the sometimes shaky base of legitimacy held by the Chinese Communist Party and its leadership.

The Beijing leadership had other foreign policy goals and ambitions apart from those related to economic development and nation building. In particular, it strove to safeguard Chinese territorial claims to disputed areas, notably Taiwan and the South China Sea. If Chinese leaders judged that outside forces were challenging important interests involving Chinese sovereignty or other sensitive issues, they were prepared to react, sometimes forcefully. Beijing's provocative military exercises in the Taiwan Strait following the Taiwan president's visit to the United States in 1995 represented a notable example. Chinese leaders also deeply resented the international isolation that resulted from the 1989 Tiananmen incident, and they worked assiduously over the next decade to end every major element of that isolation. For Beijing, President William Clinton's trip to China in 1998 capped a successful nine-year effort to end the isolation and sanctions of the 1990s.

Deng Xiaoping died in February 1997. It is now the turn of post-Deng leaders under President Jiang Zemin to determine the course of Chinese policy. Thus far, they have followed the broad outlines of the policies of the post-Mao era. They remain focused on a particularly daunting agenda of domestic economic reforms. These reforms have become even more difficult to achieve as they have run up against affected interests inside China, and adverse international circumstances, notably the Asian economic crisis. As a result, foreign affairs generally receives secondary priority, unless it impinges directly on a vital Chinese concern like

Taiwan or internal political stability.

In the short term, this broad post-Mao framework argues for continued stability, continuity, pragmatism, and moderation in Chinese foreign policy. Difficulties for the United States are likely to arise in areas where China is particularly sensitive (e.g., Taiwan, the South China Sea, Tibet, internal political dissent) or where outsiders take actions strongly antithetical to China (e.g., India's nuclear tests in 1998 were ostensibly premised on an Indian view of a threat from China). Otherwise, Beijing generally appears to see its short-term interests as well served by a foreign policy that preserves a peaceful environment conducive to economic exchange and allows China to incrementally expand its influence in Asian and world affairs.

How long this relatively benign balance in Chinese foreign policy will last is a matter of conjecture.[3] Once Chinese leaders feel confident enough in their domestic achievements, they will undoubtedly take another look at Chinese foreign policy, possibly giving more emphasis and assertiveness to longer term Chinese objectives of exerting a stronger influence in Asian and world affairs. The record of the past few years already shows some signs of greater Chinese assertiveness, or preparations for possible assertiveness, despite continued preoccupation with domestic reform and control. These include the following:

- Stepped-up diplomatic pressure against Taiwan and its supporters in the United States and elsewhere.
- Use of China's veto power in the UN Security Council to press for policy outcomes favored by China.
- Continued military buildups opposite Taiwan and continued military-backed expansion in disputed regions of the South China Sea.
- Steady increases in Chinese military modernization despite a slow down in military spending elsewhere in Asia.
- More prominent and assertive Chinese political actions over such sensitive world issues as the Middle East Peace Process, the South Asian nuclear crisis, the Korean peninsula peace talks, and the Asian economic crisis.

Several specialists in the Clinton administration as well as many people in Congress and elsewhere saw Chinese assertiveness behind Beijing's strong condemnation and warnings in 1999 over U.S. plans regarding missile defense for the United States and for East Asia. The People's Republic of China (PRC) Foreign Ministry, in an unusually detailed statement by its spokesman on January 21, 1999, laid out China's position in opposition to U.S. announced or reported efforts in these areas.[4] Specifically, the statement noted the following points:

- China's "grave concern" over Defense Secretary Cohen's announcement the previous day of plans to develop a national missile defense (NMD) system for the United States and theater missile defense (TMD) systems for East Asia and possibly elsewhere, and to seek revision of the Anti-Ballistic Missile (ABM) Treaty in order to carry out these efforts. The spokesman said these decisions would have "wide-ranging and far reaching negative impacts on the global and regional strategic balance and stability," would promote missile proliferation, and would violate the ABM Treaty, which China strongly supports.

- China's belief that U.S. cooperation with Japan and other countries to develop TMD systems to protect U.S. forces and allies in East Asia or other regions would have a serious adverse impact on the security and stability of these regions.

- China's "special emphasis" on Taiwan. The spokesman asserted that any supply of TMD equipment or technology to Taiwan would be considered a move that seriously infringes on China's sovereignty and territorial integrity and would "certainly meet with strong opposition from the Chinese people."

U.S. media reports noted the dilemma the Clinton administration faced in not wishing to seriously alienate China and possibly upset its engagement policy with the PRC as it pursues missile defense options supported by Japan and others abroad as well as by the U.S. Congress.[5] Among the many actions taken by the 105th Congress in support of greater U.S. missile defense efforts, the FY-1999 Defense Authorization Act required a Defense Department report to Congress laying out a TMD framework to protect U.S. forces and allies in Asia and the Pacific. The FY 1999 Defense Appropriations Act required a Defense Department report to Congress on the military balance in the Taiwan area. That report was released on February 17, 1999, and discussed the growing PRC ballistic missile capability against Taiwan. The House of Representatives also passed a resolution urging U.S. missile defense cooperation with Taiwan.[6] Following Secretary of State Albright's early March 1999 visit to Beijing to discuss the dispute over missile defense and other issues, Chinese officials increased their public criticism, with the foreign minister and the premier denouncing the plans.[7]

Chinese reactions suggested that the United States may face serious difficulties regarding China if the United States develops and deploys missile defense systems at home and in East Asia, and especially if it supports ballistic missile defense efforts in Taiwan. Most notably, China may see little choice other than to increase nuclear-capable and conventional missile testing, development and deployment-- thereby challenging U.S. interests in curbing missile development, and reducing the numbers of nuclear arms. Beijing may even feel compelled to resume nuclear testing in order to develop weapons better able to penetrate missile defenses. There is a distinct possibility of military tension in the Taiwan area. Some U.S. observers judged that Chinese leaders, at bottom, were not being assertive on this issue, but were reacting strongly to U.S.-backed initiatives that challenged fundamental Chinese interests, especially regarding Taiwan.

U.S. concern with these possible developments was being weighed against the many perceived benefits for the United States, U.S. forces overseas, and U.S. allies and associates of the proposed NMD and TMD systems, and the possible U.S. sharing of such systems with Taiwan. U.S. advocates of these approaches urged going forward as a means of increasing the protection of the United States and its allies despite Chinese criticism and opposition. Some in this group also believed that high-level PRC criticism was designed to intimidate the United States, and therefore judged that giving in to PRC pressure would send the wrong signal about U.S. determination to play a leading strategic role in Asian affairs. Others sought to reassure China that it is not the target of the new systems, perhaps even offering to share information about the systems with China. Although Beijing is thought to be interested in learning about missile defenses, this benefit may not be sufficient to offset the negative impact of the missile defense systems in the United States and East Asia on Chinese missile forces and missile modernization. Some observers suggested the United States could endeavor to compensate China for this impact on Chinese security concerns with gestures in other areas. The possibilities included more liberalized U.S. civil technology transfer policies, easing Chinese market access to the United States, stronger support for China's entry into the World Trade Organization (WTO), stronger U.S. backing for Beijing's position vis-à-vis Taiwan, and other steps. Of course, each of these gestures would have consequences for other kinds of U.S. interests and would arouse opposition from certain sectors.[8]

There are fundamental disagreements among U.S. policy makers on what these and other signs of Chinese assertiveness might mean for U.S. interests and what policies the United States should adopt in response. A prevailing view among Clinton administration policy makers focuses on China's increasing power and influence in world affairs and its implications for U.S. interests. Ironically, many of the administration's critics in Congress, the media, and elsewhere also focus on China's increasing power and influence, though they see different implications for U.S. interests from those seen by Clinton administration policy makers.

Believing fundamentally in the utility of economic engagement and globalization, President Clinton in early 1999 argued[9] that these economic forces will move Chinese policies in the "right direction" as far as U.S. interests are concerned. The president's engagement policy is designed to foster economic opening and growth that are expected to make Chinese leaders more interdependent internationally, and therefore more inclined to support world norms backed by the United States. Greater economic growth and openness in China is also expected to lead to social changes and ultimately political pluralism and democracy in China.

Given China's great importance, in the president's view, it is imperative that the United States endeavor to deal constructively with rising Chinese power as it gradually changes, presumably for the better, under the influence of economic engagement and globalization. Also, China's rise poses a variety of economic and other opportunities for U.S. trade, investment, and other activities, according to the president.

Many administration critics in Congress and elsewhere argue that U.S. economic engagement with China must be accompanied by a rigorous U.S. political and strategic agenda designed to press, and force if necessary, Chinese policies to move in directions acceptable to the United States. Some members in the administration also support this approach. In short, these advocates judge that if the United States does not vigorously protect and promote its wide-ranging interests in relations with China, the outcome could be a U.S.-nurtured Chinese economic power that will be used to suppress the Chinese people, maintain political authoritarianism, and promote assertive policies in Asian and world affairs contrary to U.S. interests.[10]

This study argues that perhaps both of these U.S. views are flawed because they both give too much emphasis to alleged Chinese power and influence. The record laid out here shows, at bottom, a very preoccupied Chinese regime, worried about its ability to govern. At one level, the PRC government appears to have considerable influence in world affairs, but a careful review of all major areas around China's periphery shows that China has not been effective in getting others to do what it wants in important areas. Cases in point include North Korea's wariness, Japan's defense relations and theater missile defense cooperation with the United States, most Taiwan policies, ASEAN wariness of China and Beijing's fear and weakness in the face of recent events in Indonesia, India's nuclear weapons programs, and radical Islamic movements using Central Asia as a base to support violence and resistance in China.

Thus, U.S. and other interested readers are invited to review the case made here to see for themselves whether current U.S. policy overemphasizes China's importance, either positively or negatively. Once that judgment has been made, realistic U.S. policy should analyze Chinese power and influence in relation to U.S. power and influence. If there is a marked asymmetry between the two powers, and the judgment is that China's leaders are not in a position to adopt markedly assertive, disruptive, or otherwise important actions in world politics, perhaps the conclusion should be that the United States should not appear so assiduous or concerned in dealing with China. It may be argued that China needs the United States much more than the United States needs China, and that adroit U.S. policy should not fritter away this profound advantage with an overly solicitous or overly confrontational policy toward Beijing.

Notes

1. For a review of the Maoist era in Chinese foreign policy, see among others, John W. Garver, *The Foreign Policy of the People's Republic of China*, Prentice Hall, Englewood Cliffs, NJ, 1993.

2. See, among others, Samuel Kim (ed.), *China and the World*. Westview Press, Boulder, CO, 1998. Denny Roy, *China's Foreign Relations*, Roman & Littlefield, Lanham, MD, 1998.

3. See, among others, Richard Bernstein and Ross Munro, *The Coming Conflict with China*, Knopf, NY, 1996 and Andrew Nathan and Robert Ross, *The Great Wall and Empty Fortress*, Norton, NY, 1997.

4. "Spokesman expresses 'grave concern' over NMD, TMD," *Xinhua*, January 21, 1999, carried by FBIS internet version.

5. *New York Times*, January 22, 1999.

6. Reviewed in *Taiwan: Recent Developments and U.S. Policy Choices*, CRS Issue Brief 98034 (updated regularly).

7. See especially Premier Zhu Rongji's press conference remarks of March 15, 1999, carried by *Xinhua*.

8. Reviewed in *China and U.S. Missile Defense Proposals, Reaction and Implications*, U.S. Library of Congress, Congressional Research Service (CRS) Report RS 20031, March 17, 1999.

9. *New York Times*, February 27, 1999.

10. Reviewed in *East Asia and the Pacific: Issues at the End of the 105th Congress*, Congressional Research Service (CRS), The Library of Congress, Report 98-931, November 19, 1998.

Chapter 1

China's Changing Conditions

The general development of contemporary China and the current policy priorities of Chinese leaders are determined to a considerable degree by trends in Chinese economic, political, and social conditions, and by salient influences in Chinese military affairs and Chinese foreign policy. Leading Chinese government concerns focus on managing China's rapidly changing economic and social conditions while sustaining political authoritarianism and strengthening military power.[1]

Present conditions in China include the following:

- A vibrant but still troubled *economy*. The economy seems poised to continue to grow substantially in the years ahead, although there are many major difficulties, including the recent Asian economic crisis.
- A less divided central *political leadership*. Chinese leaders are less at odds than in the past over issues of policy (that is, economic reform and political control) but face some uncertainty over how to reach decisions following the passing of senior leader Deng Xiaoping. Economic reforms have created serious political frictions between and among the central and local authorities. On balance, political trends reflect continued movement away from the ideological leadership of the Maoist period to one emphasizing practical competence and technical expertise.
- A *society* with apparently fewer strong advocates for the prevailing political system than in the past and with many segments anxious about significant aspects of government policy. The regime's ability to deal effectively with such societal discontent is markedly weaker than in the

1

past, especially because of corruption and cynicism among many officials at all levels.

- A *military* more streamlined, professionally inclined, and less tied to local political interests than in the past. The People's Liberation Army (PLA) remains the center's ultimate coercive lever against social discontent and resistant local authorities, and it could provide the margin of decision in the event of a serious political struggle among civilian leaders in Beijing.
- A *foreign policy* somewhat more assertive than in the recent past but still premised on cooperation with China's neighbors and important developed countries (including the United States). Such cooperation is a key ingredient in the regime's economic modernization program—the main determinant of the political success or failure of the Beijing government.

There is a variety of possible outcomes and implications for U.S. interests. For example, increasingly effective political administration and reform with continued successful economic modernization would be generally compatible with U.S. interests in greater economic opportunity, foreign policy cooperation, and political liberalization in China. Alternatively, Chinese administration, economic vitality, and internal cohesion could degenerate, limiting U.S. economic opportunities, challenging U.S. interests in stability in East Asia but also diminishing potential threats from a strong China. China could also develop formidable economic power while retaining authoritarian political control, emerging as a world power less interested in accommodating U.S. interests than in opposing them.[2]

Changing Conditions

Deng Xiaoping's death on February 19, 1997, created some uncertainty at the center of political power in China. Current Chinese leaders are often jealous of each other's power and prerogatives, and there are continuing signs of jockeying among them for advantageous leadership positions. The Chinese Communist Party's Fifteenth Congress was held in Beijing on September 12-18, 1997. Jiang Zemin emerged stronger than before, backed by a generally technocratic and economically pragmatic leadership. Li Peng retained his position as second in party seniority; Zhu Rongji rose to number three in the pecking order and appeared in line to become prime minister the following year. Former number-three party leader Qiao Shi was forced to follow precedent for his age group and to retire from the Central

Committee. The military no longer had an officer on the seven-member Standing Committee, though two senior officers were members of the Politburo. The congress stressed anticipated policy lines in favor of gradual economic reform, including reform of state-owned enterprises, criticism of corruption within party ranks, greater reform of political administration, including more emphasis on the "rule of law," and adherence to recent foreign policy openings and activism.

China's Ninth National People's Congress, held in Beijing March 5-19, 1998, selected Zhu Rongji as prime minister to lead government efforts over the next few years to streamline bureaucracy, reform state-owned enterprises, and reform ailing financial institutions.[3]

The U.S.-China summit in June 1998 highlighted for Chinese audiences President Jiang Zemin's power and authority as he reportedly was responsible for the unprecedented live telecast of President Clinton's remarks to a nationwide Chinese audience. President Jiang, on July 22, 1998, ordered the Chinese military to end its practice of recent years of augmenting the defense budget through military-controlled economic enterprises. Large-scale floods in central and northeastern China caused Chinese leaders to curtail their annual policy deliberations at the seaside resort of Beidaihe in August.

To revitalize the flagging economic growth, Beijing in early September 1998 issued $12 billion worth of bonds to support widespread infrastructure projects during the rest of the year, strengthened foreign exchange controls in order to sustain the value of its currency, the yuan, and appeared to slow the streamlining of tens of thousands of money-losing state-owned enterprises in order to avoid potentially disruptive large-scale unemployment. Chinese growth was said to be 7.8 percent in 1998. Statistical discrepancies suggested that actual growth was lower. The value of the yuan remained steady, though some believed that an increase in Chinese export subsidies was having the effect of a Chinese currency devaluation on Asian exporters struggling to compete with Chinese manufacturers in global markets.

Beijing leaders promised to continue in 1999 their efforts to stimulate domestic demand and promote exports in order to keep growth high (the goal was around 7.5 percent) and avoid devaluation of the yuan. They also voiced a tough line on political dissent, crushed an incipient democracy movement, and suppressed publications challenging government-approved norms.[4]

A sharp struggle for political power in Beijing would complicate existing problems of governance caused by rapid economic growth, social change, realignment of central and local power, and other factors. Although there are now more institutional mechanisms influencing Chinese leadership decisions, personalities and particular connections remain central in determining power in China. The current generation of Chinese leaders, headed by President and party chief Jiang Zemin, has narrower bases of political power than Deng and other leaders of his generation had. Nonetheless, they may be able to manage internal differences smoothly. Since the end of the Maoist period, there has been less controversy as the range of debate has narrowed in Beijing over policy, doctrine, and personnel. Indeed the pragmatic and technically competent leaders of today mark a further step away from the often fractious infighting over ideological and other political issues that characterized the Maoist period.

Economic Modernization

This remains a fundamental determinant of the future of China. Post-Mao leaders have recognized that their hold on power rests heavily on their ability to achieve concrete economic success and to make life materially better for the vast majority of the Chinese people. They are aware that they have little of Mao's prestige as a successful revolutionary and nationalist leader, and that the absolute hold of communist ideology on the minds of the Chinese people is a thing of the past. Performance counts, and economic performance is the linchpin of the continued political legitimacy of the communist leaders in China.[5]

Bad statistical reporting notwithstanding, Maoist China had quite respectable (over 8 percent annually) rates of economic growth on average. It achieved much in drawing China out of its largely agrarian roots and produced an impressive array of industrial and technological establishments. In the course of these efforts, however, tens of millions lost their lives. Waste and inefficiency reached such a point in the late 1970s that a consensus emerged among post-Mao leaders on the need to move away from state-controlled development and to open China more to the outside world. What followed was basically a pragmatic, trial-and-error approach to developing China into a more modern and efficient market-centered economic power.

Efforts focused first on rejuvenating the stagnant rural economy, resulting in several years of rapid growth, which, by the mid-1980s, had doubled the income of the average farmer. Dominated by large state-controlled enterprises, the urban economy posed a more difficult management problem. Nonetheless, progress in the direction of greater decentralization and reliance on market forces has been evident since the 1980s. Chinese officials now claim that roughly 80 percent of commodities in China are distributed through market channels at prices largely set by market forces.

Reliance on decentralized decision-making—a feature of economic reform efforts—has given local authorities a greater say in economic matters. Prior to the reform, economic policies were largely inflexible and dictated from Beijing or from provincial capitals. The reforms have given local officials greater leeway to adapt policies and implementation to fit their own conditions.

This combination of decision-making autonomy and entrepreneurial incentives has been a key to the success of the economic reform effort. Investment and trading connections, together with management expertise from Hong Kong, Taiwan, and other overseas Chinese communities, have also been major factors. Since the early 1980s, China's economy has grown at an average of nearly 9 percent a year in real terms. Living standards for much of the Chinese population have improved steadily over the past decade and a half, and consumer goods and food supplies are abundant throughout much of the country.

Beijing's trial-and-error approach to economic reforms has not been without significant drawbacks. For instance:

- In many cases, the regime has delayed the hardest reform steps—such as closing money-losing state factories or trimming surplus workers from state enterprise payrolls—out of fear of social unrest;
- Reforms have widened the gap between rich and poor regions of the country;
- Reforms notwithstanding, substantial bureaucratic interference in the market survives. Local officials still distort market economic development, create new layers of red tape, and occasionally erect interprovincial trade barriers;
- Local decision-making authority has been accompanied by rising levels of corruption;
- Despite substantial reform over the past decade and a half, the government at least until recently has had problems in tuning China's economy to achieve stable long-term growth. Economic cycles in China have tended to be severe. To curb economic overheating, Beijing has sometimes stepped in with blunt measures—such as cutting off new lending—when inflation and other unwanted side effects emerged.

In the late 1970s and 1980s, there was strong debate from often widely varied perspectives in the Chinese leadership on how to handle contradictions, bottlenecks, dislocations, and other consequences flowing from China's economic development and reform. Today, the leadership appears more united on how to handle these problems.

China's recent annual rates of economic growth have been 12.8 percent

(1992), 13.4 percent (1993), 11.8 percent (1994), 10.2 percent (1995), 9.7 percent (1996), and 8.8 percent (1997). (While not directly connected with it, the economic growth has accompanied a comparable rise in the U.S. trade deficit with China, which has become the second largest U.S. trade imbalance, after that with Japan.) Inflation was a big problem (21.7 percent) in 1994, but came down to around 1 percent in 1997.

~ On balance, the economic fundamentals of the Chinese economy appear reasonably good.[6] China has the natural resources, the human capital, and access to foreign technology, capital, and markets to sustain the growth rates of the past decade into the next century. However, China continues to face major economic impediments, including inadequate transportation and electric power systems, large population growth, an insufficiently developed business law system, and inadequate fiscal control mechanisms.

The Asian economic crisis beginning in 1997 affected China's calculus in several ways, notably complicating Beijing's plans to spend the next three years focusing on reforming the tens of thousands of money-losing state-owned enterprises (SOEs). The Chinese economy was protected from immediate negative fallout from the crisis because its currency was not convertible, it holds the world's second largest reserve of foreign exchange, its large international debt mainly involves long-term commitments, and the vast majority of investment in China comes from the 40 percent domestic savings rate. Nevertheless, because of Asian currency devaluations and related events, China faced stiffer competition from other Asian exporters, fewer opportunities for intra-regional trade and investment, and a greater need to revamp previous plans for SOE reform, which called for merging many of China's enterprises into large conglomerates not unlike the now discredited chaebols of South Korea. Beijing appeared concerned that the weak Chinese banking and finance system might prompt instability as was seen elsewhere in the region. Chinese leaders began financial reforms while striving to maintain growth and control of national economic policies.[7]

Political Problems

Political problems, especially perceived differences among the leadership elites in Beijing, have traditionally been given pride of place in Western analyses of contemporary China. During the Maoist period, Chinese leadership differences often were wide ranging and had broad implications for China's internal and foreign policies. They often reflected strong differences over ideology.

Following the death of Mao and the rise of more pragmatic and technically competent Chinese leaders bent on economic modernization and reform in the late 1970s, debate among Chinese leadership elites focused more on the dynamics of nation building. Some groups favored the central government's retention of considerable control over the economic development process. This strategy would result in slower economic growth in the interest of avoiding socially disruptive developments. In particular, some worried that continued state control was needed to ensure that China remained self-sufficient in grain production and avoided the wide disparities in wealth seen in some capitalist countries.[8]

Others favored greater reduction in state control in order to spur economic growth. They argued that more rapid economic growth over the long run would help Chinese authorities deal more effectively with social and other dislocations stemming from economic and other changes.

Over time, the range of this debate over nation building and economic reform has narrowed. Opinion has largely supported the continued economic reform noted above. It has also reflected caution over political change, seen in Chinese decisions since the crackdown on political dissent in 1989.

The above does not imply that Chinese leaders will remain unified in the period ahead. In particular, it remains to be seen exactly how central leaders will handle their continuing differences, especially over how to distribute the limited number of senior leadership positions among a larger group of aspirants, now that the elder statesmen headed by Deng Xiaoping have passed away. Perceived signs of leaders' jostling for power have included occasional attacks on high-level administrative corruption, public complaints against administrative malfeasance during China's annual session of the National People's Congress, and prominent activity by or on behalf of senior leaders thought to have been retired from politics. President Jiang Zemin has appeared to make progress in establishing his leadership position. In the process, he has endeavored to accommodate the interests of important political groups, including the military.[9]

Economic reforms in recent years have been accompanied by a large-scale devolution of authority from central party and government organs to provincial and other local authorities who are taking the lead in promoting flexible schemes to foster economic growth. This opens the possibility that local authorities will become so influential as to undermine and eventually challenge central authority. Premier Zhu Rongji has taken measures to guard against these eventualities while strengthening central control, especially over key economic decisions.

Provincial authorities have been given greater control over personnel appointments in their jurisdictions; greater authority to approve imports, exports, and foreign investment projects; greater access to tax revenues and to the profits of state enterprises; and greater power over domestic investment decisions. Provincial leaders, always able to lobby the center on matters of policy and resource allocation, are sometimes able to evade or even defy decisions they disagree with.

The decentralization of political power in China has been a disorderly process. Yet it is easy to exaggerate the implications for China's future. In particular, prospects for the political fragmentation of China—sometimes cited in Western press reporting and some China experts' analysis about China—appear fairly remote. The central government still controls the allocation of economic resources that are critical to most of the country's provinces. The party's central personnel apparatus appoints the top officials at the provincial level, and central leaders still control the People's Liberation Army and the public security apparatus. Meanwhile, the Chinese authorities have been somewhat effective in using local elections, in which non-Communist Party-approved candidates sometimes campaign freely and win posts in local administration, to allow local people to have a voice in running their own local affairs.[10] This has the benefit of reducing public dissatisfaction with the current administrative system. Alongside these political factors favoring unity must be placed the emergence of an economic system that is more highly integrated nationally than ever before, and the popular nationalistic ideal of China as a nation-state. Meanwhile, in late 1998 central authorities took tougher measures to curb political dissent and strengthen political and social stability.

Social Trends

A focal point of analytical concern in the West has been the nature of state-society relations in China. If there is going to be a big change in direction in Chinese policy and practice, many analysts believe it will be ignited by friction between the regime's injunctions and conflicting trends in society. Exacerbating this is widespread discontent with official corruption and growing disparities in wealth.[11]

There has been considerable evidence of discontent in both rural and urban areas.[12] Many city-dwelling intellectuals, workers, and others are thought to have been seriously alienated from government authority following the repression of the Tiananmen demonstrations of 1989. Urban dwellers also include the largest groups in society whose benefits are being fundamentally challenged by the economic reform policies. In the country-side, the terms of trade and government procurement practices for agricultural goods have taken a disadvantageous turn for farmers after the high growth in peasant income fostered by government policies in the late 1970s and early 1980s. Chinese and Western media report that local officials responsible for purchasing grain and other mandated crops have sometimes used their allocations of cash to speculate in real estate or local enterprises, instead of paying the farmers. They have provided peasants with "IOUs" for their crops—a practice that has set off a number of peasant demonstrations and riots.

In the past, the center could endeavor to deal with such problems through party channels, weeding out corrupt or abusive local officials in order to ensure continued effective government. Current conditions in China make such an approach less likely to succeed. Reformers in Beijing are following policies that tacitly endorse the widespread entrepreneurship shown by local officials. Corruption and misuse of funds have reportedly become so broad in scope and so widespread that there may not be enough untainted cadre or local officials uninvolved in these practices to replace or sanction the errant local cadre members.

Behind this state of affairs rests a widespread cynical view of power and politics in China. In the past, the Marxist-Leninist-Maoist vision had created an important incentive to motivate party-government cadre members to remain loyal to central discipline. Today that ideology is widely viewed as bankrupt and has often been replaced by a more self-serving mentality. Against this backdrop, Chinese officials have appeared nervous about social order and have clamped down on political dissent. They also have used propaganda themes appealing to nationalistic and patriotic sentiment in order to foster a more cohesive and pliant populace.

Military Trends

The People's Liberation Army (PLA) remains the ultimate instrument of central control over society and an important potential lever to be used by central authorities to impose their policies on possibly resistant localities. At the same time, the PLA remains important as a possible arbiter should central, civilian policy makers reach an impasse on sensitive decision points involving domestic or foreign policies.[13]

The army today is leaner, led by more professionally competent officers, and less inclined to identify with local interests than in the past. The PLA went through a series of important changes and reforms under Deng Xiaoping's leadership. At the Fourteenth Party Congress in 1992, PLA leaders thought to have strong political ambitions were demoted in ways designed to strengthen the principle of civilian control of the military and to reduce the chances of the emergence of a rival base of power. The consensus on the policies of economic reform and political authoritarianism reached at the congress and at later leadership meetings also suggests that the PLA leadership is prepared to adhere to and support current policies.

Analysts remain unwilling to rule out military involvement in politics. The death of Deng Xiaoping has removed the leader with the most civilian and military prestige. Some believe that politically ambitious PLA leaders may try to revive their political fortunes following Deng's death. Jiang Zemin has worked hard to build his support among the military leaders, but analysts are unsure if this has produced more or less civilian control over the military. In recent years, PLA leaders have been successful in gaining a greater share of the government budget for defense spending. Their share may increase following the decision of July 22, 1998, for the PLA to end its involvement with profit-making enterprises. The PLA also influences Chinese policies involving national security issues like the defense of Chinese claims to Taiwan and the South China Sea.[14]

Chinese Foreign Policy

This changed markedly during the Maoist period (1949-1976). It moved from reliance on the USSR and strident opposition to the United States to a posture of strong opposition to both the United States and the USSR, and finally to an approach that relied strategically on reconciliation with the United States to deal with the danger posed by the Soviet threat. After Mao died, Chinese leaders emphasized domestic policies of development that required markedly increased economic interaction abroad. This gave added impetus to Beijing's desire to sustain good relations with the West and to avoid disruptions around its periphery that would complicate its drive toward modernization.[15]

Major changes have taken place in the international power configuration since the late 1980s (for example, the collapse of the Soviet Union and the socialist world system centered on it) and in China (for example, the Tiananmen incident), but Chinese foreign policy continues to adhere to the general outlines established in the years after Mao's death. As long as China remains preoccupied with internal developments, and international actors avoid initiatives seen as posing fundamental challenges to the Chinese leadership, Beijing seems likely to continue following the relatively narrow range of policies that it has adhered to for almost twenty years.

Several trends have characterized the Chinese approach to foreign affairs in the post-Mao period:

- Chinese leaders now face a security environment along China's periphery that is less likely to be disrupted by a major international power than at any time in the past;
- Regional security trends have been generally compatible with China's primary focus on internal economic modernization and political stability;
- Ideological and leadership disputes have had less importance for Chinese foreign policy than in the past;
- Reinforcing the narrower range of foreign policy choices present among Chinese leaders, Chinese foreign policy has become somewhat more driven by economic relations with other countries, especially the Western-aligned, developed countries, than in the past.

On the other hand, there remains the distinct possibility that outside forces (for example, the United States, Japan, India, and Taiwan) may adopt policies that challenge fundamental Chinese interests and prompt a strongly assertive Chinese response. Thus, for example, Beijing has threatened repeatedly that it would forcefully stop any Taiwanese movement to declare Taiwan an independent country. It has also reacted strongly to U.S.-Japanese efforts to strengthen their bilateral alliance, and to India's nuclear tests in May 1998. In 1999, China reacted strongly to U.S. plans to build a national ballistic missile defense system and to step up cooperation with Japan to build a theater ballistic missile defense system in East Asia, and to reported U.S. plans to help Taiwan defend itself against ballistic missiles.[16]

Moreover, Chinese leaders are well aware of China's rising international power and influence. At times, they appear prepared to use them in asserting Chinese interests in sensitive areas like Taiwan, the South China Sea, and elsewhere. While conforming to some internationally accepted norms, Chinese leaders also continue to resist some U.S. and other international efforts to curb Chinese sales of arms, sophisticated technologies, and other materials to Pakistan, Iran, and other areas to which the United States is sensitive. They strongly resist U.S. pressures with regard to China's treatment of dissidents and other human rights issues. And they say they will retaliate against U.S. economic sanctions related to Chinese infractions of market access, intellectual property rights, and other standards. Beijing's emphasis on nationalistic and patriotic propaganda themes reduces China's flexibility in sensitive foreign policy issues with the United States and other countries. India's nuclear tests of May 1998 represented the most serious foreign policy crisis faced by the post-Deng Xiaoping leadership.

China reacted very critically to India's actions but avoided strong commitments that would have adversely affected economic modernization.

Possible Outcomes and General Implications

After the Tiananmen incident and the subsequent collapse of communist regimes in Europe and elsewhere, it was common to hear the view that the communist regime in China was destined for collapse. Other observers warned of major retrogression in Chinese economic reforms, speculating that Beijing would feel compelled in the face of domestic and foreign pressure to revert to the autarchic development policies of the Maoist past. These would reduce Chinese interdependence with other countries and presumably would reduce China's incentive to avoid disruptive behavior in interaction with its neighbors and other world powers.[17]

On balance, China's record in the 1990s has undercut the more extreme near-term predictions of collapse or retrogression. The authorities in Beijing have presided over a period of unprecedented growth in the Chinese economy. This growth has not only benefited many in China but has come at a time of often lackluster growth in several other parts of the world. The result has been a period of unprecedented international investment in and interaction with the Chinese economy. When combined with Beijing's general avoidance of major controversy and selectively accommodating posture in world affairs in recent years, the result has been to erode foreign sanctions and to enhance the international and domestic legitimacy of the Chinese leaders. The success of China's continued economic reform has also undermined the arguments of those conservative Chinese leaders who might be inclined to press for a more autarchic development strategy and a more assertive, less accommodating posture in world affairs.

Nevertheless, analysis of key determinants reveals a wide range of possible outcomes for China over the next few years. A positive scenario posits increasingly effective political administration and reform along with powerful economic modernization. Alternative outcomes are of two kinds. One sees a series of developments leading to the degeneration of government effectiveness and authority with a number of negative effects on China's economic and social development. Another sees China developing formidable economic power while retaining strong authoritarian political control. This raises the possibility of an emerging Chinese economic and military superpower, less interested in accommodation with the outside world and unfettered by the political checks and balances that accompany less authoritarian political structures.

Transformation

In this scenario, the decentralization of political and economic decision-making power is managed effectively, resulting in continued development and stability. China may adopt aspects of a federal political system, in which the federal (national) and state (provincial) governments amicably share revenue, power, and the tasks of governance. The revenue base and macroeconomic control of the central government would improve with an overhaul of the financial and taxation system. Price reform and a return to private property could stir greater rural and urban productivity. In the "best case," the political system might shift toward strengthening the legislature and increasing press freedom, though there are few historical antecedents for this. In the long term, there would also be room for reconciliation between the government and society as human rights are respected and the rule of law is established to check arbitrary abuses of power. As the economic power of the individual grows in China, the groundwork for a civil society and pluralistic politics would be strengthened. Expansion of foreign trade and investment could lead to China's closer integration with the international community, and perhaps greater willingness to abide by international norms on human rights, trade, and weapons proliferation issues, which are important to the United States.

Implications for U.S. Interests

Continued economic modernization and emerging political reform would provide growing opportunities for U.S. investors and traders, while holding the promise of political change compatible with U.S. values. The expansion of foreign economic contacts could also lead to greater consensus and cooperation on strategic and foreign policy issues such as weapons nonproliferation, technology transfer, and regional security. A China focused on domestic stability and economic development might more often than not pursue policies designed to reduce regional conflicts that are important to the United States, including tensions on the Korean peninsula and territorial disputes in the South China Sea. Chinese observers and Western analysts often judge that Beijing in this scenario would still have very great difficulty in meeting U.S. interests regarding political values, such as human rights. The political reforms that may accompany the economic changes are seen as likely to be slow in developing.

Degeneration

The leadership in Beijing could engage in a prolonged power struggle that cripples the government. Delay in needed economic and political reforms could produce greater decay, discontent, and difficult problems in the longer run. Major economic problems could grow, widening income gaps and fueling inflation, leading to rampant social instability. Corruption could swell to distort development and breed organized crime. Environmental problems, national disasters, infrastructure and energy bottlenecks, and fiscal crises could also lead to economic breakdown. Continued repression or brute coercion could contribute to social apathy or hostilities. Weak and divided civilian as well as military authorities could also induce separatist protests in areas like Xinjiang and Tibet, provoking ethnic conflicts. An insecure Chinese government might be unable to participate responsibly in the United Nations or credibly negotiate international agreements.

Implications for U.S. Interests

Such economic and political conditions would substantially reduce trade and investment opportunities for the United States. The danger of possible large-scale Chinese refugee flows to neighboring countries and China's overall strategic weakness would pose major problems for the countries in the region and for the U.S. interest in regional stability. U.S. interests in human rights and economic progress for the people of China would be substantially set back.

Some would argue that this negative transition for China might ultimately be in the interests of the United States. It could so undermine the communist regime in China as to foster its overthrow, leading presumably to a more effective, representative regime or to two or more such regimes.

Economically Powerful Authoritarianism

This outcome assumes that authorities in China will be successful in modernizing the Chinese economy and use that success to shore up authoritarian political structures at home. Not only would this result in continued political repression and human rights abuses, but China's economic power would also be of such a size and scale as to make most foreign powers reluctant to confront Beijing on most issues. Thus, Chinese leaders inclined to adopt more assertive, nationalistic policies would have a freer hand to pursue their objectives and be less concerned that trading partners would shun economic opportunities in China if Beijing violated international norms. The continued strong state direction of the massive

Chinese economy would presumably give Beijing important incentives to use its economic power to manipulate the terms of trade and investment in critical economic sectors in international commerce.

Implications for U.S. Interests

Chinese economic prosperity would continue to attract important world attention, including that of the United States. Beijing would be in a position to mobilize this economic power against American interests. Chinese leaders would presumably continue the repressive authoritarian measures of the past. In international affairs, Beijing would probably be less deferential to U.S. and allied concerns regarding security issues, trade practices, and the like. Over the longer term, an economically powerful and politically authoritarian China could hold sufficient power and harbor sufficient substantial differences with the United States to pose the most serious single international threat to U.S. interests in Asian and world stability in the twenty-first century.

Given the trends—especially the dynamic economic growth—prevalent in China in recent years, specialists have been inclined to predict some version of "economically powerful authoritarianism" or "transformation" as the most likely of the three scenarios to define China's future. Some others nonetheless find plenty of evidence of internal friction and administrative decay, seeing "degeneration" as the most likely outcome over the next decade. The major complications of the Asian economic crisis for China's future make it even more difficult to predict with much certainty which path will be followed. Outside observers are often put in a position of having to watch events unfold in order to determine the likely outcome and its implications for the United States.

Notes

1. For a recent review of Chinese government concerns, see *Current History*, September 1998, entire issue. See also weekly coverage of Chinese government concerns in *The Far Eastern Economic Review*.

2. For opposing views discussing these possible outcomes, see Richard Bernstein and Ross Munro, *The Coming Conflict with China*, New York: Knopf, 1997; Andrew Nathan and Robert Ross, *The Great Wall and Empty Fortress*, New York: Norton, 1997.

3. See discussion in Joseph Fewsmith, "Jiang Zemin Takes Command," *Current History*, September 1998, pp. 250-256.

4. For discussion, see *China's Changing Conditions*, Washington, D.C.: Library of Congress, Congressional Research Service (CRS) Issue Brief 97049 (updated regularly), pp. 2-3.

5. For background on economic trends in post-Mao China, see, among others, Nicholas Lardy, *China in the World Economy*, Washington, D.C.: Institute for International Economics, 1994; Barry Naughton, *Growing out of the Plan: Chinese Economic Reform, 1978-1993*, Cambridge, England: Cambridge University Press, 1995; The World Bank, *China 2020: Development Challenges in the New Century*, Washington, D.C.: World Bank, 1997.

6. For a strongly negative view of the recent Chinese economy, see "Will China Be Next?" *Economist*, October 24, 1998, pp. 17-18; "Red Alert," *Economist*, October 24, 1998, pp. 23-26.

7. See, among others, Maurice Meisner, *Mao's China and After: A History of the People's Republic*, New York: Free Press, 1986.

8. See, among others, Joseph Fewsmith, *Dilemmas of Reform in China: Economic Debate and Political Conflict*, Armonk, N.Y.: M. E. Sharpe, 1994.

9. Fewsmith, "Jiang Zemin Takes Command," pp. 250-256.

10. Tyrene White, "Village Elections: Democracy from the Bottom Up?" *Current History*, September 1998, pp. 263-267. See also Anne F. Thurston, *Muddling toward Democracy*, Washington, D.C.: U.S. Institute of Peace, Peaceworks 23, 1998.

11. For recent treatments of such social issues, see David Shambaugh, ed., *Is China Stable? Assessing the Factors*, Washington, D.C.: Sigur Center for Asian Studies, 1998, pp. 73-141.

12. See articles by Dorothy Solinger and Thomas Bernstein, in *Is China Stable?* ed. Shambaugh, pp. 73-110.

13. See, among others, "A Strategic Approach to Understanding the PLA: The Staunton Hill Conference," in *China Strategic Review* 3, no. 1 (spring 1998): 1-191.

14. See, among others, Hans Binnendijk and Ronald Montaperto, eds., *Strategic Trends in China*, Washington, D.C.: National Defense University Press, 1998.

15. For background, see John W. Garver, *Foreign Relations of the People's Republic of China*, Englewood Cliffs, N.J.: Prentice Hall, 1993; Thomas Robinson and David Shambaugh, eds., *Chinese Foreign Policy: Theory and Practice*, Oxford: Oxford University Press, 1994.

16. People's Republic of China (PRC) Foreign Ministry spokesman, *Xinhua*, January 21, 1999, carried by Foreign Broadcast Information Service (FBIS), Internet version.

17. For competing views of China's future and what it might mean for U.S. interests and stability in East Asia, see, among others, Bernstein and Munro, *The Coming Conflict with China*; Nathan and Ross, *The Great Wall and Empty Fortress*; Ezra Vogel, ed., *Living with China: U.S.-China Relations in the Twenty-First Century*, New York: Norton, 1997; and World Bank, *China 2020*.

Chapter 2

Current Chinese Policy Priorities:
The Primacy of Domestic Concerns

In the era following the death of Mao Zedong (d. 1976), Chinese Communist Party (CCP) leaders have focused on economic reform and development as the basis of their continued survival as the rulers of China. Support for economic liberalization and openness has waxed and waned, but the overall trend has emphasized greater market orientation and foreign economic interchange as critical in promoting economic advancement, and by extension, supporting the continued CCP monopoly of political power. For a time, the leaders were less clear in their attitudes toward political liberalization and change, with some in the 1980s calling for substantial reform of the authoritarian communist system. Since the crackdown at Tiananmen in 1989, there has been a general consensus among the party elite to carefully control dissent and other political challenges, allowing for only slow, gradual political change that can be closely monitored by the authorities.[1]

In foreign affairs, post-Mao leaders retreated from the sometimes strident calls to change the international system, and worked pragmatically to establish relationships with important countries, especially the United States and Japan, but also China's neighbors in Southeast Asia and elsewhere, who would assist China's development and enhance Beijing's overall goal of developing national wealth and power.[2]

The collapse of Soviet communism at the end of the cold war posed a major ideological challenge to Chinese leaders and reduced Western interest in China as a counterweight to the USSR. But the advance of China's economy soon attracted Western leaders once again, while the demise of the USSR gave China a freer hand to pursue its interest, less encumbered by the long-term Soviet strategic threat.

Against this backdrop, Chinese leaders in 1997 were anxious to minimize problems with the United States and other countries in order to avoid complications in their efforts to appear successful in completing three major tasks for the year:[3]

- The July 1, 1997, transition of Hong Kong to Chinese rule;
- The reconfiguration of Chinese leadership and policy at the Fifteenth CCP Congress in September 1997, the first major party meeting since the death of senior leader Deng Xiaoping in February 1997;
- The Sino-U.S. summit of October 1997, which China hoped would show people in China and abroad that its leaders were now fully accepted as respectable world leaders following a period of protracted isolation after the 1989 Tiananmen crackdown.

Generally pleased with the results of these three endeavors, Chinese leaders headed by President and party chief Jiang Zemin began implementing policy priorities for 1998. At the top of the list was an ambitious three-year effort, begun in earnest after the National People's Congress (NPC) meeting in March 1998, to transform tens of thousands of China's money-losing state-owned enterprises (SOEs) into more efficient businesses by reforming them (for example, selling them to private concerns, forming large conglomerates, or other actions).[4]

Consequently, Beijing has embarked on major programs to promote economic and administrative efficiency and protect China's potentially vulnerable financial systems from any negative fallout from the Asian economic crisis. Thus, at the NPC meeting in March 1998, it was announced that government rolls would be drastically cut in an effort to reduce inefficient government interference in day-to-day business management. And China's new premier, Zhu Rongji, initiated sweeping changes in China's banking and other financial systems designed to reduce or eliminate the vulnerabilities seen elsewhere in Asia.

As a result of the September 1997 party congress and the March 1998 NPC meeting, a new party-government team was in place, managing policy without the guidance and guidelines set by such powerful leaders of the past as Mao Zedong and Deng Xiaoping. There were problems reaching consensus on the power-holding arrangements made at the party and people's congresses, but on the whole, top-level leaders seem to be working smoothly together pursuing Chinese policy interests.

Making collective leadership work is an ongoing challenge for China's top leaders. The People's Republic of China (PRC) has traditionally been dominated by one senior decision maker. Periods of collective leadership, notably after Mao's death in 1976, were short and unstable. President Jiang Zemin has gained in stature and influence in recent years, but his power still does not compare to that exerted by Mao and Deng. When it comes time for Jiang and his senior colleagues to retire in a few years, a renewed struggle for power and influential positions by up-and-coming leaders remains a distinct possibility. If a major economic, political, or foreign policy crisis emerged before then, leadership conflict over what to do, how to do it, and who to do it could be intense.

There is little sign of disagreement over the recent policy emphasis on economic reform. The ambitious plans for economic reform, especially reform of the SOEs, are needed if China's economy is to become sufficiently efficient to sustain the growth rates seen as needed to justify continued communist rule and to develop China's wealth and power. The reforms also exacerbate social and economic uncertainties, which reinforce the regime's determination to maintain a firm grip on political power and levers of social control. By late 1998, instability caused by economic change and growing political dissent prompted the PRC leadership to initiate significant suppression of political dissidents and related activities. Observers judged that the repression would last at least through 1999 and possibly for the duration of the economic reform efforts.[6]

Against this background, foreign affairs generally remains an area of less urgent policy priority. Broad international trends, notably improved relations with the United States, support the efforts by the Chinese authorities to pursue policies intended to minimize disruptions and to assist their domestic reform endeavors. The government remains wary of the real or potential challenges posed by the recent Asian economic crisis, by Taiwan, by efforts by Japan and the United States to increase their international influence in ways seen as contrary to Beijing's interests, by India's great power aspirations and nuclear capability, and by other concerns. In early 1999, the PRC voiced special concern over the implications for China's interests of U.S. plans and reported plans to develop and deploy theater ballistic missile defense systems in East Asia.

Domestic Reform

As money-losing SOEs are being consolidated, sold, or streamlined, many workers are losing their jobs. While some find other jobs, many are unable to duplicate the mixture of income and benefits they had received from SOEs. In particular, the SOEs are often responsible for providing housing, disability and old-age support, health care, and schooling for the workers and their families. Meanwhile, the government streamlining plan announced at the NPC promises to remove around four million government employees from their positions, though many are likely to find jobs in related nongovernment agencies, institutes, and enterprises.[7] Not surprisingly, there has been an upsurge of unauthorized demonstrations, strikes, and some riots as a result of the layoffs. The authorities generally avoid Tiananmen-type tactics to deal with these events.[8] If possible, they attempt to "buy off" or accommodate the demonstrators by providing funds to restore some jobs or benefits. Meanwhile, the People's Armed Police—much expanded and better trained since 1989—has proven much more adroit at crowd control. Of course, as the reform of SOEs and other efficiency measures move into higher gear in 1998 and later years, the authorities presumably will have less flexibility to reinstate jobs and benefits, and the scope of demonstrations may tax the abilities and discretion of the police.

The Asian economic crisis has diverted Chinese leadership attention from SOE and other reforms in several ways. Initially, Chinese leaders thought China would not be seriously affected by the crisis because of the factors noted above: its currency is not convertible, it holds over $130 billion in foreign exchange reserves, most of its foreign debt is medium- and long-term debt, and most investment in China comes from domestic savings (the rate of such savings in China is 40 percent of an individual's overall income). As it deepened and spread, the crisis preoccupied Chinese leaders with such issues as the following:

- The need to support Hong Kong's economic stability;
- How to deal with growing competition in international markets from exports from Asian countries that have markedly devalued their currencies;
- How to compensate for the loss of Asian investment in China, especially investment that was counted on to purchase some ailing SOEs, and Chinese investment losses in Asian countries;
- How to revise plans to consolidate SOEs into Korean and Japanese-style conglomerates, which are now viewed with disfavor following the Asian crisis;
- How to speed reform of China's weak banking and finance systems to avoid a crisis similar to those occurring elsewhere in the region.[9]

As part of efforts to smooth foreign relations in order to focus on problems at home, Beijing has given high priority to expressing Chinese interest in human rights issues. Beijing has signed the UN Covenant on Economic and Social Rights, has signed the UN Covenant on Political and Civil Rights, has conducted numerous diplomatic dialogues with foreign groups, and has released a few dissidents. Such actions have the effect of encouraging dissidents and others in China seeking faster political change to press their case, often during such events as major party or NPC meetings. Thus, former party chief Zhao Ziyang wrote a letter to the September 1997 party congress calling for a reevaluation of the Tiananmen incident—a particularly divisive political issue. He wrote a similar letter in June 1998, immediately prior to the U.S. president's visit to China. Others are arguing against the authoritarian controls of the present regime in articles and tracts published in China, or published abroad and sent back to China via fax and Internet.[10]

The pressures for political reform and an improvement in human rights come both from within the elite and from outside the Chinese establishment. Many within the elite recognize that China will be unable to root out the prevailing corruption—a major threat to the legitimacy of the CCP—without establishing mechanisms for a more accountable administration such as a freer press, freer elections, and greater adherence to the rule of law. There is also the view that political reform and more accountable government are needed if China is to avoid the weaknesses of "crony-capitalism" that were so graphically illustrated elsewhere in the region during the Asian economic crisis. The increasingly well-to-do Chinese entrepreneurs and intellectuals outside the state-controlled system often clamor for greater representation in government decision-making. And it is widely held that regime legitimacy suffers as long as Beijing is unable to come to grips with the unjust verdicts on the Tiananmen incident. Meanwhile, outside the elite there are dissidents seeking to take advantage of the Chinese government's human rights diplomacy and image-building abroad to push for changes in the still coercive PRC regime. They sometimes strive to use the discontent of millions of unemployed and others who have suffered as a consequence of economic changes.[11]

The current Beijing leadership consensus is likely to resist such calls for change. Beginning in November 1998, the authorities arrested and imprisoned numerous dissidents and curbed the freedom of publications and some religious activities. The suppression was expected to last through 1999, and perhaps for the duration of the reforms. Meanwhile, ethnic dissidents, including some using violent means, also are pressing separatist cases; they are meeting stern repression, including frequent executions, by the authorities in Xinjiang and Tibet.[12]

China's Ninth National People's Congress (NPC)

Chinese leaders have been forthright in articulating their policy priorities in major party and government meetings. The most comprehensive recent review of their policy concerns came during deliberations at the 1998 Ninth National People's Congress. Held in Beijing in March 1998, the congress established government leadership and policies that would guide Chinese developments for the next five years. Following the broad policy guidelines set up and leadership selections made at the Chinese Communist Party's Fifteenth Congress in September 1997, the NPC set an ambitious agenda, giving priority to development issues involving broad economic reform and government streamlining.[13]

Results

Leadership

As expected, the congress reelected party leader Jiang Zemin as president, while Li Peng, number two in the party hierarchy, retired as premier and became head of the NPC. Third-ranking party leader Zhu Rongji was elected premier. Consistent with the congress' emphasis on streamlining government, the number of vice premiers and state councilors was reduced.

Zhu was clearly the "star" of the congress, especially during his masterful performance at a press conference at the end of the meeting, broadcast live by Chinese television, in which, for an hour and a half, he handled with aplomb and without notes questions that were often tough and sensitive. (The press conference was broadcast live by Chinese television, something that Chinese leaders almost never allow. For example, Chinese television carried no live coverage of Jiang Zemin's various activities in the United States in October-November 1997. There was always a time delay, presumably to allow for editing, if needed.)[14] Jiang's decision to allow live media coverage of his press conference with President Clinton in Beijing in June 1998 caused a major sensation among Chinese and Western journalists.[15]

Zhu has had overall responsibility for Chinese economic policies in recent years, and his focus remained on economic reform. He presumably was a driving force behind the congress' decisions to cut government ministries, reduce government interference in economic management, and reform ailing SOEs and the weak financial system.

Zhu's subordinates in running the economy included several officials close to him, notably newly appointed state councilor and secretary-general of the State Council, Wang Zhongyu, and the head of the People's Bank of China, Dai Xianglong. But also on the economic team were senior Vice Premier Li Lanqing and state councilor and former foreign trade minister Wu Yi, who were not in Zhu's camp and clashed with him on policy issues in the past.[16]

Jiang Zemin appeared more successful than Zhu in seeing officials close to him rise to prominence at the congress. All four vice premiers were closer to Jiang than to Premier Zhu. The newly selected vice president, party Politburo standing committee member Hu Jintao, a former party leader in Tibet, was singled out by Jiang as a rising star of the next generation. (Hu is about fifteen years younger than Jiang and Zhu.) Hu's selection for the vice presidency departed from past practice in which the post was reserved as a sinecure for aging leaders. Among other things, Hu was expected to assist Jiang Zemin in meeting China's increasing needs to travel abroad for negotiations and visits. Hu's initial trips as vice president were to South Korea and Japan in April 1998, for example.[17]

Outgoing premier and new NPC chairman Li Peng had few major allies in the new government line up. Li was close to Luo Gan, a Politburo member and state councilor who was rumored to be in line to preside over the party's political-legal commission—a leadership body that establishes policy for public security and judicial and legislative agencies. At the NPC, Li had good relations with some newly appointed leaders, but the incumbent senior NPC vice chairman, Tian Jiyun, was a liberal-leaning reformer long at odds with Li's more conservative orientation.[18]

There was general continuity in the leaders selected to direct defense and foreign policy. Jiang Zemin remained head of both the party and of the government military commissions, and the vice chairmen are Generals Zhang Wannian and Chi Haotian. Chi was retained as defense minister, despite his age (sixty-nine), presumably because other leading candidates like General Staff Department head Fu Quanyou did not have the diplomatic skills to manage China's increasingly active military diplomacy. Zhang Wannian missed the NPC meetings and was reported to be ill. He had to postpone a visit to the United States in May.

Qian Qichen retired as foreign minister but remained a Politburo member and vice premier. His successor, Tang Jiaxun, was the vice foreign minister dealing with Asian affairs. Tang was a close associate of Qian, who retained strong influence in setting Chinese foreign policy.

Policy Agenda

Premier Zhu summarized China's policy agenda, focused on achieving more efficient economic development, as a "one-three-five" program.[19]

"One ensuring"—Zhu said that current conditions in China and the

regional economic crisis required China to grow by 8 percent annually and to hold inflation to under 3 percent. He also stressed that China's currency would not be devalued in 1998 and that China would strongly support the Hong Kong currency's fixed value (the "peg") relative to the U.S. dollar. To offset losses caused by the regional economic crisis, Zhu said China would rely on more spending on infrastructure, high technology, and housing, though he and NPC documents eschewed any reference to Chinese investment of $750 billion, a prediction made by Vice Premier Li Lanqing at the international economic summit at Davos, Switzerland, in February 1998.[20]

"Three putting in place"—Zhu said this involved reforming the SOEs, the ailing financial system, and the size and scope of government over the next three years. This highly ambitious program has focused on the following areas:

- Revamping, privatizing, and consolidating the tens of thousands of money-losing SOEs. Not only is this a major economic challenge, but it directly affects the welfare, housing, schooling, and pensions of millions of workers and their families.
- The Chinese banking and financial regulation system has many of the same weaknesses seen elsewhere in Asia, and it is widely seen as insolvent. China is protected from immediate danger from the Asian economic crisis. But Zhu and other leaders recognized that the current system is a drag on rational development and a danger to future stability.
- Government rolls at the central and provincial level generally were slated to be cut in half over the next three years as Beijing moves drastically to curb the government's role in the day-to-day management of enterprises and the economy while strengthening the government's ability to manage macroeconomic levers. Heralding the sweeping reorganization and streamlining, leaders at the NPC decided to cut the previous forty ministerial-level organs down to twenty-nine. Most of those eliminated were ministries and organizations involved in the management of specific industries.

"Five Reforms"—This will involve increasing the efficiency of the management of China's grain reserve system, which is bursting at the seams with surplus grain purchased by government subsidies; reducing administrative influence and allowing the market to determine investment choices; reforming the urban housing system—that is, moving away from subsidized to free-market housing, reforming medical care, and moving to greater

reliance on income and other taxes rather than ad hoc fees to fund government activities.

Issues

Leadership

The party and government lineup resulting from the Fifteenth Party Congress in September 1997 and the NPC in 1998 raised a number of questions and revealed possible indicators regarding leadership power and policy:[21]

- How well would Zhu Rongji work with vice premiers and state councilors who were closer to Jiang Zemin and who in some cases have clashed with Zhu on policy issues in the past? Would Zhu continue to exert direct day-to-day oversight of the economy, or would he delegate that responsibility to senior Vice Premier Li Lanqing, who differs with Zhu on some issues?
- Would Zhu broaden his responsibilities to play a leading role in foreign policy, as did the previous premier, Li Peng? If so, how would he interact with Jiang Zemin and Vice Premier Qian Qichen, both of whom play central roles in leading groups in the party dealing with foreign affairs and policy toward Taiwan and Hong Kong?
- Would Li Peng, perhaps through his close association with Luo Gan, move to control policy-making dealing with public security and judiciary and legislative matters? If so, how would this affect Chinese policy dealing with dissent and other human rights issues?
- Defense policy-making appeared well established, with Jiang Zemin, backed by Zhang Wannian and Chi Haotian, in the lead. But leadership maneuvering could result from the protracted illness or death of Zhang Wannian.

Policy Agenda

U.S. and Chinese analysts remained uncertain about the ambitious reform program laid out at the NPC.[22] Sustaining 8 percent growth has run up against lost markets in Asia for Chinese goods and lost Asian investment in China because of the Asian economic crisis. Eighty percent of outside investment in China had come from Asia, according to Premier Zhu.

While few doubted that there would be strenuous efforts to downsize the government, experienced analysts pointed out that Zhu's plan was the fourth major government streamlining announced since the early 1980s; in each previous case government rolls had grown, not decreased. Most analysts consulted for a CRS study agreed that this time would be different,[23] but adding millions of government employees to those seeking new jobs at a time of major SOE consolidation and reform seemed likely to pose a formidable challenge to China's social stability.

Meanwhile, plans to reform the SOEs and the ailing financial system had been considered for some time and appeared reasonable, provided related reforms moved in tandem with them. For example, provisions needed to be made to support pensions for experienced workers from SOEs that are sold or otherwise go out of business. The authorities needed to consider how to allocate housing, medical care, and other benefits to these workers and their families whose benefits had previously been provided by the SOEs. Beijing has been working for years, thus far without major success, to come up with viable social security, health care, retirement, and other such systems. Meeting these challenges along with SOE and financial system reform in a three-year period represented a tall order.

Political reform received perfunctory treatment at the congress. When asked at the March 19, 1998, press conference about a possible reversal of verdicts over the 1989 Tiananmen crackdown, Zhu Rongji adhered to the standard line.[24] As a result, there was no clear indication of how the authorities would deal with the burgeoning pressure for political change. Popular dissatisfaction over official corruption heads the list of reasons for greater government accountability and reform. Despite generally adhering to the party "line," congress deputies voted negatively in large numbers on issues seen as related to the authorities' handling of corruption and favoritism. Meanwhile, activists within and outside the party took advantage of the authorities' ongoing efforts to improve China's human rights image abroad in order to press their case for greater government accountability, political freedom, and reconsideration of verdicts dealing with Tiananmen and with the case of Zhao Ziyang, the party leader removed as a result of the 1989 crisis.

Subsequent Complications of Reform

Not surprisingly, the leadership's ambitious reform agenda soon ran into a range of problems, complications, and resistance. PRC officials appeared likely to remain focused on dealing with these difficult domestic preoccupations for the next few years.

The Chinese leaders remained unified behind the top leadership choices and major policy guidelines made over the previous year. President Jiang Zemin remained the first among the senior party and government officials, and he and his colleagues were given credit for maintaining stability and improving China's international image. Jiang received positive publicity and support for his successful management of President Clinton's visit to China in June-July 1998.[25] However, Jiang did not dominate the leadership as Mao Zedong and Deng Xiaoping had done. Unexpected domestic or foreign policy crises or leadership competition for power as Jiang and his senior colleagues retire remained possible causes for serious leadership division and conflict.

Efforts to reduce and restructure government ministries and to purge an estimated four million cadre members from government jobs were meeting strong resistance. According to media reports in mid-1998, Premier Zhu Rongji had been unable to force the compliance of the many ministries under his direct control. Only two-thirds had sent him the required reports on how they would streamline operations, and most of those reports were returned because they did not meet the established standards for cutting personnel. Meanwhile, some senior cadre members who had been let go had moved to related private sector enterprises and had used their influence and connections to benefit themselves and their enterprises, often at the expense of the broader public good. The trend added to widespread public cynicism about endemic corruption in government and related enterprises.[26]

Housing reform added to the public perception of corruption as some government offices distributed apartments under their control to their cadre members at very cheap prices. Other government offices used their own funds to purchase apartments on the market, and then distributed them as a fringe benefit. One report claimed that "flats are being given away according to seniority and special connections. Worse, large numbers of officials and their spouses are getting four or five apartments."[27]

The administration also made little headway in dealing with the millions of laid-off workers from government ministries and SOEs. During a major leadership conference in May 1998 on unemployment, social security, and retaining, the leadership proposed a "three-pronged strategy" with money for creating new jobs to come from central government coffers, local budgets, and SOE funds. Unfortunately, the central government had few funds to spare and many of the SOEs were basically bankrupt. Sometimes, the central authorities proposed that the unemployed consider unorthodox methods such as working on farms, starting businesses in interior provinces, or seeking jobs overseas. But the actual conditions of the period included large-scale rural unemployment or underemployment, recession in the interior provinces, and the collapse of overseas job opportunities because of the Asian economic crisis.[28]

Sustaining the planned 8 percent growth rate was critically important to allow Beijing to deal effectively with the wide range of problems associated with rising unemployment. The economy grew at a 7.8 percent annual rate in 1998, a figure seen as too high by some outside experts. Massive, prolonged midyear floods in central China and in the northeast threatened to shave at least 1 percent off China's projected growth for the year.[29] In September the government resorted to large ($12 billion) bond issues to collect funds for infrastructure projects that would promote growth. Despite continued foreign investment, the pace of overall investment was sluggish, and export growth halted as China encountered tougher price competition for markets.[30]

Chinese leaders' worries over managing the complications of their ambitious government and economic reforms were mirrored in the mounting challenges posed by progressives and dissidents encouraging political reform. Anniversaries in mid-1998 of such events as Deng Xiaoping's 1978 campaign to "emancipate thought" and "seek truth from facts," the founding of Beijing University, the 1919 May 4th movement, and the 1989 Tiananmen incident prompted liberal intellectuals within the elite to press for greater changes. Some believed that party leader Jiang Zemin had authorized a limited rehabilitation of liberal reformers who had fallen from power over the Tiananmen crackdown, as well as a more moderate attitude toward student leaders such as Wang Dan.[31] Wang was released on medical parole to the United States in early 1998. But Jiang was in the lead in urging tighter control of dissent by the end of the year.

More broadly, as a result of the party and state congresses over the past year or two, developing "democratic politics" and the "rule of law" was back on the official agenda, after a nine-year hiatus. The immediate pursuit of political reform focused on government downsizing and economic legislation. Top leaders wanted to delay discussion of serious systemic political reform until much later, possibly 2010 or even 2020, when China had attained a higher stage of development. There were no known major initiatives to protect human rights or promote democracy, but a renewal of debates similar to those of the late 1980s over comprehensive reform of the Leninist system of party control of government, military, and social organizations was beginning to appear.[32]

Factors Favoring a Democratic Trend

Senior PRC leaders' talk about democracy was partly tactics aimed at improving China's international image, evading censure at the annual meeting of the UN Human Rights Commission in Geneva, and improving the atmosphere for President Clinton's June 1998 visit, but it also reflected important new dynamics at work among the political elite:[33]

- Popular dissatisfaction with official abuse and corruption was a driving force behind political reform. The NPC session in March 1998 stressed the theme of controlling corruption through the rule of law. A significant minority of delegates rejected the reports by the outgoing Supreme Court and Procuratorate and opposed the new choice for procurator-general, because they did not adequately address the problems. Delegates reportedly demanded measures to prevent corrupt officials from taking advantage of impending economic and organizational reforms. Media commentary on "grass-roots democracy" programs, including village direct elections, stressed the need to hold abusive officials accountable to the people.

- A growing middle class expanded with government downsizing. Many state cadre members moved into the professions and business, and their interests shifted from upholding bureaucratic privilege to holding officials accountable and creating a level playing field for non-bureaucratic actors. Many are quite knowledgeable about how to work the system and have a strong commitment to political reform.

- The Asian economic crisis has underscored for many in China the grave danger of unregulated "crony capitalism" and the practical necessity for democracy in Asia. The fact that the "tigers" riding out the storm have the strongest legal system (Hong Kong) and/or democratic politics (Taiwan) has nudged PRC analysts to look more closely at these political-economic systems for potential application to the mainland. The demise of the authoritarian Suharto regime in Indonesia underlined the point. The official argument that stability is a prerequisite for state enterprise reform now faces a counterargument that only democratic reform can provide sufficient accountability to save China from political and economic crisis.

- The priority attached to achieving progress toward peaceful reunification with Taiwan and maintaining confidence in Hong Kong resulted in pressure to show movement toward democratization. It was clear to many in China that independence for Taiwan would continue to gain support unless the island people were convinced that the mainland is making changes to its political system.

- Heightened global competition into the next century has produced a major new high-tech drive, spearheaded by President Jiang Zemin and Premier Zhu Rongji through a new Politburo leading group on science and education. Press reports on reform spoke starkly of a "critical moment for China's destiny"—either join the "fast lane" in global development or slide into the "slow lane." Chinese media cited an outmoded political system as a major drag on competitiveness. This theme was reinforced, albeit only implicitly, in a report by the Academy of Sciences warning that China must reverse a "severe brain drain problem" (for example, more than a third of Beijing University graduates had left the country) if it was to catch up with the "recent rapid development of global information technology."[34]

- Improved prospects in U.S.-China relations made it easier for reformers to experiment with "Western" concepts and pursue expanded exchanges in sensitive areas. Official legal cooperation, for example, allowed legal reformers to push for change without being labeled "tools of containment."

Factors Impeding a Democratic Trend
  ➤ Political reform will continue to be inhibited by a number of factors:

- [Different views of democracy and rule of law.] China's leaders remain committed to "socialist democracy" as a variant of the Asian model of authoritarian government and market economics.[35] They want only marginal, even glacial, changes to their highly managed, "consultative" feedback system. Jiang Zemin seems to define democracy as educated leadership. Progressives occupying midlevel bureaucratic or professional positions favor a much larger dose of elitist democracy for utilitarian reasons—accountable government would improve economic efficiency and help reverse the brain drain.[36] Both groups are wary of a growing strain of populist democracy focused on the suffering of those marginalized by reform. Political dissidents who have no faith in top-down approaches work on grassroots social organizing of a sort greatly feared by the government, especially as working-class anger rises against managers and officials who profit from state enterprise reorganization. There is a split, however, between those who call for democratic revolution and those who pursue increasingly sophisticated tactics to pressure the government to abide by the constitution, the law, and international covenants.
- [Politics of Tiananmen. Just as in 1989 when the people blamed corrupt officials for profiteering that drove inflation, so NPC delegates have complained that workers are laid off for the good of enterprises while managers of the enterprises accept large bribes, leading to enterprise collapse. Leaders may be forced to consider further marginal revision of the verdict on Tiananmen. (They now speak vaguely of "political disturbance" rather than "counter-revolutionary turmoil.") Some suggested using a trial (for corruption) of the former mayor of Beijing to further defuse the issue by blaming him for "misleading" Deng Xiaoping and other leaders with his reports on the students' motives and plans. Li Peng, still second-ranking party leader, would feel threatened by this, and the leadership would certainly split over bolder gestures to

exonerate former party chief Zhao Ziyang and provide amnesty for exiles, even though doing so would shore up regime legitimacy and help reverse the brain drain.

- Complex generational dynamics. Technocrats now in power, shaped by the Soviet command system, have difficulty relating to the younger Chinese on whom they must rely for advice and staffing to deal with complex socioeconomic and international problems. The youngest of these, in their 20s and 30s, have a practical and competitive mindset, an orientation to the future, disdain for outmoded talk of Marxism and revolution, and a strong individualist, antiauthoritarian strain. Although they share nationalistic goals with their elders, they are more open to fulfilling them through full immersion in global regimes that set new parameters for China's political and economic options. Jiang and Zhu, with their strong personal attachments to two of China's premier universities, may prove flexible enough to gain the support of this rising urban elite of professionals and entrepreneurs. But they will find it hard to accommodate the in-between "Cultural Revolution generation" of former Red Guards and younger siblings who were sent to the country-side for the decade preceding Mao's death and are now in their forties and fifties. This group bears strong grievances against the party-state, as shown by their leadership in the dissident community backing populist change. A significant turning point came with the stepped-up suppression of political dissidents, unauthorized publications, and related activities beginning in November 1998. Jiang Zemin, Li Peng, and others strongly endorsed the suppression.

U.S. and Chinese observers thought that the firm emphasis on tighter political control would continue through 1999 and possibly longer because of a number of factors:

- Regime concern over growing unemployment and related social instability as a result of SOE and government bureaucracy streamlining;
- A perceived need to curb dissidents emboldened by Beijing's endorsement of UN human rights covenants and China's multifaceted dialogues with the United Nations, the United States, and others in the West;
- Regime concern that major decennial anniversaries in 1999 (for example, the eightieth anniversary of the 1919 May 4th movement, the tenth anniversary of the 1989 Tiananmen incident of June 4, 1989, and the fiftieth anniversary of the establishment of the PRC on October 1, 1949) could provide catalysts for disruptive behavior.[37]

Trends in Military Affairs

There has been more continuity and less controversy over recent military policies and developments than over policies and developments dealing with economic and political reforms and related social stability. China's 1998 defense budget increased official defense spending by about 13 percent—a real increase of some 8 percent. But this was only part of the story, with additional revenue coming from other ministerial allocations and from PLA commercial enterprises. In mid-1998, Jiang Zemin announced a major shift in policy, calling on the PLA to cut its ties with commercial enterprises. The severance of ties was reported as completed in December 1998, though many details regarding compensation, employee transfers, and other issues remained to be worked out. Estimates of the total allocations for the PLA range widely, with some putting the figure at more than Japan spends on defense. But even the lower estimates contrast with cutbacks elsewhere in Asia as a result of the economic downturn. As China sustains its defense spending, it will make relative gains. But it still finds it hard to keep up with constantly changing military technologies, and China will not be a match for U.S. or Japanese armed forces for decades.[38]

Changing Philosophy

Lessons from allied operations in the Middle East and from the U.S. reaction to the Taiwan Straits crisis of 1996 prompted the PLA into reconsidering its strategy. The philosophy of a people's war of attrition has given way since the mid-80s to one of "active defense," for which the PLA aims to develop (albeit from a low base) a high-tech rapid deployment capability with a streamlined command structure, advanced information warfare (including better surveillance capability), and high-performance precision-guided munitions.

With no current threat to China's land borders, the PLA's priority is to build up its maritime force-projection and strategic-missile capability to provide military options for successfully blockading or invading Taiwan should diplomacy fail; to reinforce sovereignty claims in the South China Sea; and to deter others, particularly the United States, from interfering in China's maritime and other areas of interest.

Restructuring

The army aims to reduce the standing force by 500,000, bringing it down to 1.6 million by the year 2000. While the force is large in global terms, only a few divisions will be prepared for rapid deployment. The navy has introduced modern Russian Kilo-class conventional submarines and is planning to acquire Sovremenny destroyers—complete with supersonic antiship missiles and helicopters after 2000. The air force is buying more long-range Russian SU-27 fighters and reportedly is interested in the greater-capability SU-30 multirole aircraft, as well as the latest air-to-air missiles. Combined with plans for airborne surveillance, in-flight refueling, and both cruise and ballistic missile developments, these new acquisitions would provide a significant offshore deterrent capability to support China's interests in the region. And China aspires to an aircraft carrier—though operationally it could not do this for over a decade.

China faces significant problems in modernizing its military. The defense budget is stretched by the size of the force and will allow only incremental improvements. The PLA—hampered by low education levels, undeveloped tactics, and often primitive logistic support—is having difficulty assimilating high-tech equipment. Problems exist in indigenous design, development, manufacture, and support for technologically sophisticated systems—indigenous weapon platforms and systems are often poor in quality and unreliable—and China remains reliant on Russia and others for support.

The critical aspects of modern maritime warfare that China has yet to master include joint war fighting doctrine, combined operations, anti-submarine warfare capabilities, shipborne air defense, and replenishment at sea. Lack of proficiency in these skills would work to China's disadvantage in any naval engagement.

Looking to the future, China's push for a modern, effective fighting force, commensurate with its global standing, will yield results only slowly. And it is some way yet from possessing the capability to sustain a deployed force offshore—for example in Taiwan—though it will have, within a few years, a modest maritime capability to support its sovereignty claims. Even so, the PLA's modernization will generate concern, especially as nearby countries affected by the economic crisis apply the brakes to their own modernization plan. This in turn will highlight the importance of the U.S. security commitment to the Asia-Pacific region.

Politics in the PLA have been managed relatively smoothly. PLA elders Liu Huaqing and Zhang Zhen retired at the Fifteenth Party Congress and have been succeeded by Chi Haotian and Zhang Wannian, though the latter do not have the senior party rank (Politburo Standing Committee membership) enjoyed by Liu Huaqing.

Ongoing reform efforts included the appointment of a respected technocratic civilian minister to direct the Commission for Science, Technology, and Industry for National Defense (COSTIND). The new director, Liu Jibin, was a vice minister of finance and seems to have a mandate to curb abuses in the purchasing of military equipment and in entrepreneurial activities by the PLA. Jiang Zemin's subsequent injunction against PLA involvement with business underlines this reformist trend.[39]

Recent Directions in Environmental Policy

Usually getting relatively little attention as Chinese leaders focus on the need for rapid economic development, environmental concerns have received more priority from Beijing authorities in recent years. In 1998, Chinese officials took pains to focus on problems in rural areas and linked environmental issues with family planning.[40]

China's environment—not good to begin with—has deteriorated alarmingly during two decades of unbridled economic growth. Only belatedly has the government paid attention to the ecological consequences. Leaders have begun to take the problem seriously.

Premier Li Peng, declaring his intent to be the environmental premier, raised the issue's profile over the past decade. Premier Zhu Rongji's commitment to environmental issues remains to be tested, but among his first acts was to upgrade China's EPA to ministerial status as the State Environmental Protection Administration (SEPA), not an easy step during a major government downsizing.

SEPA chief Xie Zhenhua has called for tightening law enforcement and establishing a public supervision system, setting long-term goals of marked improvement by 2030 and a healthy environment by 2050. He faces an uphill battle. In late 1997 the government announced it had allocated about $22 billion for pollution control and environmental protection during the years 1998-2000, but independent assessments estimate it will cost much more just to clean up the mess left behind by lax enforcement of existing regulations.

Environmental officials have begun focusing attention on rural areas, where pollution is virtually uncontrolled. Township and village enterprises discharge half of all industrial pollutants, according to Chinese studies, and only 40 percent of their industrial waste water is treated, compared with 80 percent in big urban plants. In the years 1996-1997 China shut down some 65,000 small factories, concentrating on such major polluters as leather, printing and dyeing, coking, and paper mills.

In 1998 Chinese leaders held a number of conferences devoted to addressing jointly the problems of environment and population. President Jiang, Li Peng, and other top officials told the fora that there must be no slackening of efforts to control population growth; officials estimate China's population will reach 1.6 billion by 2050. Symbolizing the continued high priority of this effort was the retention of the State Family Planning Commission, despite a major reduction in the number of government ministries.

With family planning largely institutionalized and highly effective among urban residents, Chinese officials have turned their attention to rural areas and rural migrants to big cities. Increasingly, officials and experts see the control of rural population growth and emigration to urban areas as intimately tied to local development and poverty alleviation efforts. Development, in turn, has exacerbated environmental problems, necessitating a more comprehensive approach.

Economic development and changing social norms also affect old methods of enforcing family planning. Though quotas and coercive measures still prevail in many poor or remote areas, leaders have pressed for a shift from coercion to improved education, provision of services, and voluntary compliance.

In sum, post-Deng leaders are preoccupied with a wide range of pressing domestic concerns. Many of these concerns are aggravated by international developments, notably the Asian economic crisis. On the whole, the generally pragmatic and more technically competent Chinese leaders of today have made progress in their reform initiatives, but there is almost no chance that they will finish the jobs they have set out for themselves. Meanwhile, economic reforms and social change have added to internal pressures for political change. The top PRC leaders are disinclined to allow significant political change as they deal with numerous economic and social problems. The renewed suppression of dissent in late 1998 underlined the PRC leadership's determination to maintain "stability" as it endeavors to sustain economic momentum and social order amid sometimes grim regional and global economic conditions. There is little sign of serious division among senior PRC leaders at present, though the likelihood of factionalism and conflict would probably increase if China faced a major internal or foreign policy crisis; as the Jiang Zemin generation retires in a few years, up-and-coming leaders also may dispute over leadership positions and influence.

Notes

1. See, among others, Andrew Nathan, *China's Transition*, New York: Columbia University Press, 1998.

2. See, among others, Denny Roy, *China's Foreign Relations*, Lanham, Md.: Rowman & Littlefield, 1998.

3. Chinese officials and specialists repeatedly noted these tasks during meetings in Beijing and Washington in 1997.

4. See, among others, Barry Naughton, "China's Economy: Buffeted from Within and Without," *Current History*, September 1998, pp. 273-278.

5. Western media continue to probe for signs of such leadership division. See, in particular, coverage of reported PRC leadership maneuvers in frequent articles by Willy Wo-Lap Lam in the *South China Morning Post*.

6. Consultations with U.S. and PRC officials, Beijing, January 7-10, 1999.

7. See, among others, "Breakthrough Must Be Effected in State Enterprise Report," *People's Daily*, January 13, 1998; "A Major Issue Affecting the Overall Situation," *People's Daily*, editorial, May 17, 1998.

8. See, among others, Dorothy Solinger, "The Potential for Urban Unrest," in *Is China Stable? Assessing the Factors*, ed. David Shambaugh, Washington, D.C.: Sigur Center for Asian Studies, 1998, pp. 73-92.

9. For conflicting assessments of how Chinese authorities have been dealing with these problems, see Trish Saywell, "Steady as She Goes," *Far Eastern Economic Review*, October 1, 1998, pp. 70-72; Lung Hua, "Key Topics for Beidaihe Meeting," *Hong Kong Hsin Pao*, July 22, 1998, p. 15; and "Will China Be Next?" *Economist*, October 24, 1998, pp. 17-18.

10. For background, see Geremie Barme, "Spring Clamor and Autumnal Silence: Cultural Control in China," *Current History*, September 1998, pp. 257-262. See also Benjamin Kanlim, "Toppled Chinese Leader Issues Tiananmen Plea," *Reuters* (internet version), June 24, 1998.

11. See Margaret Pearson, "China's Emerging Business Class: Democracy's Harbinger?" *Current History*, September 1998, pp. 268-272; Susan Lawrence, "False Dawn," *Far Eastern Economic Review*, October 1, 1998, pp. 26-27; Elizabeth Rosenthal, "U.N. Rights Official, Back from China, Sees Better Attitude," *New York Times*, September 16, 1998.

12. June Teufel Dreyer, "The Potential for Instability in Minority Regions," in *Is China Stable?* ed. Shambaugh, pp. 123-141.

13. In addition to Western media coverage at the time of the congress, see, among others, "China's Ninth National People's Congress—Results, Issues and U.S. Policy Concerns," Congressional Research Service (CRS), Library of Congress, Washington, D.C., March 24, 1998, pp. 1-9.

14. See "Zhu Rongji's News Conference," Beijing Central Television Program One Network in Mandarin, March 19, 1998, carried by U.S. Foreign Broadcast Information Service (FBIS) (internet version).

15. See "Fact Sheet: Achievements of U.S.-China Summit," White House, Washington, D.C., June 29, 1998 (internet version).

16. In addition to sources noted above, see Willy Wo-Lap Lam, "Zhu Tightens Grip on Power," *South China Morning Post*, April 19, 1998, p. 5.

17. Willy Wo-Lap Lam, "Jiang Zemin, Hu Jintao to 'Expand' Influence," *South China Morning Post*, March 17, 1998, p. 3.

18. "China's Ninth National People's Congress," p. 2.

19. This is based on Zhu's lengthy March 19, 1998, news conference. See note 14, above.

20. "Li Lanqing Addresses Davos Economic Meeting," *Xinhua* (internet version), January 31, 1998.

21. See, among others, David Shambaugh, "The Chinese Leadership: Cracks in the Facade?" in *Is China Stable?* ed. Shambaugh, pp. 23-34; Richard Baum, "The Fifteenth Party Congress: Jiang Takes Command?" *China Quarterly*, vol. 153, March 1998; and H. Lyman Miller, "Preparing for Change with Promises of Continuity,"

Chinese Business Review, January-February 1998.

22. For perspectives on these issues, see "China's Economic Prospects" and "The Political System," in Han Binnendijk and Ronald Montaperto, eds., *Strategic Trends in China*, Washington, D.C.: National Defense University Press, pp. 33-46.

23. See "China's Ninth National People's Congress," p. 4.

24. "Zhu Rongji's News Conference."

25. See Nancy Bernkopf Tucker, "A Precarious Balance: Clinton and China," *Current History*, September 1998, pp. 243-249.

26. Reviewed in *China: Recent Policy Priorities—Implications for U.S. Interests and Policy Goals*, Washington, D.C.: Library of Congress, CRS Report 98-802F, September 23, 1998, p. 11.

27. See, among others, *The South China Morning Post*, May 20, 1998.

28. "Jiang Zemin: Laid Off Workers Top Priority," *Xinhua* (internet version), May 14, 1998.

29. The floods were a central feature of Western media coverage of China during July and August 1998.

30. On recent economic trends, see especially weekly coverage in the *Far Eastern Economic Review*.

31. See Geremie Barme, "Spring Clamor and Autumnal Silence," *Current History*, September 1998, pp. 257-262; Margaret Pearson, "China's Emerging Business Class: Democracy's Harbinger," *Current History*, September 1998, pp. 268-272; and Tyrene White, "Village Elections," *Current History*, September 1998, pp. 263-267.

32. For background, see the discussion by Carol Hamrin, David Shambaugh, and other prominent U.S. China experts at the conference, "Is China Unstable? Assessing the Factors," Sigur Center, George Washington University, Washington, D.C., June 19, 1998. The conference papers are published in *Is China Stable?* ed. Shambaugh.

33. The following analysis replays that seen in *China: Recent Policy Priorities,* pp. 13-14, which was taken largely from presentations by Carol Hamrin and others at the Sigur Center conference noted above. See also, among others, Michael Laris, "Chinese Scholars Speak Out on Rights Issues," *Washington Post,* September 8, 1998; Willy Wo-Lap Lam, "Jiang Walking a Tightrope," *South China Morning Post,* July 1, 1998, p 19; Willy Wo-Lap Lam, "Beijing Said Cool on Forming Plan for Political Reform," *South China Morning Post*, July 11, 1998, p. 7; Willy Wo-Lap Lam, "Clean Government Crusade," *South China Morning Post*, July 22, 1998, p. 19.

34. Cited in *China: Recent Policy Priorities*, p. 13.

35. See especially Susan Lawrence, "False Dawn," *Far Eastern Economic Review*, October 1, 1998, pp. 26-27.

36. See Bruce Dickson, "Political Instability at the Middle and Lower Levels," in *Is China Stable?* ed. Shambaugh, pp. 35-50.

37. Consultations, Beijing, January 7-10, 1999.

38. This section is a synthesis from Hans Binnendijk and Ronald Montaperto eds., *Strategic Trends in China*, Washington, D.C.: National Defense University Press, 1998; "A Strategic Approach to Understanding the PLA: The Staunton Hill Conference"; *China Strategic Review* 3, 1 (spring 1998), entire issue; and *China: Recent Policy*

Priorities, pp. 14-16.

39. See, among others, *Washington Post*, July 23, 1998, p. 1.

40. See "PRC UN Envoy Shen Guofang on Sustainable Development," *Xinhua* (internet version), April 30, 1998; Chen Fengying, "Environmental Protection—A Key to Sustainable Global Development," *Contemporary International Relations*, Beijing, November 1997, pp. 12-23; Zhao Shaoqin, "Clean Coal to Combat Pollution," *China Daily*, September 28, 1998; Shen Bin, "Vehicle Emissions Policies Force Polluters off Roads," *China Daily*, September 28, 1998. Also see publications in the *China Environment Series*, Washington, D.C.: Woodrow Wilson Center, 1998, especially Kenneth Lieberthal, "China's Growing System and Its Impact on Environmental Policy Implementation." See also Elizabeth Economy, *The Case Study of China*, Cambridge, Mass.: American Academy of Arts and Sciences, 1997; and Vaclav Smil and Mao Yushi, *The Economic Costs of China's Environmental Degradation*, Cambridge, Mass.: American Academy of Arts and Sciences, 1998.

Chapter 3

Relations with the United States

Chinese policies and practices interact most directly with U.S. interests and policies in the realm of foreign affairs. Although Chinese leaders' recent policy priorities focus on domestic development and stability, and China's generally cooperative approach to foreign affairs is rooted in these domestic determinants, Chinese foreign policies and behaviors are often critically important to the United States. Thus, this study examines in detail Chinese policies and practices toward the United States and other world powers and regions, as well as other salient aspects of Beijing's recent approach to foreign affairs, before arriving at a concluding assessment as to what Chinese priorities mean for U.S. interests and policies.

Once it became clear to Chinese leaders that the strategic basis of Sino-American relations had been destroyed by the end of the cold war and the collapse of the Soviet Union, and that political relations would take a long time to return to normal after the trauma of the Tiananmen incident, Chinese leaders worked throughout the 1990s to reestablish "normalized" relations with the United States on terms as advantageous as possible to China. Consistently suspicious of U.S. intentions and well aware of fundamental ideological, strategic, and other differences with the United States, Chinese officials settled on a bifurcated view. This held that U.S. leaders often saw their interests as well served by cooperating with China, and would extend the hand of "engagement" to the Chinese government. But U.S. leaders were also seen as suspicious of Chinese intentions and influence, and determined to "contain" China's rising power and block China's assertion of influence in world affairs. The Chinese emphasis on cooperating with the "soft" U.S. "hand" of engagement or reacting to the "hard" U.S. "hand" of containment varied in the 1990s, though the trend since 1996 has been to emphasize the positive and minimize the negative on the part of both the Chinese and U.S. administrations.[1] It is important to note that Chinese officials often explicitly recognize that the division between perceived U.S. "engagement" and U.S. "containment" is too stark, and that in fact U.S. policy toward China is made up of a number of positive and negative incentives. They often add that specific U.S. policy actions toward China contain elements of both "engagement" and "containment." In short, the terms engagement and containment appear to be used by Chinese officials not so much to indicate specific U.S. policy approaches but rather to indicate positive and negative features of U.S. policy toward China. Nonetheless, Chinese officials continue to refer regularly to the so-called "two hands" of U.S. policy—engagement and containment.

Presidents George Bush and Bill Clinton were clear about U.S. differences with China in several key areas. The United States was determined to expend such a vast array of resources on defense that it would remain the world's dominant power, and also the dominant military power in East Asia, for the foreseeable future. The United States would continue to provide strong support, including sophisticated arms, to Taiwan; and the United States endeavored to use growing government, commercial, and other nongovernmental contacts with China, as well as other means, to foster an atmosphere promoting political pluralism and change in the authoritarian Chinese communist system. For its part, Beijing strove for a post-cold war world order of greater "multi-polarity"; China would be one of the poles and would have greater opportunity for advantageous maneuvering than in a superpower-dominated order. China strove for a gradual decline in U.S. power and influence in East Asia and globally. And Beijing called for cutbacks in U.S. military sales and other support to Taiwan in order to help create advantageous conditions for the reunification of the island with the "motherland." Finally, the Chinese Communist Party leaders were determined to maintain the primacy of their rule in the face of economic, social, and political challenges at home and abroad, including challenges supported by the United States.

A critical problem for Chinese leaders in dealing with the United States in the 1990s involved mixing their strategies and goals with those of the United States in ways advantageous to China. In general, the Chinese approach focused on trying to work constructively with U.S. power, concentrating on areas of common ground and minimizing differences wherever possible. This was difficult to achieve, especially when U.S. policy concentrated on the stark differences between the United States and China over human rights, Taiwan, weapons proliferation, and trade issues. In some instances, Chinese officials would choose to confront the United States with threats of retaliation if the U.S. pursued pressure tactics against China. For the most part, however, Chinese leaders bided their time, endeavoring to avoid complications that would ensue from protracted confrontation with the United States. At bottom, they believed that China's growing economy and overall international importance would steadily win over international powers to a cooperative stance with China, and encourage politically important groups in the United States, especially business groups, to press for an accommodating U.S. approach to China. Following this general line of approach in the 1990s, Beijing managed to end its diplomatic isolation stemming from the Tiananmen incident, isolated the Clinton administration advocates of conditioning most favored nation (MFN) tariff treatment for China, and prompted the president to end this policy in 1994. And with the Sino-American summits of 1997 and 1998, Beijing clearly established the Chinese leaders as legitimate and respected actors in world affairs.

Chinese officials have been under no illusions as they have been dealing with what they have called the "two hands" of U.S. policy in the 1990s—the hand of "engagement" and the hand of "containment." But as they have repeatedly made clear to Western specialists and others, Chinese officials have seen it as in Chinese interests—whether they have liked it or not—to try to get along with the United States,[2] for the following reasons:

- Strategically, the United States has remained the world's sole superpower and poses the only potential strategic threat to Chinese national security for the foreseeable future. A confrontation with such a power would severely test Chinese strength and undermine Chinese economic and political programs.
- As the world's leading economic power, the United States has markets, technology, and investment important for Chinese modernization. It has also played an important role in international financial institutions heavily involved in China; Western financial actors and investors have viewed the status of U.S. relations with China as an important barometer determining the scope and depth of their involvement in China.
- Internationally, establishing cooperative relations with the United States facilitates smooth Chinese relations with Western and other powers that are close to Washington. Antagonistic U.S.-China relations would mean that China would have to work much harder, and presumably offer more in the way of economic and other concessions, to win over such powers.
- The United States continues to play a key strategic role in highly sensitive areas around China's periphery, notably Korea, Japan, the South China Sea, and especially Taiwan. Cooperative U.S.-Chinese relations allow Beijing to continue to focus on domestic priorities with

reasonable assurance that its vital interests in these sensitive areas will not be fundamentally jeopardized by antagonistic actions by the United States. Indeed, good U.S.-China relations tend to increase Chinese influence in these areas.

On balance, the record of Chinese relations with the United States in the 1990s shows considerable achievement for China. Beijing reestablished extensive high-level contacts with the U.S. administration and saw the end of most Tiananmen-related sanctions against China. By 1998, the Clinton administration appeared sincerely committed to pursuing a policy of generally accommodating engagement with China. U.S. administration officials endeavored to work closely with the Chinese administration to reduce differences over U.S. world primacy, the U.S. strategic posture in East Asia, U.S. support for Taiwan, and U.S. support for political pluralism in China. Chinese officials took satisfaction in the fact that the improvement in U.S.-China relations resulted much more from marked shifts toward accommodation of China's rising power and influence by the U.S. administration than from the adjustments made by the Chinese government in dealing with issues sensitive to the United States.[3]

While there were differing assessments among Chinese officials of the status and outlook of U.S.-Chinese relations, the prevailing view in 1999 was one of caution. There remained plenty of evidence that U.S. policy continued to have the hard hand of containment to go along with the seemingly accommodating engagement. Political forces in the United States, many interest groups, and the media still lined up against Chinese interests on a range of human rights concerns, strategic issues, Taiwan, and economic questions. Many Chinese officials remained suspicious of the ultimate motives of some members of the Clinton administration as well. As a result, Beijing remained privately wary as it continued to seek advantages by building cooperative relations.

Recent Relations

The Clinton administration's decision in 1993 to condition MFN status for China on progress in human rights issues posed a major problem for China. It was met indirectly by the rapid growth of the Chinese economy, which attracted a strong U.S. business interest, and the interest in turn of many U.S. visitors from Congress and the administration concerned with the growth of the U.S. economy and economic opportunity abroad.

By early 1994, Chinese officials were well aware that proponents for continuing human rights conditions on MFN treatment for China had become isolated in the administration, centering on the State Department. Earlier visits to China and other Chinese interaction with U.S. departments concerned with business, notably Treasury and Commerce, had made clear the private reservations among senior officials in these departments about the human rights linkage to MFN status. Moreover, U.S. business groups had moved into high gear in warning that conditioning MFN treatment could jeopardize U.S. access to the burgeoning Chinese market.[4]

Sino-American disagreements over human rights conditions in China and MFN status rose sharply during Secretary of State Warren Christopher's March 11-14, 1994, visit to Beijing. The debate called into question key elements of the Clinton administration's policy toward China. In particular, it cast doubt on earlier expectations that progress in narrowing U.S.-Chinese differences on human rights would lead to a Clinton administration decision to renew MFN tariff treatment for Chinese exports to the U.S. by the required deadline of June 1994. The MFN tariff status was widely seen as an essential ingredient in the rapidly growing U.S.-Chinese economic relationship (annual trade was then worth over $30 billion; U.S. investment was worth over $3 billion).[5]

The secretary went to Beijing to discuss human rights and other issues in part to make clear to the Chinese government what the United States expected China to do in order to meet conditions set out in a May 1993 U.S. executive order. That order granted MFN treatment to China for a year and said that the Chinese government had to meet specific conditions regarding human rights in order for President Clinton to grant MFN status for China in 1994.

Before and during Secretary Christopher's visit, Chinese leaders appeared defiant in the face of U.S. human rights requirements. Most notably, Chinese security forces detained prominent dissidents immediately prior to the secretary's arrival and also detained some Western journalists covering interaction between prominent Chinese dissidents and the Chinese security forces. In public interchange during the secretary's visit, Chinese leaders strongly warned against U.S. use of trade or other pressure to prompt changes in China's human rights policy.

China's public stance raised doubts about whether or not the Clinton administration would renew MFN trade status for China. It posed a serious dilemma for the administration as it attempted to balance American concerns about human rights conditions in China with American commercial and other concerns that would be jeopardized if MFN status were withdrawn.

The widely publicized, tough Chinese stance upset an earlier expectation that events were moving the Clinton administration toward renewal of China's MFN status. Although he entered office on a political platform sharply critical of Beijing's human rights and some other policies, President Clinton subsequently moderated his stance, allowing the renewal of MFN treatment for China in 1993 with certain human rights conditions. Later, the president and other administration officials adhered to a policy of "engagement" with the Chinese leaders. This involved renewed high-level exchanges long sought by China, including President Clinton's meeting with Chinese President Jiang Zemin in Seattle in November 1993. The expectation was that these exchanges would prove useful in reassuring Chinese leaders regarding American intentions, while providing a high-level channel through which to make clear to Beijing the U.S. expectations on human rights and other sensitive issues.

Members of Congress also engaged in intensive exchanges with Chinese leaders, with unprecedented numbers of members traveling to China during congressional recess periods in late 1993 and 1994. Many used their interaction to reinforce the administration's efforts to reassure Chinese leaders of U.S. intentions while making clear what was expected of China in order to allow U.S. renewal of MFN treatment.

Against this backdrop, a widely held U.S. expectation was that the extensive exchanges and other actions would prompt Chinese actions sufficient to meet the conditions set forth in the 1993 executive order and allow renewal of MFN treatment for China. Clinton administration officials repeatedly emphasized their view in late 1993 and 1994 that China had not yet done nearly enough to meet the conditions set forth in the executive order. They held out the hope that Chinese leaders would build on earlier measures—improve human rights conditions and take steps to meet the requirements of the executive order.

China's tough public posture during the Christopher trip was due to several reasons:

- The U.S.'s "didactic" style. Prior to his arrival in Beijing, Secretary Christopher went on record several times voicing U.S. concerns that China must meet specific human rights conditions in order to assure U.S. MFN treatment. Reportedly, this prompted Chinese leaders to react strongly to such overt outside "pressure."
- Shattuck's meeting with Wei Jingsheng. Prior to the secretary's visit, Assistant Secretary of State for Human Rights Affairs John Shattuck traveled to Beijing for talks on human rights concerns. While there, he met privately with leading dissident Wei Jingsheng. Wei subsequently disclosed the meeting to the media. Chinese officials reportedly were infuriated by this meeting, which they would not have approved. The detention of dissidents prior to Secretary Christopher's visit was

designed to prevent such a meeting taking place between the U.S. secretary and Chinese dissidents.

- The National People's Congress and perceived dissident activism. The secretary's visit coincided with the annual session of China's National People's Congress, and with a perceived increase in actions by Chinese political dissidents like Wei Jingsheng to push for political change. It also occurred against a backdrop of heightened Chinese sensitivity to the maintenance of strict political order and stability as a result of leadership uncertainties, including the frail health of senior leader Deng Xiaoping and the difficulty Beijing was encountering in controlling some of the economic, social, and other side effects of rapid economic growth (for example, corruption, inflation, and unequal distribution of wealth). Consequently, Beijing was inclined to clamp down on dissidents who might "disrupt" the public order.

- Chinese bargaining tactics. Most importantly, Chinese leaders perceived that the time was right to press the United States to alter its human rights policy, especially the linkage with MFN renewal. In particular, they saw the Clinton administration leaders as divided on the issue, with U.S. commercial officials—strongly backed by the U.S. business community—emphasizing the importance of continued close U.S.-Chinese economic relations. They saw members of the U.S. Congress as much more supportive of maintaining MFN treatment for China than in the recent past—a change stemming in part from the numerous congressional visits to China to observe and benefit from the vibrant economic conditions there. Meanwhile, U.S. political allies but economic competitors like Japan, Germany, and France were sending high-level officials to China, underlining their willingness to help fill the vacuum of economic opportunities in China should U.S.-Chinese economic relations falter with a withdrawal of MFN tariff treatment. As a result, Beijing used a tough stance during the Christopher visit to isolate those in the U.S. government favoring linkage of MFN treatment and human rights conditions and force U.S. leaders to change their policy or lose the considerable economic opportunities in the Chinese market.

Chinese officials were generally pleased with President Clinton's May 26, 1994, decision to "delink" the U.S. granting of MFN treatment to China from U.S. consideration of Chinese human rights practices. They also welcomed votes in the House of Representatives on this issue on August 8, 1994, that appeared to support the president's new policy. Chinese commentators were anxious for the United States and China to take advantage of the improved atmosphere in bilateral relations to push for more far-reaching and comprehensive progress in the U.S.-Chinese relationship. From the Chinese perspective, progress was seen to involve the organizing of more and higher-level official visits; further easing of bilateral tensions over trade, proliferation, and human rights questions; easing of U.S. technology transfer restrictions concerning China; and avoiding U.S. policy initiatives on sensitive issues for China such as greater U.S. support for Taiwan and Tibet.[6]

U.S. officials placed more emphasis on the need to "solve problems" and to make further concrete progress on continued differences in Sino-U.S. relations before comprehensive forward movement in the relationship would be possible.[7] They emphasized that the two sides faced a host of trade problems (for example, mounting Chinese trade surpluses with the United States, intellectual property issues, market access problems, etc.), concerns over divergent human rights policies and practices, and strategic policy differences. These problems, along with strong U.S. domestic political sensitivities about China, made it appear unlikely that U.S. leaders would respond fully to Chinese calls for active U.S.-Chinese leadership efforts to push the relationship forward to a new stage of comprehensive cooperation.

Chinese Views of U.S. Motives, 1994

Chinese officials and other commentators at this time gave mixed assessments of the U.S. insistence on dealing with the problems of the relationship, and the seeming American reluctance to move forward comprehensively in Sino-American relations.[8] On the one hand, some Chinese commentators tended to agree with a number of U.S. observers in emphasizing the difficulties the Clinton administration faced in attempting to reconcile many competing interests in the United States in order to establish clear priorities and goals in U.S. foreign policy generally and policy toward China in particular. These difficulties were seen as lying behind the apparently mixed signals coming from the administration about China in the previous year, with some U.S. officials emphasizing the need for China to meet U.S. demands on human rights improvements, trade, and other issues; and others seemingly emphasizing the importance of close cooperation with China for American economic well-being and security interests in Asian and world affairs.

On the other hand, there appeared to be a widely held belief among Chinese officials that U.S. policy reflected, at bottom, a fear of China's growing economic, political, and military strength. In this view, U.S. policy was said to be designed to "hold back" or "impede" China's progress toward greater wealth and power. Specific examples cited to support this view of allegedly sinister U.S. motives included recent U.S. policy initiatives in support of Taiwan and Tibet, which were said to weaken China's national cohesion; the U.S. refusal to speed Chinese entry into the Generalized Agreement on Traffic and Trade (GATT) unless certain conditions were met; U.S. opposition to the Chinese bid to host the year 2000 Olympic Games; U.S. support for the "illegal" activities of Chinese dissidents; some U.S. observers' emphasis on China as a possible security threat to nearby countries and areas; and alleged U.S. support for a policy of "peaceful evolution" for China—a policy designed to bring down the Communist Party regime there through incremental, nonviolent means.

Chinese commentators and officials holding this view were not persuaded by arguments from Americans that this Chinese perspective had little justification in fact. Chinese officials and U.S. experts resident in China said that this kind of negative, conspiratorial view of U.S. policy toward China was widely prevalent among Chinese officials at senior levels and supporting intellectuals and experts. It was asserted that the political atmosphere in Beijing was such that Chinese observers who disagreed with this view of U.S. motives were unable or unwilling to challenge the premises and factual basis of the believers in conspiracy, who reportedly enjoyed senior-level official backing.

The Lee Teng-hui Visit—Impact on PRC Views of the United States

Chinese views of U.S. policy took a turn for the worse following President Clinton's reversal of past policy in permitting Taiwan President Lee Teng-hui to make an ostensibly private visit to Cornell University in June 1995. Beijing responded to Lee's visit with strongly worded protests, suspension or cancellation of a number of important dialogues with the United States, suspension of most important ongoing dialogues with Taiwan, and widely publicized military exercises, including ballistic missile tests, near Taiwan. China's invective was accompanied by dark warnings of what China would do (that is, invade Taiwan) if Taiwan were to move toward de jure independence, and admonitions suggesting that Beijing foresaw a protracted cold war with the United States over Taiwan and a number of other issues.[9]

U.S. efforts to reassure Beijing about U.S. intentions and Beijing's reassessment of the costs and benefits of its hard line against the U.S. and Taiwan led to some thawing in U.S.-PRC relations, though PRC pressure against Taiwan continued. An October 24, 1995, meeting between U.S. President Bill Clinton and China's President Jiang Zemin proceeded smoothly despite earlier wrangling over the protocol level and site of the meeting.[10] U.S. and Chinese officials endeavored to portray the session in New York's Lincoln Center as the most positive of the three face-to-face encounters between the chief executives. The meeting achieved no notable breakthrough in U.S.-Chinese relations, but it was accompanied by other tentative signs that both governments were interested in improved relations. These included China's agreement to the appointment of U.S. Ambassador-designate James Sasser, the return of China's ambassador to the United States after his abrupt withdrawal in June, and the U.S. dispatch of Assistant Secretary of Defense Joseph Nye for talks in Beijing designed to resume the high-level defense discussions that had been suspended in mid-1995.[11]

The U.S. decision despite Chinese objections to allow the Taiwan president to visit the United States in mid-1995 not only resulted in the suspended diplomatic and other official ties noted above, but reinforced existing PRC suspicions that the United States had decided to "contain" China in a new cold war in Asia.[12] This negative view of U.S. policy held that U.S. government officials basically opposed the rising power of China under Beijing's communist system and were taking a variety of measures in various policy areas, including Taiwan, in order to "hold back" China's power. Events cited by Chinese officials and other leaders of opinion to support their view ranged from U.S. statements about the security environment in East Asia and the South China Sea, statements that were seen as directed against China, to the pressure brought by the United States against China's trade practices, human rights policies, and proliferation of technology for weapons of mass destruction.

In general, Chinese officials and opinion leaders maintained that despite lively debate in the United States over many issues in policy toward China, U.S. policy makers were acting as though China's growing power posed a threat to the United States that must be countered by weakening China's strength through security, economic, political, and other measures. Presumably because senior PRC leaders were as yet unwilling to confront the U.S. leadership directly on this question, the top Chinese officials and authoritative government commentary often refrained from directly accusing the United States of this intent to "hold down" and weaken China. Nevertheless, Chinese officials and intellectuals repeatedly affirmed in private conversations with U.S. observers that senior Chinese leaders did indeed harbor such sinister views of U.S. intentions.[13]

Many Chinese officials and intellectuals traced the alleged U.S. desire to weaken and hold down China at least to the reevaluation of U.S. policy toward China following the 1989 Tiananmen massacre and the concurrent collapse of the Soviet Empire and the end of the cold war. At that time, they claimed, U.S. leaders took a number of measures in the form of economic, military, and political sanctions against China that were designed to help bring down Beijing's communist system. U.S. leaders were not seen as fearful of China's power under Beijing's communist rule; rather, they expected the

Chinese regime in a few years time would be swept away by the same forces of history that had removed their ideological comrades in Europe and elsewhere.

This did not happen as anticipated, and the PRC began to grow at a remarkable rate of economic development beginning in 1992 and continuing into the 1990s. China's economic growth was accompanied by greater military power, successful expansion of China's foreign relations, and greater self-confidence and assertiveness by Chinese leaders at home and in Asian and world affairs. In response, the Chinese claimed, the U.S. began to step up its efforts in a wide range of areas to curb the growth of China's power. From this viewpoint, the evidence of such U.S. efforts included the following:

- Stronger U.S. support for Taiwan, Tibet, and Hong Kong as entities separate from PRC control. U.S. support for the Taiwan president's visit and provisions on Taiwan, Hong Kong, and Tibet in concurrent U.S. foreign policy legislation (for example, H.R. 1561, S. 908) were viewed as designed to keep the PRC preoccupied with protecting China's sovereignty and territorial integrity and to reduce its ability to exert influence elsewhere.
- Pressure on Chinese trade and other economic practices. The years 1994-1995 saw strong U.S. efforts to press Beijing to observe intellectual property rights, to open its markets to outside goods and services, and to meet strict conditions before gaining entry into the World Trade Organization (WTO). Chinese leaders apparently saw these steps as being designed to help to keep the PRC economically weaker and less influential than it would otherwise be.
- Restrictions against the export of military-related and other high technology to China and pressure on China to restrict its sales of technology and equipment that could be used for weapons of mass destruction. For example, the United States maintained its own technology restrictions against China and warned others (including Russia) about the dangers of arms or military technology sales to China—steps interpreted by Beijing as designed to keep China from becoming militarily stronger.
- Warnings against Chinese assertiveness in Asia. The Clinton administration's February 1995 statement about the security environment in East Asia[14] was seen in Beijing as implicitly critical of China's assertiveness and lack of transparency in flexing its military power in the region. At the same time, the administration articulated a security approach to the region that gave renewed emphasis to Japan as the center of U.S.

attention in the face of regional uncertainties—a statement also viewed with some suspicion in China.[15] In May 1995, the administration stated a stronger position on U.S. interests in the South China Sea—a statement coming after China had caused serious concerns in the region by taking unilateral military action in South China Sea islands claimed by others. Meanwhile, Congress was considering legislation (H.R. 1561, S. Res. 97) that took aim at China's assertive actions in the South China Sea. Some in Congress added that the United States should move ahead to full diplomatic relations with Vietnam as a way to counter PRC expansion.[16]

U.S. analysts differed on the importance of such conspiracy-based Chinese views on U.S.-China relations.[17] On one side were those who judged that Chinese government leaders were deliberately and cynically manipulating Chinese opinion for ulterior motives. Thus, Chinese criticism of the United States was seen as part of a broader effort by PRC leaders to use nationalism and nationalistic themes, which enjoyed widespread support in China, to fill the ideological void caused by the collapse of world communism, and to help shore up the sagging prestige of the PRC leaders in the wake of the Tiananmen massacre. In particular, by associating the policies and practices of the Beijing regime with Chinese nationalism, PRC leaders were able to portray criticism of those policies by the United States and others as affronts to the Chinese nation and the Chinese people. This could have the side effect of alleviating the need to deal with the substance of complaints.

Meanwhile, another perceived ulterior motive of Chinese officials was to put the U.S. side on the defensive. In particular, U.S. officials anxious to restore a meaningful dialogue with China would, presumably, be expected to "prove" their intentions with some gestures designed to show the Chinese that their conspiratorial view of U.S. policy was not correct. Of course, such gestures would involve unilateral U.S. steps of benefit to China. Chinese leaders were said to have used similar techniques against Japan in the 1970s and 1980s—whipping up sometimes strident media campaigns against Japan's alleged "militarist" designs against China and the rest of Asia until Japan agreed to several billions of dollars of grants or low-interest loans for China. Once the money was promised, the charges of Japanese "militarism" subsided.[18]

A very different view came from U.S. analysts who saw the Chinese leaders' conspiratorial view of U.S. policy as misguided but genuine. They believed it reflected a combination of U.S. pressures on China, the suspicious view of the outside world held by many Chinese leaders, and the pressures of domestic Chinese politics during a period of leadership succession. The latter pressures were thought to incline PRC leaders to adhere to more narrow, somewhat chauvinistic views of foreign powers, especially those like the United States with an ability to threaten Chinese interests. U.S. analysts argued that this Chinese perception had now reached a point where PRC leaders were convinced that the U.S. government was "out to get them" and would almost certainly interpret future U.S. policy actions toward China along those lines.

U.S. specialists with extensive contacts with Chinese officials and experts in China and the United States generally supported the latter view of China's intentions with the following points:

- The Clinton administration's reversal on the Lee Teng-hui visit was said to have undermined those in the Chinese leadership arguing for a more moderate approach toward the United States. As most of China's American specialists had reportedly predicted that the administration would stick to its declared policy and not allow Lee to visit, they were discredited when the U.S. president reversed the policy and allowed Lee to come. The way was then open for advocates of a more suspicious view of U.S. intentions to pursue a harder line toward the United States.
- The administration's reversal also prompted most PRC specialists on the United States to "play it safe" and go along with the strongly negative view of U.S. policy at the time, even though personally they may not have agreed with the negative view.
- Finally, Lee's determination to visit the United States appears to have undermined PRC President Jiang Zemin's efforts in January 1995 to encourage a dialogue with Taiwan's leaders on the basis of a flexible-sounding PRC eight-point proposal. In the view of PRC specialists, Jiang's "flexible" approach on Taiwan was now seen as naive, as PRC leaders began to view Lee Teng-hui as determined to pursue Taiwan's independence from the mainland.

Results of the Crisis Over Taiwan—1996

While keeping its deep suspicion of U.S. intentions within limits and showing more outward moderation to the United States in late 1995, Beijing kept up heavy pressure, including intimidating military exercises, against Taiwan. The exercises were timed to coincide with Taiwan's legislative elections in December 1995 and presidential elections in March 1996. Because of the escalating pressure on Taiwan and other factors, the Clinton administration—under strong congressional and media pressure—reversed its virtual silence on the Chinese exercises near Taiwan. Escalating U.S. official statements in February 1996 led to a large show of force by two U.S. aircraft-carrier battle groups in the Taiwan area in March 1996. Following Lee Teng-hui's impressive 54 percent showing in a field of four candidates in the March 1996 elections, the PRC halted its provocative military exercises and the U.S. forces withdrew without incident.

Beijing derived mixed lessons from the experience. On the positive side, Chinese officials claimed several achievements resulting from the PRC's forceful reaction to the Lee Teng-hui visit to the United States:[19]

- It intimidated Taiwan, at least temporarily, from taking further assertive actions to lobby in the U.S. Congress and elsewhere for greater international recognition;
- It prompted second thoughts by some pro-Taiwan advocates in Congress as to the wisdom of pursuing their agenda at this time;
- It resulted in heightened sensitivity by the Clinton administration regarding PRC policy toward Taiwan, including official U.S. assurances to the PRC that any future visits by Taiwanese leaders would only occur under exceptional circumstances;
- It caused at least some pro-independence advocates in Taiwan to reassess their previous claims that the PRC was bluffing in its warnings against Taiwan's independence, and to adjust their claims that a PRC attack on Taiwan, even if prompted by a unilateral Taiwanese declaration of independence, would result in U.S. military intervention on the side of Taiwan;
- It dampened the enthusiasm of some international officials to have their governments follow the U.S. lead in granting greater recognition to Taiwan's government and leader.

At the same time, Beijing appeared to have overplayed its hand in pressing the United States for "concrete" pledges against Taiwanese official visits and in pressing Taiwan's people to abandon Lee Teng-hui in favor of a leader more committed to reunification with the mainland. Beijing also appeared to recognize that it was not productive to accuse the United States of attempting to contain China and shun dialogue with the United States until the United States proved otherwise. Such accusations merely strengthened the hands of those U.S. officials who were deeply suspicious of, or hostile to, the Chinese government and weakened the arguments of U.S. officials in the Clinton administration and Congress who argued for a more flexible, moderate U.S. approach to China. Given China's perceived need to sustain a working relationship with the United States for the foreseeable future, Beijing officials tried through President Jiang's meeting with

President Clinton and other means to find and develop common ground in U.S.-China relations while playing down bilateral differences to some degree.

In the wake of the October 24, 1995, Clinton-Jiang summit meeting in New York, Chinese officials privately made known China's interest in sustaining a "smooth" relationship with the United States in general and the Clinton administration in particular.[20] Some Chinese and U.S. officials said that whereas Beijing had appeared prepared in mid-1995 to freeze contacts with the Clinton administration, awaiting the results of the 1996 U.S. elections, Beijing now appeared to have judged that endeavoring to work constructively with the current U.S. government was in China's best interests. In particular, U.S. and Chinese officials said that Beijing now saw the prospect of a possibly difficult year ahead in the U.S.'s China policy as a result of initiatives from a wide array of critics of the Chinese government in the U.S. Congress and the media, and the possibility that China policy might become a contentious issue in the 1996 presidential campaign, with a possible negative impact on China's interests. As a result, officials believed that Beijing had decided to attempt to work more closely with the Clinton administration.

Beijing also appeared determined to do a better job of working with the U.S. Congress. Jiang Zemin told U.S. reporters in mid-October 1995 that lobbying Congress would be an important priority in the year ahead, and Chinese specialists also said that the PRC would put more effort into winning greater understanding and support from other U.S. sectors, notably the media and business.[21]

Following the Taiwan Strait crisis of 1995-1996, the Clinton administration also tried harder to find common ground to sustain a longer-term engagement with China through high-level communications and face-to-face meetings. Newly appointed U.S. Ambassador James Sasser delivered a letter (one of several reported letters from President Clinton to senior Chinese leaders) in early 1996 that prompted Chinese leaders to send the PRC State Council's senior foreign policy expert, Liu Huaqiu, to Washington for extensive talks with National Security Adviser Anthony Lake and other senior officials.

Continued signs of U.S.-China frictions in 1996 included sensitive negotiations over reports of alleged PRC transfers of nuclear weapons technology to Pakistan, disputes over intellectual property rights (IPR) infractions, and the annual debate in Congress over the president's decision to grant most favored nation (MFN) tariff treatment to China. The first two issues were dealt with through negotiation. The annual debate in Congress ended without reversing the president's decision; a June 27, 1996, vote in the House failed by a wide margin to reverse the president's action.[22]

U.S. Engagement—1996-1998

There appeared in 1996 increasing, albeit still tentative, signs that U.S. policy toward China—long pulled in different directions by a variety of competing interests and concerns—was coming together in a clearer, more coherent way. There was less debate than in the recent past pushed by single issue advocates demanding that their interest be the top priority of U.S. policy toward China. There was more awareness of China's rise as a great power, of the multifaceted challenges this posed for U.S. interests, and of the need for the United States to establish carefully crafted, effective policies and contingency plans to deal with these challenges.[23] Evidence of the more serious, sober, and attentive U.S. approach to China could be seen in the following examples:

- President Clinton's more carefully balanced use of positive and negative incentives in dealing with China issues in 1996. The show of force in the Taiwan Strait and the president's tough stance on intellectual property rights provided a counterweight to the administration's renewal of MFN treatment and its agreement with Beijing over the sale of nuclear-related equipment to Pakistan;
- Senator Bob Dole's major policy speech on Asia on May 9, 1996, which avoided any wide difference from the overall direction of Clinton administration China policy, though he castigated the administration's "inept" handling of the U.S.-China relationship in the previous three years;
- Secretary Christopher's first major address on China, May 17, 1996, which laid out a rationale for continued close, attentive U.S. efforts dealing with the rise of China's power and influence;
- President Clinton's subsequent willingness to take the initiative in publicly discussing issues of China policy, despite the expectation that he would not do so based on his past reticence and the sensitivities of U.S. election-year politics;
- The administration's decision to send National Security Adviser Anthony Lake to China in early summer 1996, paving the way for a U.S.-China summit meeting. Undersecretary of Defense Walter Slocombe also visited Beijing in late June, reenforcing a recently resumed high-level Sino-U.S. defense dialogue interrupted by the crisis over Taiwan;
- President Clinton's reported dispatch of several private letters and messages to senior Chinese leaders, reassuring them of U.S. intentions;
- Growing evidence that important congressional leaders were willing to give voice to the notion that the idea of the United States "punishing"

China through withdrawal of MFN privileges or other means needed to be replaced by a more carefully crafted, serious effort by the United States to "deal" with China's rise.

Following the U.S. presidential and congressional elections in 1996, Chinese officials[24] suggested that President Clinton's victory and the moderate rhetoric on China policy coming from congressional leaders since then indicated that U.S. domestic politics might be less of an obstacle than in the past in what the officials saw as the U.S. president's efforts to improve U.S.-China relations. Echoing a refrain often heard from Chinese media, the PRC officials urged that leaders of the two countries "seize the opportunity" of the currently more favorable situation to move relations forward. They judged that Chinese leaders had taken steps to improve the atmosphere in bilateral relations by muting past public references to alleged U.S. schemes to "contain" China's rising power, and by acknowledging in conversations with U.S. counterparts that China's administration, like the U.S. administration, believed that Sino-U.S. confrontation was not good for either side, and that Beijing desired a stable and predictable relationship with the United States.

The Chinese officials in late 1996 noted that numerous issues continued to complicate Sino-U.S. relations and that leaders on both sides were often suspicious and wary. During the anticipated ministerial and higher-level meetings between the two countries over the next few months, they expected that the U.S. side would continue to raise differences over human rights, trade issues, and weapons proliferation concerns, and that Chinese leaders would continue to raise issues over Taiwan. They advised that neither side should take actions that would upset the still delicate balance in U.S.-Chinese ties.

Chinese officials were optimistic by early 1997 that there would be substantial progress in U.S.-China relations that year, and they were subsequently surprised by the vehemence of the U.S. debate that impeded progress by midyear. In early 1997, they saw President Clinton, Vice President Gore, and senior administration officials as strongly committed to a policy of "engagement" with Chinese counterparts. This seemed likely to provide the impetus for U.S.-Chinese agreements on China's entry into the World Trade Organization (WTO), possible U.S. consideration of granting permanent MFN status for China, and other issues during high-level U.S.-Chinese exchanges planned for 1997 and 1998. The Clinton administration was seen as backed strongly by many U.S. businesses with interests in China's advancing economy, by U.S. strategists who judged that U.S. policy needed to deal constructively with China's rising power and influence in Asian and world affairs, and others. The Chinese officials acknowledged that the U.S. media appeared to remain critical of the Chinese government, that U.S. public opinion continued to view it negatively, and that a number of U.S. groups critical of Chinese government policies and practices on issues of human rights, trade, and proliferation of weapons remained active.

Chinese officials were concerned by the Clinton administration's weakened public commitment to the engagement policy as a result of the campaign contribution controversy highlighted by the U.S. media in late 1996 and early 1997. Most damaging from the Chinese officials' perspective were charges in the U.S. media that the Chinese government had been involved in funneling campaign contributions to U.S. candidates with the intention of winning their support for favorable U.S. trade or other treatment of China.[25] As a result, President Clinton, Vice President Gore, and other administration leaders were seen, for a time, to have adopted a lower-key public posture in defense of the engagement policy with China. At the same time, U.S. critics of the engagement policy were seen to use the controversy to launch a varied attack on China's policies and practices and on the Clinton administration's approach to China issues.

In mid-1997, Chinese specialists were not certain how long the current U.S. debate would last.[26] They were disturbed by what they saw as "partisan" elements in both the U.S. Democratic and Republican parties allegedly using the debate over China policy for partisan reasons. Thus, they charged that some of the U.S. criticism of Vice President Gore over China policy reflected a design by certain elements within the Democratic Party to use China issues to weaken Mr. Gore's standing in the party and his chances to serve as the party's presidential candidate in 2000. Some Republican politicians were thought to hold to a similar reasoning in their criticism of Mr. Gore's China policy. Meanwhile, according to Chinese specialists, some Republican activists, who adhered strongly to the socially conservative agenda of the religious right, were said to be using China issues against some leaders in the Republican Party who were seen as not suitably conservative on social and other issues important to these activists. Chinese specialists suspected that these partisan charges might continue well after the 1997 debate on MFN treatment for China and become a fixture of U.S. domestic politics for the next few years.

Chinese officials did not appear seriously alarmed as to the likely impact of the U.S. policy debate on basic Chinese interests. They expected U.S. MFN treatment for the PRC to continue. A common view of Chinese officials was that it was natural for U.S. opponents of forward movement in U.S.-China relations to become more active in reaction to the Clinton administration's engagement policy and high-level meetings with Chinese leaders. The Chinese officials claimed to be confident that China's rising power and influence in world affairs, and its willingness to cooperate with the United States on issues of importance to both countries, made it unlikely that the U.S. opponents of the engagement policy would have a serious, lasting impact on U.S.-China relations.

Events over the next year appeared to bear out the Chinese assessments. On the one hand, the Clinton administration followed through on plans for extensive U.S.-China summit meetings, which capped the Beijing leaders' decade-long effort to restore their international legitimacy after the Tiananmen incident. The results redounded to the benefit of the presiding Chinese leaders, especially President Jiang Zemin, who was anxious to carve out a role as a responsible and respected international leader, as part of his broader effort to solidify his political base of support at home.

Basically satisfied with the anticipated results from smooth summit meetings with the U.S. president, Beijing saw little need to take the initiative in dealing with continuing U.S.-China differences over issues like human rights, trade, and weapons proliferation. It was the U.S. side that felt political pressure to achieve results in these areas. Responding to repeated U.S. initiatives to reach agreements at the summit meetings on these kinds of questions, Chinese officials took the opportunity to make demands of their own, especially regarding U.S. policy toward Taiwan. At the same time, Beijing was willing to marginally improve its human rights practice, and it curbed nuclear and cruise missile exchanges with Iran, for the sake of achieving a smoother, more cooperative U.S.-China relationship.

The sudden revival of sometimes partisan debate over China policy in Washington in mid-1998 surprised but did not upset the basic calculations of Chinese officials. In sum, Chinese officials were well pleased with the progress they had made in normalizing relations with the United States from the low points after the Tiananmen incident of 1989 and the confrontation over Taiwan in 1995-1996. The progress had been made largely by changes in U.S. policy toward China, and with few concessions by Beijing in key areas important to China. The summits of 1997 and 1998 represented the capstone of this normalization effort, in effect strongly legitimating the PRC leaders at home and abroad—a key Chinese goal after the Tiananmen incident. Once this was accomplished, Chinese leaders could turn to their daunting domestic agenda with more assurance that the key element of U.S.-China relations was now on more stable ground.

Of course, Chinese leaders had few illusions about U.S. policy. They saw plenty of opportunities for continued difficulties. U.S. behavior continued to fit into a pattern of engagement and containment—the "two hands" of U.S. policy. The main trend was toward greater engagement, but there remained many forces in Congress, in the media, and among U.S. interest groups prepared to challenge any forward movement in U.S.-China relations. And the fact remained that although it was clearly in China's interest to cooperate with the United States under current circumstances, the two countries continued to have fundamentally contradictory interests over the international balance of influence, the U.S. strategic role in East Asia, U.S. support for Taiwan, and U.S. support for political change in China.

Notes

1. See, among others, Robert Ross, "The Strategic and Bilateral Context of Policymaking in China and the United States," in *After the Cold War*, ed. Robert Ross, Armonk, N.Y.: M. E. Sharpe, 1998, pp. 3-39; Nancy Bernkopf Tucker, "Clinton's Muddled China Policy," *Current History*, September 1998, pp. 243-249; Steven Levine, "Sino-American Relations: Practicing Damage Control," in Samuel Kim, ed., *China and the World*, Boulder, Colo.: Westview Press, 1998; Ezra Vogel, ed., *Living With China*, New York: Norton, 1997; and Kim Holmes and James Przystup, eds., *Between Diplomacy and Deterrence: Strategies for U.S. Relations with China*, Washington, D.C.: Heritage Foundation, 1997.

2. Chinese officials have repeatedly used this kind of language in personal conversations with the author and other U.S. China specialists in recent years. It is reported, for example, in "Sino-U.S. Summit Watch," Congressional Research Service (CRS) memorandum, Library of Congress, Washington, D.C., May 11, 1998, pp. 5-6; and "China-U.S. Relations: Issues on the Eve of the MFN Debate—the View from Beijing," CRS memorandum, Library of Congress, Washington, D.C., June 10, 1997, pp. 7-8.

3. See, among others, "Sino-U.S. Relations Gradually Warm Up," *Ta Kung Pao*, June 1, 1998, p. A2; "Experts Appraise Sino-U.S. Relations," *Jie Fang Jun Bao*, June 1995, p. 5; Wang Jisi, "Deepen Mutual Understanding and Expand Strategic Consensus," *Renmin Ribao*, June 16, 1998, p. 6; Tao Wen Zhao, "Hurdles Cannot Stop Momentum of Improvement," *Wen Wei Po*, October 23, 1997, p. A7; "A New Phase in the Development of Sino-U.S. Ties," *Renmin Ribao*, editorial, November 5, 1997; "Questions and Answers at Qian Qichen's Small-Scale Briefing," *Wen Wei Po*, November 4, 1997, p. A6; and Li Hongqi, "Expand Common Understanding," *Xinhua*, December 31, 1998.

4. See, among others, Robert Sutter, *U.S. Policy toward China: An Introduction to the Role of Interest Groups*, New York: Lanham, Md.: Rowman & Littlefield, 1998, pp. 47-65.

5. This assessment of the background and implications of Secretary Christopher's visit to China is taken from "Trip Report on Visit to Beijing, March 29-April 2, 1994," CRS memorandum, Library of Congress, Washington, D.C., April 6, 1994, pp. 1-4. For background, see sources cited in note 1, as well as David M. Lampton and Alfred Wilhelm, eds., *United States and China: Relations at a Crossroads,* Lanham, Md.: University Press of America, 1995; and David M. Lampton, "America's China Policy in the Age of the Finance Minister: Clinton Ends Linkage," *China Quarterly*, vol. 139, September 1994, pp. 597-621.

6. This assessment of Chinese and U.S. views during this period is taken especially from "Sino-U.S. Relations: Status and Outlook," CRS memorandum, Library of Congress, Washington, D.C., August 15, 1994, pp. 1-6. For background and analysis, see sources in note 1.

7. "Sino-U.S. Relations."

8. "Sino-U.S. Relations," pp. 2-3.

9. See, among others, Harvey Feldman, "Cross Strait Relations with Taiwan: Implications for U.S. Policy," in Holmes and Przystup, eds., *Between Diplomacy and Deterrence,* pp. 141-149.

10. *New York Times*, October 25, 1995.

11. This section is taken largely from "Crisis in U.S.-China Relations—Possible Outlook for 1996," CRS memorandum, Library of Congress, Washington, D.C., March 18, 1996, pp. 1-9.

12. See, among others, *China Policy: Crisis Over Taiwan 1995—A Post Mortem*, Washington, D.C.: Library of Congress, CRS Report 95-1175F, December 5, 1995, pp. 1-13.

13. For an account of Chinese officials' private remarks on U.S.-China relations during this period, see, among others, the Congressional Research Service memoranda cited above, along with additional memoranda titled and dated as follows: "China's Relations With the U.S.—The View from Beijing, December, 1995," December 29, 1995; "Taiwan-Mainland China Relations: Status and Outlook," July 17, 1996; "U.S.-China Relations: Outlook and Specific Issues," August 8, 1996; "Beijing's Foreign Priorities—An Update," September 17, 1996. These memoranda capture the findings of interviews with over a hundred Chinese officials.

14. U.S. Department of Defense, *United States Security Strategy for the East Asia-Pacific Region*, Washington, D.C.: February 1995, p. 32.

15. *Washington Post*, February 19, 1995.

16. For background, see *Vietnam*, Washington, D.C.: Library of Congress, CRS Issue Brief 93081 (updated periodically).

17. See discussion in *China's Sinister View of U.S. Policy: Origins, Implications and Options*, Washington, D.C.: Library of Congress, CRS Report 95-750S, June 26, 1995, pp. 1-5.

18. See, among others, Allen Whiting, "Sino-Japanese Relations," *World Policy Journal* 8 (winter 1990-1991): 107-134.

19. This is based on interviews with sixty Chinese officials and specialists during this period. See also *China Policy: Crisis Over Taiwan 1995—A Post-Mortem.*

20. This is taken from *China Policy: Crisis Over Taiwan 1995—A Post-Mortem.*

21. *U.S. News and World Report*, October 23, 1995, p. 72.

22. Discussed in *China-U.S. Relations*, Washington, D.C.: Library of Congress, CRS Issue Brief 94002 (updated regularly).

23. See, among others, Robert Sutter and James Przystup, "U.S.-China Relations: Issues and Options," in Holmes and Przystup, eds., *Between Diplomacy and Deterrence*; Tucker, "Clinton's Muddled China Policy"; and Ross, "Strategic and Bilateral Contest."

24. This section is based especially on interviews with a hundred Chinese officials and specialists, in Beijing and Washington, D.C., 1996-1998.

25. For background, see, among others, *Congressional Quarterly Weekly Report*, April 25, 1997, pp. 967-972.

26. Discussed particularly in "China-U.S. Relations: Issues on the Eve of the MFN Debate—The View from Beijing," CRS memorandum, Library of Congress, Washington, D.C., June 10, 1997, pp. 1-8.

Chapter 4

Relations with Russia

In the wake of the end of the cold war and collapse of the Soviet Union, China's relations with Russia have continued to develop in positive and constructive ways that minimize remaining differences and allow Beijing and Moscow to use the image of their closer cooperation to boost their respective leverage, especially against the United States. For Beijing, the "strategic partnership" with Moscow provides the model for Chinese efforts to ensure stable relations with neighbors and major world powers, and has added benefits, especially sophisticated Russian arms. Chinese leaders show keen awareness of the limits of Russian economic strength and political stability; they do not allow rhetorical and political gestures in support of Russian-Chinese assertiveness and independence against the West to get in the way of the continuing strong Chinese interest in maintaining a close working relationship with the United States and its allies and close associates.[1]

Background and Recent Developments

China and Russia have had a long and often troubled history. Czarist Russia's expansion into the Far East came largely at the expense of the declining Chinese Empire. Nineteenth-century treaties saw vast stretches of territory formerly under Beijing's rule become part of the Russian Empire. China's internal weakness and political dislocation during the first half of the twentieth century provided opportunities for Lenin and Stalin to seek allies and foster revolutionary movements favorable to the USSR. Soviet involvement was often ham-handed and, on occasion, worked against the immediate interests of the communist guerilla movement in China led by Mao Zedong.[2]

Seeking economic support and strategic backing in the face of an indifferent or hostile West, Mao Zedong's newly formed People's Republic of China concluded an alliance with Stalin's USSR in 1949. After many weeks of hard bargaining, the alliance was signed on February 14, 1950. The alliance relationship was essential to China's security and its military, economic, and social development in the 1950s. Soviet aid, advisers, and guidelines were key features fostering the changes under way in China. But steadily escalating differences arose over strategy toward the United States and international affairs, the proper ideological path to development, and the appropriate leadership roles of Mao and Khrushchev in the world communist movement. Soviet aid was cut off in 1960. Polemics over strategy and ideology led to more substantive disputes over competing claims to border territories. Armed border clashes reached a point in 1969 at which the Soviet Union threatened to attack Chinese nuclear installations, and Chinese leaders countered with a nationwide war preparations campaign against the "war maniacs" in the Kremlin. Party relations were broken, trade fell to minimal levels, and each side depicted the other in official media as a dangerous international predator.

The start of Sino-Soviet talks on border issues in October 1969 eased the war crisis, but each side continued preparations for a long-term struggle against its neighboring adversary. As the weaker party in the dispute, China attempted to break out of its international isolation and gain diplomatic leverage against perceived Soviet efforts at intimidation and threat. Beijing's opening to the Nixon administration was an important element in this policy. The Soviet Union continued its previous efforts to build up military forces along the Sino-Soviet and Sino-Mongolian borders in order to offset any perceived threat from China. It also pursued this course to provide a counterweight against any Chinese effort to exert pressure on countries around China's periphery that were interested in developing closer relations with the USSR (for example, India, Vietnam).

The death of Mao Zedong in 1976 and the gradual emergence of a more pragmatic leadership in China reduced the importance of ideological and leadership issues in the Sino-Soviet dispute; but the competition in Asia again reached a crisis in 1979. China countered Soviet-backed Vietnam's invasion of Cambodia by launching a limited military incursion into Vietnam. The Soviet Union responded with warnings and large-scale military exercises along China's northern border. China also denounced the Soviet invasion of

Afghanistan in 1979 and sided with the U.S.-backed anticommunist guerrillas in Afghanistan.[3]

Subsequently, both countries attempted to moderate the tensions. Soviet leader Brezhnev made several public gestures calling for improved economic, government, and party relations with China before he died in 1982. This prompted the start of a series of political, economic, technical, and cultural contacts and exchanges.

By 1982, the Soviet leadership concluded that their post-1969 strategy toward China (including the massing of forces along the eastern sector of the border and a media campaign of denunciation) had backfired. The post-1972 normalization of China's relations with the United States and Japan and the signing of the 1978 China-Japan friendship treaty showed a strategic convergence among the United States, China, and Japan, which added to the Soviet defense burden and worsened the security environment on its long, remote, and thinly populated eastern flank. To undo this problem, Brezhnev and later leaders held out an olive branch to the Chinese leadership. Political contacts and trade increased and polemics subsided, but real progress came only after Mikhail Gorbachev consolidated his power and made rapprochement with China an urgent priority. In particular, Gorbachev was prepared to make major changes in what China referred to as the "three obstacles" to improved Sino-Soviet relations: Soviet troops in Afghanistan, the buildup of Soviet forces along the border (including the deployment in Mongolia), and the Soviet-backed Vietnamese military occupation of Cambodia.[4] Motivated by a desire to repair relations with China, to ease the defense burden on the Soviet economy, and to reciprocate China's reduction of its 4 million troops to 2.95 million from 1982 to 1986, the Soviet government announced in 1987 that a phased reduction of its troops (roughly sixty-five thousand in total number) from Mongolia would be initiated with the aim of eliminating the deployment by 1992.[5] The Soviet formations in Mongolia had been kept at a higher level of readiness than others along the border, and the Chinese had long viewed them as a first-echelon strike force aimed at Beijing. In December 1988, Gorbachev announced at the United Nations that Soviet conventional forces would unilaterally be reduced by five hundred thousand. Soviet spokesmen later clarified that, of the total, one hundred and twenty thousand would come from the troops arrayed against China, and that remaining Far Eastern units would progressively be reconfigured in a defensive mode. In late 1989, following Gorbachev's visit to Beijing in May, Chinese and Soviet officials began negotiations on reducing forces along the border, and during Chinese Prime Minister Li Peng's visit to Moscow in April 1990, an agreement was reached on governing principles regarding force reductions. By the time the

Soviet Union collapsed in 1991, five rounds of talks on force reductions had been conducted.

The reduction of the conventional threat to China was complemented by the 1987 U.S.-Soviet Intermediate Nuclear Forces (INF) treaty under which Moscow, accepting the concept of a "global zero," dismantled all its medium- and intermediate-range nuclear missiles, including 180 mobile SS-20s that were based in Asian regions of the USSR.

Meanwhile, the USSR agreed under the April 1988 Geneva Accords to withdraw its combat forces from Afghanistan by May 1989, and encouraged Vietnam to evacuate its troops from Cambodia by the end of 1989.

High-level political contacts helped to alter the adversarial character of Sino-Soviet relations, the most important being the visits of Eduard Shevardnadze and Gorbachev to Beijing in 1989 and of Li Peng and Chinese Communist Party General Secretary Jiang Zemin to Moscow in 1990 and 1991, respectively. Talks on resolving the border dispute, which had been derailed by the Soviet invasion of Afghanistan, resumed in 1987. A treaty delimiting the eastern sector of the border was signed in May 1991. These military and political transformations in Sino-Soviet relations were supplemented by a significant growth in trade—especially along the border—and agreements providing for thousands of Chinese workers to be employed in construction projects in Siberia and the Soviet Far East.[6]

Chinese leaders welcomed Gorbachev's military withdrawals from around China's periphery, and the collapse of the USSR in 1991 removed the Soviet military threat that had been the central focus of Beijing's strategic planning since the 1960s. The changes came at a time when Chinese leaders were beleaguered in the face of national and international resentment over their handling of the Tiananmen Square demonstrations of 1989. Representing one of the few surviving communist regimes in the post-cold war world, Chinese officials were especially suspicious of Boris Yeltsin and his proposed democratic reforms, which were anathema to Chinese leaders determined to maintain the Communist Party's monopoly of political power. Nevertheless, more pragmatic consideration of the national interests of China and Russia saw Yeltsin and Chinese leaders continue the process of gradually improving relations begun in the 1980s.

Political Relations

The ideological grounds for polemics between Moscow and Beijing were basically removed in the Gorbachev years—party-to-party ties were reestablished during the 1989 Deng Xiaoping-Gorbachev summit. The end of Communist Party rule in Russia and the reforms that China has embarked upon since 1978 rendered the old schismatic disputes about "revisionism," "social imperialism," and "hegemonism" irrelevant. Beijing's poor human rights record and its use of force to suppress the Tiananmen demonstrations were criticized by Russians but have not become major problems in government-to-government relations. Also, unlike the United States, Russia has not allowed its expanded economic ties with Taiwan to offend Beijing. Meanwhile, progress on resolving Russo-Chinese border disputes continued. The May 1991 eastern sector border agreement was followed by the signing of an agreement in September 1994 on the western sector of the border. As a result, except for some small areas, the entire Russo-Chinese border was delimited.[7]

Both countries have maintained the momentum of political contacts at the highest levels. Yeltsin visited Beijing in 1992, 1996, and 1997, and Prime Minister Viktor Chernomyrdin in 1994 and 1997. President Jiang Zemin visited Moscow in 1994, 1995, 1997, and 1998, and Prime Minister Li Peng in 1994, 1996, and 1998. Prime Minister Zhu Rongji visited Moscow in February 1999. In addition, there have been numerous meetings between the foreign ministers, defense ministers, and economic officials of both countries.

Military Issues[8]

In 1992, Yeltsin's government completed the withdrawal of troops from Mongolia initiated by Gorbachev in 1987. By May 1996, Russia reportedly had cut a hundred and fifty thousand troops from its Far Eastern deployment, and the Pacific Fleet had been reduced by 50 percent from its 1985 level. At the eighth round of negotiations on force reductions along the border in December 1992, both sides agreed that their formations would be pulled back one hundred kilometers from the border. Offensive weapons (tanks, strike aircraft, artillery, and tactical nuclear weapons) are to be reduced in the two hundred-kilometer zone that results.

Efforts to reduce forces and institute confidence-building measures (CBMs) along the border became multilateral with the addition of the Soviet successor states, Kazakhstan, Kyrgyzstan, and Tajikistan—all of which share borders with China—to a joint Commonwealth of Independent States (CIS) delegation. Guidelines, including force reductions, warnings preceding military exercises, and the attendance at exercises of observers from the signatories, were incorporated in an agreement signed by the leaders of the four CIS states and China in Shanghai during Yeltsin's April 1996 visit.

A joint declaration signed at the end of Yeltsin's visit to China in December 1992 called for reducing troops along the border to "a minimal level" and for increased contact between Chinese and Russian military personnel. Each party also pledged to eschew the use of force against the other, including the use of force in the domain of third countries, and to refuse to enter any "military and political alliances directed against the other Party, or sign with third countries any treaties or agreements detrimental to the state sovereignty and security interests of the other Party."[9]

In July 1994, the Russian and Chinese defense ministers agreed on measures (such as preventing accidental missile launches, ending the electronic jamming of communications, and establishing signals to warn aircraft and ships in danger of violating the other side's border) to reduce the danger of inadvertent military escalation. In September 1994, the two sides agreed to the principle of no-first-use for nuclear weapons and to re-target nuclear missiles away from each other's territory. In May 1994, Chinese warships from the North China Fleet visited Vladivostok. Units of the Russian Pacific Fleet called at Qingtao that August. Local Chinese commanders have also visited Russian military districts.[10]

Russian Arms Sales[11]

China has become the largest customer for Russian arms, having purchased $2 billion worth in 1994 alone.[12] Major purchases in recent years include two hundred Su-27 fighter-ground attack aircraft, fifty T-72 tanks, one hundred S-300 surface-to-air missiles, ten Il-76 transport aircraft, several *Kilo*-class (diesel-electric) submarines, and two Sovremenny-class de-stroyers.[13] Moscow is also providing China with technology to improve the accuracy of surface-to-surface and air-to-air missiles, and training in Russia for personnel who will operate the weapons purchased. Several of the sales have been difficult. The Su-27 transaction has been in the works since 1992, and the first twenty-four aircraft were delivered in 1992. Additional deliveries were held up by a dispute over China's desire to pay for two-thirds of the cost through barter. Although precise details of how the dispute was settled are unavailable, after the visit to Russia in December 1995 by Chinese military leader Liu Huaqing, the way was finally cleared for the delivery of the forty-eight Su-27s, and an agreement was reached (reportedly worth $2 billion) allowing China to manufacture this high-capability aircraft under license.

At bottom, these sales reflect a pragmatic marriage of important bilateral needs. For Russia, arms sales to China supply much-needed hard currency and consumer goods from China, provide orders for severely distressed Russian defense industries, and reduce the tendency of the United States, Japan, and others to take Russia for granted in the post-cold war Far East. Russia's political disarray also facilitates these arms sales, as reduced central control from Moscow gives defense industries more independence to make such deals. For China, the Russian equipment is relatively cheap, compatible with the existing Chinese inventory, and comes without political or other preconditions. Both Russian and Chinese leaders are sensitive to concerns in the United States and Japan, and among Asian governments along China's periphery, that the Russian transfers could substantially add to China's power projection and alter the prevailing military balance in East Asia. In general, Russian and Chinese officials say that China has a long way to go before it can use the recently acquired Russian weapons effectively or project its augmented power in ways that would seriously upset the military balance in the region.[14] There is debate in the West over when and if such weapons will alter the regional balance.

Economic and Societal Changes

Trade between the two countries has grown substantially from a low base. In 1985, Sino-Soviet trade was $300 million. Russian-Chinese trade peaked in 1994 at $7 billion, and cross-border trade, which resumed in 1982 and is conducted largely in barter,[15] accounted for a third of the volume, although its proportion is falling in accordance with the desire of both governments. China became Russia's second largest trade partner after Germany.[16]

Along the economically more important eastern section of the Russo-Chinese border, roads and rail connections link nineteen working border checkpoints between the two sides, with two more planned. In addition, direct postal and telephonic links have been created between northeastern China and the Russian Far East. Russia has also signed contracts to build nuclear and hydroelectric power plants in China.

Problems caused by an influx of Chinese into the Russian Far East, particularly those who remain in violation of visa regulations, led Russia and China to work out a more stringent visa regime in 1994. But the problem of Chinese migration into the Russian Far East is likely to persist. Both countries face the unprecedented challenge of managing the movement of what could be millions of people across a long border. Russia, in particular, cannot afford to pump large sums of money into securing that border more effectively. There is a structural supply-and-demand dynamic at work: the high population density and unemployment that obtains on the Chinese side stimulates people to cross into the Russian Far East, which has traditionally suffered from severe labor shortages. The entire eastern third of Russia (east of Lake Baikal, a territory almost the size of the continental United States) has fewer than twenty million inhabitants—and its population is shrinking as people remigrate toward Russia's European heartland. This is exacerbated by economic distress in the Russian Far East that is worse than in most other regions, including severe food and energy shortages and wage arrears.

Yeltsin-Jiang Summits

The extent of Sino-Russian cooperation—and its clear limits—have been well illustrated during the frequent formal and informal summit meetings between the top leaders. Chinese media coverage of Russian President Boris Yeltsin's November 9-11, 1997, visit to China suggested that Beijing continues to seek a broader and firmer foundation for its post-Soviet relationship with Russia but that the conditions for doing so are limited. As in their treatment of past China-Russia summits, the media this time signaled Beijing's intention to use its relations with Russia as a counterweight to U.S. global influence.[17]

Reflecting China's interest in moving Sino-Russian relations forward, despite continuing obstacles, Yeltsin's visit followed the pattern of previous Sino-Russian summits in the post-Soviet era, the meeting portrayed as the latest step in a continuous process of improving relations. Echoing Beijing's assessment of PRC President Jiang Zemin's visit to Russia in April 1997—which PRC media described at the time as "remarkably successful" and occurring in a "sincere and friendly" atmosphere—the joint statement issued at the end of Yeltsin's visit said that his meeting with Jiang on November 10 was a "complete success." *Xinhua* also cited the two leaders as praising their "strategic cooperative partnership" and quoted Jiang as asserting that bilateral relations are based on a "solid political foundation" whose "system of regular meetings" between top leaders constituted an improvement in relations.

Similarly, the joint statement itself played up the "active development" of bilateral relations and stressed the "important role" played by the four previous Sino-Russian joint statements in "implementing" the partnership. The statement went on to "reconfirm" what it called the "especially significant" principles contained in the previous statements, namely (1) strengthening "trust and mutual respect" for sovereignty and "noninterference in each other's internal affairs"; (2) regularizing high-level visits and setting up "consultation mechanisms"; and (3) "strengthening mutual coordination on major international issues."

While the agenda of Yeltsin's visit was less weighty than that of Jiang's visit in April—which included a joint pronouncement on the "multi-polarization of the world," the signing of a five-nation agreement on border forces reduction, and the formal establishment of a Sino-Russian committee for friendship, peace, and development—it nevertheless included the additional step of resolving remaining border issues and attempted to expand the scope of bilateral economic cooperation. Reflecting these goals, the joint statement asserted that the two sides had "settled" most outstanding border issues and reached agreements on cooperation in a number of areas, including "large-scale" cooperation in energy extraction and production, financial and investment relations, science and technology, transportation and communications, and "military technology."[18]

Progress on Border Issues

PRC media portrayed the signing of agreements on Sino-Russian border issues as the major accomplishment of the summit, claiming that border conflicts were a thing of the past and playing down remaining disputes. For example, the joint statement asserted that "all issues" concerning demarcation of the "eastern sector" of the Sino-Russian border had been "settled" and that the demarcation of the eastern border has for the first time been "marked on the ground."[19] Although the statement said nothing about remaining differences over disputed frontier islets on the Amur and Ussuri rivers, the French News Agency, *AFP*, quoted a Chinese Foreign Ministry spokesman as saying it is "entirely possible" to find a "settlement" of this issue.[20]

In addition, a November 10 *Xinhua* report on the visit also stated that Chinese and Russian officials had signed an agreement on "guiding principles" for joint economic utilization of "individual islets" in "border rivers and surrounding waters," although it did not specify the islets or rivers concerned.[21]

The joint statement was more cautious in commenting on the "western sector" of the border. Describing this sector as being "about 55 km" in length, it said that the two sides "declared their readiness" to implement demarcation work "within an agreed time frame" and to continue talks aimed at a "fair and rational" solution of "certain outstanding issues."

The strongest indication that Beijing did not intend to allow differences over borders to sour future Sino-Russian relations came in remarks by Jiang at his meeting with Yeltsin. According to *Xinhua*, Jiang glossed over any remaining border disputes, saying that the signing of Sino-Russian agreements, including agreements on the demarcation of borders, is a "successful example" of "settling questions left over by history through equal consultation, mutual understanding, and accommodation."

Continuing Limits on Economic Relations

Despite persistent PRC media reports touting a great potential for expanded economic relations, reiterated by Jiang and the joint statement during Yeltsin's visit, the two sides appeared to have made little progress beyond rhetorical affirmations of their goals. *Xinhua* cited Jiang as telling Yeltsin that the two sides should make "even greater efforts" to "fully tap their respective vast potentials" and as calling for "breakthroughs" in cooperation on "large and medium-sized projects." He also urged enterprises from the two countries to "expand contacts" in order to "find partners for cooperative ventures." Similarly, the joint statement noted the "huge potential" for strengthening bilateral cooperation in nine areas that covered a broad and diverse spectrum of economic activity.

However, although *Xinhua* reported that in addition to the joint statement a number of "other documents" were signed on "economic and technological cooperation," the media were not observed to report the contents of most of these agreements, suggesting that little was accomplished in the way of concrete business deals. Reinforcing this impression, the two "memorandums of understanding" (MOU) for which some detail was provided did not go beyond general statements of purpose. According to the *Xinhua* report, Chinese Vice Premier Li Lanqing and Russian First Deputy Prime Minister Boris Nemtsov signed one MOU on the "basic principles" for laying gas pipelines and developing gas fields and another on the "basic orientation" of economic, scientific, and technological cooperation.[22]

Finally, media coverage of Jiang's talks with Yeltsin during both summits in 1997 implied that the two sides were skeptical that their bilateral trade target of $20 billion in total volume by the turn of the century would be met. For example, Jiang reportedly told Russian Prime Minister Viktor Chernomyrdin during Jiang's April 1997 visit to Moscow that he and Yeltsin had agreed on the need for both sides to "make efforts to raise" trade levels and "stand on higher ground" on the bilateral trade issue and that he hoped Russia would make a "positive study" of proposals for cooperative projects. Similarly, *Xinhua* cited both leaders as stating during the November summit that it was "entirely possible" to reach their bilateral trade targets as long as both sides made "unremitting efforts." At least one report, carried by the PRC-owned Hong Kong news service *Zhongguo Tongxun She* prior to Yeltsin's visit, implied that the trade target was unrealistic.[23]

Multipolar World, China's Standing

Building on the joint statement signed by Jiang and Yeltsin during the April summit—which pledged to "promote the multipolarization of the world and the establishment of a new international order"—PRC media commentary on Yeltsin's visit underscored China's intention to continue using its warming relationship with Russia to counter what it views as U.S. efforts to dominate the post-cold war world. Both the joint statement and Jiang's remarks to Yeltsin reiterated Beijing's current line that its newly established "partnerships" with major powers, including Russia, are necessary to ensure a global balance of power in a "new, improved international political and economic order."

For example, in discussing the Sino-Russian relationship of "friendship and cooperation," the joint statement cited recent summit meetings between China, Russia, the United States, and Japan as evidence that "state-to-state alliances" or "strategic unions" directed against a "third country" are a "thing of the past" and that "larger nations" should back the trend toward a "multipolar" world.

The statement also intimated that China and Russia are seeking these goals for altruistic motives, since, it said, neither state is pursuing "expansionist" or "hegemonistic" aims—an allusion to the United States.

Similarly, in his talks with Yeltsin at which both presidents reendorsed their two countries' "strategic cooperative partnership," Jiang made another pitch for the concept of a "new world order," noting Beijing's belief that world affairs should be decided upon by "all countries."

Jiang appeared to indirectly criticize the United States, telling Yeltsin that "great powers" should abandon a "cold war mentality," respect the "reality of a diversified world," and conform to the "trend" of "world multipolarization."

An editorial in the PRC-owned Hong Kong newspaper *Wen Wei Po* on November 10, 1997, played up the importance of the Sino-Russian "strategic cooperative partnership" and the two countries' partnerships with other countries in "preventing superpowers from manipulating and guiding international security."[24] It asserted that the "new international order" promoted by China and Russia, which opposes "hegemony and the world's centralization," serves the interests of "all countries that refuse to be controlled by others."

Prospects

The improvement of Russian-Chinese relations has continued, with Li Peng and Jiang Zemin visiting Moscow in 1998 and Zhu Rongji visiting in February 1999. The development of closer relations has caused concern among some observers in the West and in Asia. As both countries face the prospect of continued difficulties with the U.S. superpower's intention of maintaining and developing its international strategic advantage through such means as NATO enlargement and the strengthening of the U.S.-Japanese military alliance, some experts warn of an ever closer Russo-Chinese strategic alignment.[25] They see the beginnings of this structure in joint Russo-Chinese statements supporting a multipolar world, in increasing military cooperation, and in efforts by Russia and China to work together politically and diplomatically to thwart U.S. efforts at the UN Security Council and elsewhere to pressure countries like Iraq, Iran, Libya, and others to conform to international norms supported by the United States.

Others argue that there are serious limits to Russian-Chinese cooperation and major obstacles to a strategic alliance between them.[26] The condition that would be most conducive to the emergence of a Sino-Russian strategic alliance would be a crisis or rupture in Russia's or China's relations with one of the other major powers, such as the United States or Japan.[27] Absent such a development, or a mounting strategic confrontation, the limits to Russian-Chinese cooperation seem substantial and the obstacles to a strategic alliance formidable.[28]

Continued Cooperation Likely

China and Russia both find that their relations with the advanced industrial democracies, particularly the United States, remain difficult. China faces problems over human rights abuses, trade and weapons proliferation questions, the status of Tibet, and especially the Taiwan question. For Russia there are problems concerning its relations with other Soviet successor states, tension over NATO enlargement, and nuclear proliferation. Internationally, Russia supports China's position on Taiwan, and China backs Russia's opposition to NATO enlargement. Each opposes international interference in what the other views as its internal affairs. Some Chinese and Russians countries view themselves as outsiders vis-à-vis the Group of Seven (G7), which they see as the "rich countries' club." As still-developing economies, they tend to resist certain G7-supported economic and trade policies in areas such as protectionism, dumping, intellectual property rights, transparency, and government regulations.

Russia badly needs the China market to export arms and industrial products for which, for various reasons, it has relatively few other buyers who can afford to pay.[29] Food and inexpensive consumer goods from China play a vital role in helping sustain the Russian Far East. These factors helped propel China into the position of Russia's second largest trade partner. Economically, China is far less dependent on Russia. But Russia can provide China with relatively cheap advanced weapons, nuclear reactor technology, and other industrial products that might otherwise be much more costly for Beijing or unavailable for political reasons.

Both Russia and China find it helpful, to some extent, to use their improving bilateral relations for leverage vis-à-vis the West, particularly the United States. This strikes some as reminiscent of Nixon/Kissinger's famous playing of the "China card" against the Soviet Union. Moscow tends to be more explicit about this than Beijing. Many Russian officials, for example, have warned that NATO enlargement could drive Russia into much closer cooperation, even a strategic alliance, with China.

China and Russia share some other common interests that strengthen the basis of their cooperation. For example, both see the possible spread of radical Islam in Central Asia as a threat to their own domestic stability and national security.[30] Both countries desire regional stability in Asia, want to avoid any crisis on the Korean Peninsula, and wish to forestall the reemergence of Japan as a major military power.

Limits to Cooperation

Despite the broad basis for Russian-Chinese cooperation there are serious limits to that cooperation—and even more to the creation of a strategic alliance between them.

In the aftermath of the collapse of the Soviet Union and the loss of its peripheral territory and population, Russia's relative economic weakness and political instability vis-à-vis China make many Russians nervous. Russia's population (roughly 147 million) is about half that of the former Soviet Union—and the sparsely populated Russian Far East is losing people. Russia's economy has contracted significantly during the still far from

complete transition to a market economy. Industrial production may be as complete transition to a market economy. Industrial production may be as low as 50 percent of its 1991 level.[31]

With President Yeltsin's ailments and other problems, the political situation is unstable. One aspect of that instability is the difficulty Moscow has in controlling distant regions, such as Eastern Siberia and the Far East. Leaders in those resource-rich regions seek greater autonomy from Moscow and some flirt with the idea of separatism.[32] Finally, many Russians are keenly aware of the deterioration of their country's military strength. The Russian Army's remarkably poor performance in Chechnya was one indication of this.

In contrast, from Moscow's perspective, China—with its dynamic economy, huge and growing population, apparent national self-confidence and assertiveness, stable, authoritarian political system, and large and modernizing army—seems strong. Some among the Russian policy elite find Beijing's example admirable and see in China both a model to emulate and a natural ally. Others—mindful of Russia's declining power vis-à-vis China and of the history of Russia's seizure of vast territories in Eastern Siberia and the Russian Far East from China in "unequal treaties" in the later part of the nineteenth century—see China's renaissance and burgeoning power as a challenge and potential threat. Russians' nightmare scenario from this perspective is that a resurgent China might try to retake vast, thinly populated territories from a weakened Russia.

Although Russia's sale of advanced weaponry to China is widely believed to be motivated in large part by economic necessity on Russia's part and is strongly supported by the defense industrial sector, there are serious reservations in the Russian security community. Some Russian commentators question the wisdom of helping to modernize the military of a country that may well become a threat to Russian security in the future. These reservations reportedly extend to the Russian General Staff.[33]

On the Chinese side, too, there are significant limitations and constraints on cooperation with Russia. The radical swings in Soviet and Russian domestic politics and foreign policy since the mid-1980s inevitably make Russia appear somewhat unreliable in Chinese eyes. Russia's economic, political, and military weakness has been duly noted by Chinese strategic planners, who nonetheless remain vigilant for any signs of a revival of Russian strength that could affect Chinese interests in Asia.

Also, Russia is much less important economically to China than vice versa. Russia accounts for less than 2 percent of China's $300 billion in foreign trade. China's trade with and credits and investments from the G-7 countries weigh far more heavily in Beijing than does Russo-Chinese trade.

In a policy crunch, China would be loath to jeopardize its vital economic relations with the advanced industrial democracies on Russia's behalf.

In short, the markets, financing, and technology of the West and the developed countries of East Asia represent a key link in China's ongoing program of economic modernization. And economic modernization and the concrete benefits it gives to the broad masses of Chinese people are the key sources of political legitimacy for the post-Mao leaders. It is difficult to imagine circumstances in which Chinese leaders would allow closer military, political, or other ties with an economically anemic Russia to jeopardize China's vital links with the world's most important economies—unless China faced a major crisis or geostrategic confrontation with the United States or Japan.

Thus, the pattern of China's recent relationship with Russia shows Beijing giving lower priority to Moscow than in the past. Beijing seeks to keep relations with the often unstable Russia as calm as possible. It also seeks military equipment and some advanced technology. When Chinese relations with the United States, Japan, and NATO are strained, Chinese officials fall back on relations with Moscow as a possible source of political leverage against the Western-aligned states. But when Beijing's higher-priority relations with the United States and the developed powers are in reasonably good shape, Beijing tends to keep at some distance the Russians and their desire to gain Chinese support for a strong, public, anti-U.S., anti-Western stance on sensitive issues. Even though Beijing—like Moscow—says it wants to see a multipolar world order develop, with the U.S. superpower as only one power among many, it sees only limited benefits from tilting strongly toward Russia as it opposes U.S. and Western policies. It sees far more to be gained from a positive and constructive engagement with the United States and Western-aligned states—a higher priority in Chinese foreign policy.

Notes

1. For recent background, see, among others, John W. Garver, "Sino-Russian Relations," in Samuel Kim, ed., *China and the World*, Boulder, Colo.: Westview Press, 1998, pp. 114-132; Rajan Menon, "The Strategic Convergence between Russia and China," *Survival* 39, 2 (summer 1997): 101-125; Stephen Blank, *The Dynamics of Russian Weapons Sales to China*, Carlisle, Pa.: U.S. Army War College, Strategic Studies Institute, March 4, 1997; and James Clay Moltz, "Regional Tension in the Russo-Chinese Rapprochement," *Asian Survey* 35, 6 (June 1995): 511-527.

2. See, among others, John W. Garver, *The Foreign Relations of The People's Republic of China*, Englewood Cliffs, N.J.: Prentice Hall, 1993, pp. 31-112. See also Lowell Dittmer, *Sino-Soviet Normalization and Its International Implications, 1945-1990*, Seattle: University of Washington Press, 1992.

3. Robert Ross, ed., *China, The United States and the Soviet Union: Tripolarity and Policy Making in the Cold War*, Armonk, N.Y.: M. E. Sharpe, 1993.

4. This analysis draws heavily on the work of Rajan Menon. See his "Strategic Convergence."

5. For a review of the military situation, see James Clay Moltz, "Regional Tension."

6. See, among others, Stephen Uhalley, "Sino-Soviet Relations: Continued Improvement Amidst Tumultuous Change," *Journal of East Asian Affairs*, winter-spring 1992.

7. See Moltz, "Regional Tension."

8. See discussion in Menon, "Strategic Convergence"; Blank, *Dynamics of Russian Weapons Sales to China.*

9. Moltz, "Regional Tension," p. 518.

10. Reviewed in Menon, "Strategic Convergence."

11. See Blank, *Dynamics of Russian Weapons Sales to China.* Also *China's Rising Military Power*, Washington, D.C.: Library of Congress, Congressional Research Service (CRS) Report 96-66F, January, 16, 1996, pp. 18-19.

12. *Conventional Arms Transfers to Developing Nations, 1988-1997*, Washington, D.C.: Library of Congress, CRS Report 98-647F, July 31, 1998.

13. The destroyer deal was reportedly completed during Li Peng's December 1996 visit to Moscow. The Sovremenny-class destroyers are highly capable, modern vessels. They would be China's largest and most formidable surface warships. They will reportedly be equipped with the SS-N-22, a very fast antiship cruise missile designed to counter U.S.-built Aegis cruisers and destroyers, and could also threaten aircraft carriers. U.S. military officials said this purchase was China's direct response to the deployment in March 1996 of two U.S. aircraft carriers to waters near Taiwan during the tension surrounding the Taiwanese elections and Chinese military exercises and missile firings. Bill Gertz, "Pentagon Says Russians Sell Destroyers to China," *Washington Times*, January 10, 1997, pp. A1, 10.

14. Consultations with Chinese and Russian officials, Washington, D.C., Beijing, 1996-1998.

15. Chinese food, textiles, and consumer goods and Russian raw materials predominate.

16. Reviewed in Menon, "Strategic Convergence."

17. This section relies heavily on "Yeltsin China Visit," Foreign Broadcast Information Service (FBIS), *Trends*, December 2, 1997 (internet version).

18. Cited in FBIS *Trends*, "Yeltsin China Visit," December 2, 1997.

19. The joint statement was carried by Russian and Chinese media on November 10, 1997, and by FBIS.

20. Cited in FBIS *Trends*, December 2, 1997.

21. *Xinhua*, November 10, 1997.

22. Cited in FBIS *Trends*, December 2, 1997.

23. Ibid.

24. Ibid.

25. For example, Peter Rodman (a Reagan and Bush administration senior National Security Council staffer and former director of Policy Planning at the State Department) warned that "another strategic problem is looming in East Asia . . . a rapprochement between Russia and China that has disturbing geopolitical implications." ("A New Russian-China Alliance?" *Los Angeles Times*, March 25, 1996). A *Wall Street Journal* headline warned, "Russia and China Getting Together Again: Anti-Western Mood Shifts Moscow's Focus Eastward," December 30, 1995. For a fuller discussion of the threat of a Sino-Russian alliance, see Hung P. Nguyen, "Russia and China: The Genesis of an Eastern Rapallo," *Asian Survey*, March 1993.

26. See, for example, Peggy Falkenheim Meyer, "From Cold War to Cold Peace? US.-Russian Security Relations in the Far East," in *Russian Security Policy in the Asia-Pacific Region: Two Views*, ed. Stephen Blank, Carlisle, Pa.: U.S. Army War College, Strategic Studies Institute, May 1996.

27. The hypothesis here is that if Russia or China—and particularly both of them—were to become locked in protracted geostrategic confrontation and hostility with the United States and/or a resurgent Japan, this could push Moscow and Beijing to forge a strategic alliance to counter their powerful common enemy. One such scenario might arise if China and Russia, for whatever reasons, simultaneously became embroiled in conflicts with Taiwan and with some of the Soviet successor states, provoking confrontation or conflict with the United States and its allies: this could lead to a Moscow-Beijing alliance.

28. This section benefited from analysis by Stuart Goldman in *Russian-Chinese Cooperation: Prospects and Implications*, Washington, D.C.: Library of Congress, CRS Report 97-185F, January 27, 1997, pp. 8-13.

29. Most Russian nonmilitary manufactured goods are qualitatively uncompetitive on the international market. Many of Moscow's traditional customers are unable to pay in hard currency. Some traditional customers who can pay, such as Iraq, Libya, and Serbia, are inaccessible to Russia because of UN trade sanctions. Russian officials argue that Moscow would be less eager to sell arms to customers that make the United States nervous, such as China and Iran, if Washington cooperated in giving Russia a share in the arms trade with "more civilized" countries.

30. During the period of the Sino-Soviet split, Moscow and Beijing vied for influence in Central Asia. This feature of their relationship is now greatly reduced and in some respects ended.

31. See Goldman, *Russian-Chinese Cooperation*, p. 13. Others, who say that this estimate is too bleak because it does not adequately take unreported production into account, estimate that the decline in industrial production since 1991 is roughly one-quarter to one-third.

32. Russian "great-power" nationalists view these centrifugal tendencies with alarm, fearing that they weaken Russia and, some believe, increase its vulnerability to a dynamic and potentially expansionist China. For a history of the Russian Far East

and an assessment of the possibility of separatism in that region see John J. Stephan, *The Russian Far East: A History*, Stanford, Calif.: Stanford University Press, 1994.

33. See analysis in *Russian-Chinese Cooperation.*

Chapter 5

Relations with Japan

Relations between China and Japan have swung markedly in the post-cold war period. At first, both powers adjusted their bilateral relations amicably following the demise of the USSR and its strategic influence in East Asia. The rise of China's power and influence in Asian affairs in the mid-1990s, combined with Chinese military assertiveness over Taiwan and the South China Sea, coincided with a protracted period of lackluster Japanese economic performance and weak political leadership. This called into question the past disparity of the economic relationship between the two powers, added to ongoing differences over territorial, strategic, and economic issues, and strengthened the wariness and occasional antipathy between the two countries.

Some commentators predicted that more intense competition, confrontation, and possible conflict lay in the future. More balanced assessments reviewed the differences in Japan-China relations against the background of alternating tensions and cooperation between the two powers in the recent past, and emphasized the important mutual interests that continue to bind them together. These mutual interests center on strong, growing economic and strategic interdependence between Japan and China and the influence of the United States and other third parties—all of whom can be expected to work on preserving Sino-Japanese stability.[1]

The Asian economic crisis, which began in 1977, added to the preoccupations of leaders in Tokyo and Beijing with their respective domestic problems, especially economic problems. At least for the time being, neither government sought to exacerbate tensions over the array of issues that continue to divide them. Thus, they went ahead with senior leaders' meetings in Tokyo and Beijing, capped by President Jiang Zemin's November 1998 visit to Japan. They endeavored—at least outwardly—to emphasize the positive and give less public attention to important and often deeply rooted differences. But this outward moderation was accompanied by media and other comment pointing to differences over history, the U.S.-Japan alliance, Taiwan, theater missile defense in East Asia, and other important questions.[2]

Friction and Cooperation in Japan-China Relations

Relations between Japan and China became troubled in the mid-1990s. The difficulties involve territorial, strategic, and economic issues, notably the following:[3]

- Exchanges of diplomatic complaints backed by strongly worded media and other rhetoric over competing claims to islets in the East China Sea;
- Increasingly evident signs of mutual suspicions over East Asian security issues. Chinese officials and commentators took a jaundiced view of Japan's reaffirmation of its alliance relationship with the United States; Japanese strategists publicly expressed concern over China's rising power and military capabilities in the region. In 1999, the two sides differed sharply over U.S.-Japanese plans to develop a theater missile defense in East Asia. China saw the move as directed at countering Chinese as well as North Korean ballistic missiles;
- Concerns among Japanese government decision makers that China's rising economic power, fostered by Japanese aid, trade, and technology, might lead to the expansion of Chinese political, economic, and military influence in regional and world affairs in ways contrary to Japanese interests.

The disputes reflected changes in the attitudes of Japanese and Chinese decision makers, opinion leaders, and popular opinion about the status and outlook of their mutual relationship.[4]
In Japan:

- With the collapse of the Soviet Union and the end of the cold war, strategic thinkers in the Japanese government and elsewhere in Japan focused more on China's rising power as the key regional security concern for Japan for the foreseeable future.

- China's continued remarkable economic growth, along with its rising political and military standing, prompted more Japanese to view China as a rival for regional influence. This contrasted with previously prevalent Japanese views of China's relative economic backwardness and political isolation, especially after the 1989 Tiananmen incident and the resulting international sanctions imposed on China.
- Previous Japanese sensitivity and responsiveness to Chinese demands for special consideration on account of Japan's negative war record in China over fifty years ago lessened with the passage of time, the change in Japanese leadership generations, and Beijing's loss of moral standing in Japan on account of its crackdown after the Tiananmen incident and its recent bullying, intimidation, and other aggressive moves seen in military and other actions regarding Taiwan, the South China Sea, and nuclear testing.
- Undergirding Japan's more critical approach to China was a strong sense of national pride and determination among Japanese leaders and public opinion to preserve Japanese interests in the face of perceived efforts by PRC officials to use charges from the distant past and recent economic, political, and strategic issues to prompt Tokyo to give way to Chinese interests.

In China:

- Chinese strategists' long-standing concerns about Japan's impressive military capabilities increased as a result of U.S.-Japanese agreements from 1996 onwards, which to Chinese observers appeared to have broadened Japan's strategic role in East Asia and to have provided U.S. strategic support for Japanese politicians wishing to strike a military posture in the region less deferential to China than in the past.[5]
- Chinese government specialists acknowledged recent changes in Japanese attitudes toward China and judged that Beijing appeared likely to meet even more opposition and gain less support from Japan as it sought to expand its influence in Asian and world affairs.[6]
- Chinese nationalism was a focal point of government-sponsored media and other publicity for many years, especially following the Tiananmen incident and the collapse of communism in Europe and the Soviet Union at the end of the cold war. Appealing to the sense of China as having been victimized by foreign aggressors in the past, the publicity

focused heavily on the role of Japan, by far the most important foreign aggressor in modern Chinese history. The United States was another major target of Chinese nationalistic feeling, especially in response to U.S. pressure on China over a variety of policy disputes in the 1990s. The government-sponsored Chinese publicity has elicited a widespread positive response from Chinese opinion leaders and public representatives, who sometimes take the lead in criticizing Japan, the United States, or others for alleged transgressions against China's national interests or nationalistic sensitivities.

The tensions in Japanese-Chinese relations in the mid-1990s contrasted with a period of several years after the Tiananmen incident that was widely acknowledged as the most positive and cooperative period in bilateral relations since the establishment of the PRC.[7] Japan's initial response to the incident was muted. Tokyo went along with Group of Seven (G7) sanctions against China. In July 1990, however, Tokyo diverged from the rest of the G7 to announce a resumption of lending to China. Beijing strongly supported the Japanese move, which ushered in a three-year period of increasing cooperation and cordiality.

A visit to China by Prime Minister Kaifu in 1991 confirmed that Tiananmen was no longer an obstacle to a cordial relationship. The change in Japanese policy coincided with a surge of Japanese investment in China; many Japanese business leaders now judged that Chinese authorities had shown themselves capable of maintaining stability, and this encouraged Japanese investment. Japanese Prime Minister Hosokawa declared in late 1991 that Japan's relationship with China was as important as its relationship with the United States. A successful visit to China by the Japanese emperor in 1992 indicated that both sides could put the past behind them, at least for a time. More forthright expressions of regret, by Japanese leaders including Hosokawa in 1993 for past Japanese aggression against China, were also appreciated by the Chinese. Economic relations developed rapidly, with China becoming Japan's second largest destination for direct foreign investment after the United States. Official dialogues and intergovernmental cooperation expanded, including cooperation in military security matters.

In 1995, several difficult political issues surfaced in the bilateral relationship.[8] China's nuclear testing program drew strong protests from Japan, followed by the freezing of a small part of Japan's large aid program in China. Beijing responded angrily, reminding Japan again of its record of aggression in China. The fiftieth anniversary of the end of the Pacific War was also used in China as an opportunity for extensive media examination of Japan's military past.

In November 1995, Japan's alleged failure to address adequately its history of aggression was criticized in a joint press conference in Seoul by the presidents of both China and the Republic of Korea (ROK). Japanese politicians and various community leaders reacted very negatively, perceiving this as political manipulation of war history. Some commentators interpreted Japanese actions in 1995 as evidence of increased willingness to be tough with China.

Relations with Taiwan also became a more difficult bilateral issue in 1995, largely as a result of China's concerns about Taiwan's stepped-up efforts to improve its international standing. The Chinese military actions designed to intimidate Taiwan in 1995 and 1996 alarmed many people in Japan, increasing Tokyo's wariness of PRC ambitions in the region.

The mixed picture in the first half of the 1990s—three "good" years followed by two "troubled" years—was not unusual in the modern history of Japan-China relations. Roughly comparable ups and downs occurred during the 1960s, 1970s, and 1980s.[9] In the early 1960s, for instance, Beijing was stridently opposed to both the United States and the Soviet Union and sharply criticized Japan's government as a "running dog" of "U.S. imperialism" in Asia. But China faced a major economic crisis as a result of the withdrawal of Soviet economic and technical support in 1960, as well as the disastrous collapse of the Great Leap Forward by 1961-1962. In this context, Beijing proved sufficiently pragmatic to reach a five-year economic agreement with a wide-ranging group of Japanese industries—in effect making Japan the major developed country involved in the support of China's economy.

While continuing to trade with Japan even during the most disruptive years of the Cultural Revolution in the late 1960s, Beijing strove to use its nascent opening to the Nixon administration and growing pro-PRC sentiment in Japan to isolate Japanese Prime Minister Sato and his conservative Liberal Democratic Party (LDP) government over their refusal to break ties with Taiwan and establish ties with Beijing. The surprise announcement by President Nixon in July 1971 that he would visit Beijing came as a "shock" to Sato and undermined his policy toward China. Beijing kept up the political pressure on Japan until a new LDP prime minister was selected and quickly normalized relations on terms agreeable to the PRC in 1972, ushering in a period of Sino-Japanese cooperation.

As post-Mao China developed an "open" foreign economic policy in the late 1970s, Japan loomed large in China's development calculus. Japan was China's largest trading partner. Aid relations grew rapidly, and by 1982 China was the largest recipient of official Japanese development assistance. Nonetheless, Chinese discontent grew in the 1980s over what China perceived as asymmetrical aspects of the economic relationship (for example, China sold Japan coal, oil, and raw materials; Japan sold China higher-value-added machinery, autos, and other equipment; Japan avoided much direct foreign investment in China; Japan shared less technology with China than with some other, developed, countries). Combined with Chinese irritation over the refusal of Japanese officials to take what Beijing saw as an appropriately contrite posture for Japan's negative war record in China, the seeming imbalance in economic benefits led to sharp criticisms of and demonstrations against Japan by students, other opinion leaders, and some officials. Both governments moved to minimize the disputes, with Japan notably stepping up its aid efforts in China and curbing official references to the war record that were likely to elicit a sharp Chinese response.

Differences in Japan-China Relations

History[10]

Japan's aggression against China in the seventy years prior to Japan's defeat in World War II is a potent issue in mainland China. The concerns of Chinese strategists and opinion leaders, as well as broader Chinese public opinion, about a possible revival of Japanese military expansion or more general Japanese untrustworthiness remain strong. This is partly due to the fact that Japanese aggression against China was far more severe than that of any other power; and to the fact that Chinese government-supported media and other outlets have used accusations of Japanese militarism as a way to build nationalistic feeling in China, to put the Japanese government on the defensive, and to elicit concessions from the Japanese government in the form of aid, trading terms, or other benefits.

For their part, Japanese officials sometimes exacerbate bilateral difficulties by denying the facts of history or equivocating on Japan's aggression against China up to the end of World War II. While many in Japan feel genuine regret about the war, repeated reminders from China seem particularly self-serving and undermine positive feelings toward the PRC regime. Meanwhile, some Japanese commentators speculate that Beijing strives to use its rising economic, political, and military influence to exert a dominant influence in East Asia, placing Japan in a similar kind of subservient position to the one that it held in the historical order in East Asia throughout most of the two thousand-year history of the Chinese Empire.

Territorial[11]

Sino-Japanese tensions over territorial disputes involving the islets in the East China Sea have erupted several times in the past. In February 1992, for example, Beijing passed a law reaffirming China's territorial claims to the eight islets known as the Diaoyu Islands in Chinese and the Senkaku Islands in Japanese. The islets are uninhabited, but they occupy an important strategic location, and the region around them is considered highly prospective for oil resources. The Japanese government strongly and promptly protested Beijing's sovereignty law while Taiwan also subsequently reasserted its claim to the islets.

The roots of the dispute go back to the nineteenth century. Japan defeated China in a war and took control of Taiwan in 1895. Following Japan's defeat in World War II, Taiwan was returned to China. But the islets remained under U.S. control. Japan's claim to the islets appeared strengthened when the United States returned them to Tokyo's control along with nearby Okinawa in 1971. Since then, the U.S. government has endeavored to keep from taking sides in the dispute.

In the 1970s, Tokyo and Beijing agreed to put the disputed islets issue aside as they normalized diplomatic relations and signed a peace treaty addressing issues stemming from World War II. Japanese rightists built a makeshift lighthouse on one of the islets in 1978. The Japanese coast guard has patrolled near the islets and has fended off efforts by fishermen and others from Taiwan to assert claims to the islets. Renewed activities by Japanese rightists on the islets in mid-1996 precipitated a period of Sino-Japanese tension over competing territorial claims.

Meanwhile, Japan and China have also had some differences over how to resolve competing claims to offshore resources in the East China Sea.

Economic[12]

Economic relations have been troubled on several occasions despite Japan's status as China's main trading partner, main source of economic assistance, and a leading source of direct foreign investment. In particular, China in the past has sometimes resisted perceived inequities in the bilateral economic relationship. Alleged efforts by Japanese government-backed companies to dominate key sectors of China's market were an important focal point for anti-Japanese demonstrations in Chinese cities in the mid-1980s. More recently, analysts sometimes see a shift in the bilateral economic relationship, as China prospectively becomes a more important partner for Japan than Japan is for China, and as China becomes a bigger economy. Indeed, Japan is already altering the level and scope of its aid program in China, to focus on areas less challenging to Japanese industry and more compatible with other Japanese interests (for example, the environment). Also, Tokyo has not budged in the face of Chinese complaints that the combination of the requirement that they repay Japanese loans in yen and the large rise in the value of the yen in relation to the U.S. dollar and China's currency over the past decade has put a heavy additional burden on China's economic development. Meanwhile, Japanese companies have been reluctant historically to share their most advanced technology with countries like China, fearing the technology will be absorbed and used to compete with Japanese producers.

Strategic[13]

During the cold war, Japan and China were preoccupied with the military dangers posed by the Soviet Union. In recent years, the two countries have warily viewed one another as longer-term strategic concerns.

In Japan, officials and strategists worried mainly about possible social instability and political paralysis in China in the immediate aftermath of the collapse of the Soviet Empire. Like the USSR, China had lost its ideological commitment, while the Tiananmen demonstrations revealed major political and social cleavages. Beijing's subsequent rapid economic growth, continued political stability, and more assertive military and foreign policies shifted Japanese concerns more toward dealing with the multifaceted consequences of the rise of a power of China's size. In particular, Japanese officials and other strategists are said to be more concerned with Beijing's increased air and naval power abilities; the assertive stance, backed by military force, used by Beijing to deal with disputes with Taiwan and in the South China Sea; and China's nuclear testing and practices involving the proliferation of weapons of mass destruction, delivery systems, and related technology.

In China, concern has focused recently on Japan's cooperation with the United States in "revitalizing" the U.S.-Japan alliance. Chinese planners are especially attentive to U.S.-backed efforts to encourage Japanese forces to play a bigger role in dealing with military contingencies in the East Asian region. Those Chinese commentators and officials who in recent years have seen the United States as determined to hold back or contain China's rising influence in East Asia suggest that the United States is using the alliance with Japan toward this end. They charge that Japan is a willing accomplice because Tokyo fears that China's rising influence will come at its expense.

They are especially critical of recently stepped-up U.S.-Japan cooperation to develop a theater ballistic defense in East Asia. They see this as directed at China as well as against North Korea's ballistic missiles.

Domestic Politics

Political conditions in both Japan and China are fluid and leaders must assuage important domestic interests in order to stay in power. China and Japan have been part of the growing trend of national assertiveness and pride that has spread throughout East Asia in the post-cold war period.[14] In the case of China, the government has gone out of its way to stoke the fires of nationalism, in part as a way to fill the ideological void created by the failure of communism. National pride in Japan is more understated but has emerged as a strong force prompting Japanese leaders to be more assertive in pressing Japan's case over issues dealing with trade disputes with the United States, territorial disputes with China, and the acquisition of a permanent seat in the UN Security Council. As a result, compromise on sensitive issues in China-Japan relations has become more difficult.

Mutual Interests in Japan-China Relations[15]

Both the Japanese and the Chinese governments continue to give top priority to the economic development of their countries, which they believe requires a peaceful and cooperative relationship with their neighbors, notably one another. China depends heavily on Japan for economic assistance, for technology and investment, and as a market for Chinese goods. Japan is increasingly dependent on China as a market, source of imports, and offshore manufacturing base. Projections suggest that trade links will be increasingly important for both sides. In foreign investment, recent trends also suggest that Japan may catch up with and surpass the United States and Taiwan to become China's second largest source of foreign investment (Hong Kong is way ahead and likely to remain in first place in this category).

Personal exchanges between Japan and China have grown rapidly. Since the inauguration of the post-Mao reforms, over forty thousand Chinese students have studied in Japan. Japanese students visiting or studying in China numbered twenty-two thousand in 1994 alone.[16] Numerous exchange programs—some fostered by the governments—work to build mutual understanding and improved relations. Such contacts do not always result in more positive feelings toward one another. But they do promote more realistic mutual assessments that can be effective in avoiding alarmist or otherwise excessive reactions concerning the other's capabilities or intentions.

No other government involved in East Asian affairs would benefit from or be inclined to promote greater Sino-Japanese friction. The United States is determined to maintain regional stability and to solidify U.S. relations with Japan while seeking U.S. comprehensive "engagement" with China. Russia has improved its relations with China markedly in recent years; its relations with Japan remain complicated by territorial disputes and economic incompatibilities, but both sides seek regional stability and mutual development.

In Southeast Asia, the Association of Southeast Asian Nations (ASEAN) seeks to reduce tensions and build mutual trust in the region through political dialogue between ASEAN and Chinese, Japanese, and other leaders, or through Asian-Pacific nations meeting in groups such as the ASEAN Regional Forum, which deals with regional security questions.

Some observers suggest that Taiwan would benefit in its competition with the PRC by a growing split between Japan and China.[17] Presumably, Taipei would seek to side with Tokyo against Beijing. But this line of reasoning ignores Taiwan's aversion to regional tensions and conflict, which have important negative consequences for the trade-dependent island.

At times, South Korea has not been adverse to lining up with Beijing to criticize Japan's war record. Privately, South Korea officials have shown some interest in using improved relations with China to balance South Korea's strong dependence on the United States and Japan for security and economic-technological support, respectively. Such manipulation works well in a peaceful atmosphere; but increased PRC-Japan tensions would seriously complicate the regional military and economic stability that is so important to South Korea's development. Moreover, South Korea's President Kim Dae Jung appeared to put such manipulation aside as he and Japanese leaders reached close rapport during Kim's visit to Japan in late 1998.

North Korea is less concerned with development than with survival, but in this case as well it is hard to see what benefit Pyongyang would derive from exacerbated Sino-Japanese tensions. In any event, North Korea's ability to influence such policy in Beijing and Tokyo is low and on the decline.

Recent High-Level Exchanges

Visits by top-level leaders to Beijing and Tokyo in 1997 and 1998 accentuated the positive and at least outwardly tried to play down the disputes in Sino-Japanese relations.[18] Beijing was satisfied with Japanese

Prime Minister Hashimoto's fence-mending efforts during his September 4-7, 1997, "successful" state visit, judging from official Chinese press reports. Agreement on annual high-level exchanges—including visits by Premier Li Peng later in 1997 and by President Jiang Zemin in 1998, the twentieth anniversary of the peace and friendship treaty—pointed toward further improvement.

Hashimoto publicly expanded previous Japanese statements of understanding of the PRC position on the Taiwan issue and the expectation of a peaceful resolution; Tokyo pledged no support for "two Chinas" or for Taiwan's independence and declared that Taiwan, as a part of China, was not qualified to enter the UN. Beijing doubtless hoped this would prod Washington to make similar high-level statements during Jiang's visit to the United States and President Clinton's subsequent visit to China.

Beijing was mollified, if not wholly satisfied, with Hashimoto's finessing of the sensitive issue of whether the revised U.S.-Japan defense guidelines cover the Taiwan Strait. He reiterated that the "areas surrounding Japan" did not represent a geographic concept but would be defined according to the nature of a given situation; he also promised that Japan would "act cautiously" on the basis of the Japan-China treaty and the joint statement on normalization of relations.

In his talks with Hashimoto, President Jiang Zemin departed from China's rhetoric of the past decade on Sino-Japanese relations, stressing that relations should be viewed from a "strategic" perspective. Li Peng reemphasized this theme during his visit to Japan on November 11-17, 1997.[19] An authoritative *Renmin Ribao* editorial capping the visit credited him with proposing a new set of "basic principles" for Sino-Japanese relations and asserted that these were formulated by Beijing "from a long-term strategic perspective." Although heralded by *Xinhua* at the time as a new approach, Li's five principles were similar to the guidelines China has espoused for relations with other powers and with Japan in the past. The five principles are: (1) noninterference in each other's internal affairs and toleration of ideological differences; (2) "correct" handling of differences to avoid "obstacles" to improving ties; (3) expanding dialogue and exchanges to enhance trust and understanding; (4) expanding economic cooperation; and (5) developing cross-generation friendship.

As the first head of government to visit Japan since before China's crackdown on pro-democracy protestors in 1989, Li's visit carried particular symbolic importance. The *Renmin Ribao* editorial heralded Li's visit as "completely successful," stating that he had received a "warm welcome and lavish hospitality" and had "reached the expected goal" of "deepening understanding, increasing friendship, and strengthening cooperation." It also said that Li had "achieved a broad consensus" with Hashimoto on key issues and predicted that the visit would have a far-reaching impact on the "stabilization and development" of bilateral relations.

As in the authoritative media treatment of high-level bilateral visits in the past, PRC media coverage of the Hashimoto-Li exchange made it clear that economic interest remains the core component of Beijing's diplomacy toward Japan. Underscoring this theme, a *Xinhua* "roundup" on December 28, 1997, praised Japan's official development assistance to China over the past twenty years as having "contributed to China's development" and promoted Sino-Japanese "friendship." Li's trip, in particular, seemed intended as an effort to push Japanese investment and technology exchange to new levels to meet the demands of China's burgeoning economy.

During the visit, Li was portrayed as making an unusually strong bid for investment and technology transfer in a series of speeches to Japanese business and industrial circles. His strongest pitch, in a speech to Japan's federation of economic organizations, the Keidanren, touted China's economic growth and stability, including its ability to withstand the Asian financial crisis, and went on to promise to "gradually open" China's "financial, trade, and other service sectors to foreign investors." Praising the "relentless efforts" of Japanese businessmen to facilitate the expansion of Japanese investment into new fields, he declared that "the fields for cooperation are broad and the formats flexible." He also asserted that Chinese markets have undergone "profound changes" and that Japanese businessmen are able to "change their concepts, seize opportunities, and suggest conditions for competing."

During the Li Peng visit, the two sides reached formal agreements on several key issues of importance to China that had been negotiated during Hashimoto's visit to China, including an agreement on bilateral environmental cooperation, a long-awaited fishery accord, and a joint declaration on China's accession to the WTO that implied further Japanese support.

Despite Beijing's efforts to smooth over troubled waters, authoritative media made it clear that past irritants continued to fester and could easily throw relations off track again. For example, during the state visits of both Hashimoto and Li, PRC media described the atmosphere of bilateral talks as "frank and sincere"—a formulation that is used by Beijing to indicate important differences and that has been used to characterize high-level visits since the Tiananmen crackdown. In addition, while Chinese leaders toned down their rhetoric on issues of deep concern, they pressed Japan to go further in making amends for wartime aggression in China and to clear up the ambiguity over whether the Japan-U.S. security guidelines included

Taiwan. Apparently, Beijing chose not to raise the territorial dispute over the Diaoyu (Senkaku) Islands during the visits, even though on the eve of Li's trip to Japan a Foreign Ministry spokesman was quoted by the PRC-owned Hong Kong paper *Wen Wei Po* as stating that this issue, "in particular," remained a problem, claiming that the islands had been China's territory "since ancient times."[20]

Although Hashimoto was quoted during his trip to China as reaffirming Japan's one-China stance, Li Peng nevertheless warned him that Beijing would not accept any effort, "direct or indirect," to include Taiwan in Japan-U.S. "security cooperation." Jiang Zemin told him that "any more" moves by Japan on the Taiwan issue would affect the "political foundation" of bilateral ties. Similarly, both Jiang and Li reiterated to Hashimoto China's views on Japan's wartime aggression, even though they adopted a softer tone than they had used in past public statements to Japanese leaders.

As for Li's visit to Japan, authoritative PRC media portrayed him as glossing over both the Taiwan and the history issues in his talks with Hashimoto but as making more pointed comments in his remarks to other groups. In his talks with Hashimoto, he was quoted as saying that the two countries should "deal in a timely manner with whatever problems arise" and "prevent the overall development of bilateral relations from being interrupted." He went on to say that China had "taken note" of the "promises" made by Hashimoto while in China and "hopes the Japanese side will honor and carry out its promises." Although he said Hashimoto had affirmed Japan's rejection of "two Chinas" or of Taiwanese independence, he did not specifically mention China's concern over the scope of the Japan-U.S. security guidelines; and while he said that Hashimoto had made promises on "historical issues," he did not spell them out.

The visit of Defense Minister Chi Haotian to Tokyo on February 3-8, 1998—the first such high-level substantive military exchange since diplomatic relations were established in 1972—marked more forward movement, while noting continuing differences.[21] Suggesting that China viewed Chi's visit as successful in maintaining the momentum of improving ties, PRC media coverage of Chi's talks with Prime Minister Hashimoto, Foreign Minister Keizo Obuchi, and JDA Director-General Fumio Kyuma continued the generally positive spin that Beijing media had put on Sino-Japanese relations over the previous year and portrayed the establishment of military-to-military relations as a further step toward consolidating bilateral ties. Media coverage of Chi's meeting with Hashimoto, for example, was markedly upbeat and contained no reference to such thorny issues as Taiwan or Japan's wartime actions in China. A *Xinhua* report on February 5 stressed the positive nature of the relationship, quoting Chi as saying his visit was a "good beginning of the new year for bilateral ties" and showed that exchanges between the two nations have "expanded to all spheres."

Media coverage of Chi's talks with Kyuma was more explicit in linking military ties to the improvement of bilateral relations. A February 4, 1998, *Xinhua* report on their talks that day cited Chi and Kyuma as agreeing that defense cooperation is "conducive" to maintaining bilateral relations as well as regional peace and stability. The two officials also agreed on military exchanges between the People's Liberation Army and the Japanese armed forces, and Kyuma reportedly accepted "with pleasure" Chi's invitation to pay a reciprocal visit to China within the year.

Reflecting Beijing's intention to remind Tokyo of areas in which it is closely monitoring Japan's behavior, the *Xinhua* report on Chi's meeting with Kyuma also cited Chi as bringing up Taiwan and historical issues, but as referring to these issues only briefly. Suggesting that the Taiwan issue continues to worry Beijing more than other irritations in the relationship, Chi called on Japan to adopt a "more definite stance" on Taiwan in regard to the U.S.-Japan "Defense Cooperation Treaty." He adopted a softer tone on the history issue, calling on Tokyo to adopt a "responsible attitude toward history" so as to imbue Japanese youth with a "correct historical perspective."

Further progress in Chinese-Japanese relations came during Chinese Vice President Hu Jintao's extensive goodwill visit to Japan in April 1998. Beijing subsequently broadened its contacts in the more fluid and notably less pro-China political arena in Japan by normalizing relations with the Japanese Communist Party after a hiatus of thirty years; and by establishing—after a similarly lengthy wait—normal relations with the conservative Japanese newspaper *Sankei Shimbun*, the only major Japanese daily that refused to close its bureau in Taiwan in return for the opportunity to open a bureau in Beijing. China reacted calmly to the fall of the Hashimoto government in August 1998 and muted its criticism of Japan in the lead up to President Jiang's first visit to Japan in September 1998. Privately, and sometimes publicly, Chinese officials were critical of Japan's economic policies during the Asian economic crisis. Jiang Zemin reportedly postponed his September visit in order to put pressure on Japan to adhere more closely to PRC views on Taiwan.[22] Nonetheless, the visit was rescheduled for November 1998 and both governments worked to ensure a positive atmosphere for the trip.

In any event, Jiang's visit took place in late November. Gains for China included substantial added economic aid from Japan. Prime Minister Obuchi went no further than previous Japanese leaders in meeting Chinese demands on Taiwan; he notably eschewed a formal declaration similar to the so-called "three no's"—no support for "one China, one Taiwan," Taiwanese independence, or Taiwanese membership in international organizations requiring statehood—voiced by U.S. President Clinton in Shanghai on June 30, 1998. And Obuchi's remarks on Japan's past aggression in China and the U.S.-Japan defense treaty were consistent with past practice.[23]

Outlook

The past cyclical pattern of Sino-Japanese relations and an assessment of their recent status suggest a generally mixed picture of difficulties and cooperation for the future. As in the past, the relationship could be unstable for a time, with periods of warming relations followed by periods of dispute in which economic and other mutual interests are damaged to some degree. But the swings in policy are likely to be less wide than during the Maoist period, if only because present-day Chinese leaders are in general agreement that Beijing's interests are best served by working generally with the world as it is, rather than attempting to foster major change in the East Asian region or the world as a whole. For their part, Japanese leaders seem determined to adhere to the general outlines of a policy that fosters Japanese economic growth in an international environment of peace and stability.

Unsteady domestic politics in Beijing and Tokyo, rising assertiveness backed by stronger nationalistic feelings, and mutual wariness as the two powers adjust to China's rising power and influence in Asian and world affairs will head the list of factors complicating smooth China-Japan relations. But until such time as one side or the other feels strong and confident enough to risk a serious break with the other, the forces promoting economic interdependence and mutual accommodation are likely to overrule the forces of assertiveness and confrontation.

In sum, this record of alternating "good" and "bad" periods in recent Sino-Japanese relations reveals the difficulty the generally preoccupied and pragmatic PRC leaders have in dealing with a major neighboring power that is allied to a superpower with mixed intentions toward the Chinese government and that has proved enormous material benefit for the Chinese economy. At bottom, Chinese leaders are in no position to confront Japan over differences in their relationship unless Japan impinges seriously on a vital PRC concern like Taiwan. There is little positive sentiment between the two governments, but both sets of leaders place a higher priority on development and stability than they do on allowing bilateral differences to drive their relationship.

Notes

1. See, among others, Donald Klein, "Japan and Europe in Chinese Foreign Relations," in Samuel Kim, ed., *China and the World*, Boulder, Colo.: Westview Press, 1998, pp. 133-150; Banning Garrett and Bonnie Glaser, "Chinese Apprehensions about Revitalization of the U.S.-Japan Alliance," *Asian Survey* 37, 4 (April 1997): 383-402; Christopher Howe and Brian Hook, eds., *China and Japan: History, Trends and Prospects*, Oxford: Oxford University Press, 1994; Kokubun Ryosei, *Challenges for China-Japan-U.S. Cooperation*, Tokyo: Japan Center for International Exchange, 1998.

2. Chinese, Japanese, and Western media noted the highlights of Jiang's visit, which began on November 25, 1998.

3. See *Asia's Global Powers: China-Japan*, Canberra: East Asian Analytical Unit, Government of Australia, 1996; Banning Garrett and Bonnie Glaser, "Review of the U.S.-Japan Alliance and Emerging Sino-Japanese Rivalry," unpublished manuscript, September 1996; Li Zhengxin, "My Views on the U.S. Adjustments to Its Asian Strategy," Beijing, *Shijie Zhishi*, May 16, 1998, pp. 4-7; and Wang Shaopu, "The Readjustment of China-Japan-U.S. Triangular Relations," *Shanghai Shehui Kexue*, December 15, 1998, pp. 34-37.

4. These are reviewed in *Asia's Global Powers*. See also *Japan, China Relations: Status, Outlook and Implications for the United States*, Washington, D.C.: Library of Congress, Congressional Research Service (CRS) Report 96-864F, October 30, 1996.

5. See, among others, "The 1997-1998 International Situation Analysis Report," by Su Guiyou and Liu Yusheng, Beijing, *Zhongguo Xinwen She*, January 20, 1998 (internet version). See most notably "White Paper on China's National Defense," *Xinhua*, July 27, 1998 (internet version).

6. See *Japan, China Relations*, p. 2.

7. Reviewed in Kim, ed., *China and the World*, pp. 113-127. See also review in *Asia's Global Powers.*

8. See review of these and later events in *Japan, China Relations*, CRS Report 96-864F, pp. 3-4.

9. Allen Whiting, *China Eyes Japan*, Berkeley: University of California, 1989; Kim, ed., *China and the World*, pp. 113-127; A. Doak Barnett, *China and the Major Powers in East Asia*, Washington, D.C.: Brookings Institution, 1977; and Robert Sutter, *Chinese Foreign Policy: Developments after Mao*, New York: Praeger, 1986.

10. Reviewed in *Asia's Global Powers*, pp. 11-13.

11. Reviewed in *Senkaku (Diaoyu) Islands Dispute*, Washington, D.C.: Library of Congress, CRS Report 96-798F, September 30, 1996, and *East Asia: Disputed Island and Offshore Claims*, Washington, D.C.: Library of Congress, CRS Report 92-614S, July 28, 1992.

12. Reviewed in Allen Whiting, *China Eyes Japan;* and in *Asia's Global Powers*, pp. 25-80.

13. Reviewed in Banning Garrett and Bonnie Glaser, "Review of the U.S.-Japan Alliance and Emerging Sino-Japanese Rivalry." See also *Asian-Pacific Security Arrangements: The U.S.-Japanese Alliance and China's Strategic View*, Washington, D.C.: Library of Congress, CRS Report 97-375F, March 21, 1997, pp. 1-16.

14. *"Asian Values" and Asian Assertiveness*, Washington, D.C.: Library of Congress, CRS Report 96-610F, July 9, 1996.

15. Reviewed in *Asia's Global Powers*; Kim, ed., *China in World Affairs*; *Japan-China Relations*.

16. Cited in *Japan-China Relations*, p. 8.

17. Ibid.

18. This section is taken especially from an excellent review of recent Japan-China exchanges. See Foreign Broadcast Information Service memorandum, "Sino-Japanese Relations in 1997," January 26, 1998 (Internet version).

19. See "Sino-Japanese Relations in 1997," detailing media play-by-play during Li's visit.

20. Cited in "Sino-Japanese Relations in 1997."

21. FBIS *Trends*, "Defense Minister Visit Highlights Latest Move toward Further Normalization of Relations," March 5, 1998 (Internet version).

22. See, among others, "Jiang's Visit to Japan Delayed by Policy Splits," *Financial Times*, August 26, 1998, p. 5.

23. See, among others, *China Daily*, November 25-29, 1998.

Chapter 6

Relations with the Koreas and Taiwan

Korea

With the collapse of the Soviet Union and demise of East-West and Sino-Soviet competition for influence in the Korean peninsula after the cold war, Beijing adjusted Chinese relations to take advantage of economic and other opportunities with South Korea, while sustaining its position as North Korea's most important foreign ally. But the international confrontation caused by North Korea's nuclear weapons program and related ballistic missile programs, and the sharp decline in economic conditions and the rise of political uncertainty there following the sudden death of Kim Il Sung in 1994, raised great uncertainties in China about the future stability of the peninsula. In general, Chinese officials have used economic aid and continued military exchanges to help stabilize and preserve Chinese relations with the North, while working closely with the United States and South Korea in seeking a peaceful resolution to tensions on the peninsula through the so-called four-party peace talks that began in 1997. Meanwhile, China's active interest in beneficial economic relations with South Korea has continued to grow, albeit with complications caused by the sharp decline in South Korea's economic conditions as a result of the Asian economic crisis in the late 1990s.[1]

Chinese and South Korean leaders have taken a series of initiatives in recent years to markedly improve their bilateral relations. Top Chinese leaders visited Seoul, while South Korean Presidents Kim Young Sam and

Kim Dae Jung and other senior leaders visited Beijing. Trade grew markedly, as did South Korean investment in China. Beijing's delicate position, maintaining long-standing ties with North Korea while rapidly improving relations with South Korea, was tested notably in February 1997; a senior North Korean official, Hwang Jang-Yop, attempted to defect to South Korea at the South Korean mission in Beijing. Five weeks of negotiations led to a settlement in which Hwang was allowed to travel to the Philippines, where he stayed for a month before arriving in Seoul.[2]

China and South Korea have demonstrated similar motives in seeking increased bilateral contacts for economic reasons, to enhance their interests on the Korean peninsula, and to broaden foreign policy options.

Trade and Investment

Both sides have been anxious to facilitate trade and investment. Bilateral trade in 1992 was worth $5 billion. It doubled to $10 billion in 1994 and doubled again to $20 billion in 1996. By 1997, China was South Korea's third largest trading partner, after the United States and Japan. South Korea was China's fourth largest trading partner.[3]

At that time, South Korea invested more in China than in any other foreign country. The level of investment amounted to $2.7 billion in several thousand mostly small-scale enterprises centered in the nearby Chinese provinces of Shandung, Tianjin, and Liaoning. Burgeoning business ties resulted in extensive travel, especially from South Korea to China. There were seven hundred thousand South Korean visitors to China in 1996.

The Asian economic crisis of the late 1990s had a devastating effect on economic conditions in South Korea. Anxious to appear supportive of an important neighbor, trading partner, and investor, China backed International Monetary Fund (IMF) rescue plans for South Korea. China's commitment not to devalue its currency to better compete with exports from South Korea and other Asian states with devalued currencies scored public relations points in Seoul. It stood in notable contrast to Japanese reluctance to take steps to hold the decline in the value of the Japanese yen—a reluctance that allowed Japanese exporters to cut into South Korean export markets.[4]

Korean Peninsula

Closer relations with China have helped to ease South Korean concerns about Beijing's possible support for North Korean aggression against the South. They have also provided Seoul, via Beijing, with an indirect channel of information on and communication with North Korean leaders, who have generally refused to interact directly with their South Korean counterparts. Such channels of communication with and information about North Korea have helped to reassure South Koreans about trends on the Korean peninsula, including North Korea's repeated efforts to seek progress in relations with the United States at the expense of South Korea. Meanwhile, South Korean enterprises anxious to enter the North Korean market have been able to sidestep restrictions on bilateral trade and investments by working with North Korea through South Korean enterprises based in China.[5]

Chinese officials have viewed improved relations with South Korea as broadening China's influence on the peninsula. Some Chinese officials have asserted that Beijing's improvement of relations set "a good example," which should be reciprocated by the United States and Japan in moving ahead with their respective relations with North Korea. Beijing officials have judged that such "cross recognition" would markedly ease North Korea's isolation and fears, and thereby open the way to eased tensions on the peninsula. South Korean officials for many years emphasized that they opposed such U.S. and Japanese measures unless they were accompanied by improved North Korean relations with South Korea. President Kim Dae Jung, who took power in February 1998, adopted a different position on this issue in mid-1998, urging the United States and others to move forward and improve relations with North Korea.[6]

Although Chinese officials have denied it, some South Korean specialists and U.S. experts have asserted that one of Beijing's longer-term motives in improving ties with the South has been to preclude an increase in U.S. prominence on the peninsula.[7] According to this view, Chinese officials have been concerned by North Korea's apparent recent focus on relations with the United States as the central element of Pyongyang's foreign policy. The Chinese have been determined to avoid a situation in which the United States would become the dominant outside influence in both South and North Korea, and they have viewed improved relations with Seoul as a useful hedge against such an outcome.

For the time being, however, both Beijing and Seoul have stressed efforts to seek closer cooperation to deal with possible contingencies stemming from the increasingly uncertain situation in North Korea. And in this endeavor, both China and South Korea have sought close cooperation with the United States and other involved powers.

Chinese specialists have strongly affirmed their common ground with South Korea and the United States in trying to preserve peace and stability on the Korean peninsula. Chinese officials are often more optimistic than their South Korean and American counterparts about the current situation and the future outlook for the regime in North Korea. Thus, in the late 1990s, they claimed that North Korea's regime remained under Kim Jong Il's rule, was able to weather current shortages of food, energy, and foreign exchange without collapse, and was making some small headway in developing relations with and getting assistance from foreign countries. Nevertheless, Chinese specialists were clearly more concerned than in the past about the viability of the North Korean regime unless the Kim Jong Il leadership implemented some economic reforms and opened the country to more international contact. At the same time, they believed that too-rapid North Korean reform and opening could seriously destabilize the Pyongyang regime. China has continued to supply food assistance and oil to North Korea. And it has continued leadership contacts, especially by the military, with North Korea.

China supported U.S., South Korean, and other efforts to get North and South Korea to resume an effective dialogue, and to encourage the North to reform itself domestically and open itself up internationally. Notably, China has backed the U.S.-South Korean-initiated four-party talks (involving North and South Korea, the U.S., and China) as a way to ease North-South differences and to bring about a more lasting peace settlement on the peninsula. China has continued to oppose direct pressure on North Korea, judging that it could lead to a negative reaction.

Chinese specialists expect that North Korea will raise obstacles, preconditions, or other difficulties in the four-party talks and other interactions with South Korea, at least for the time being. At bottom, the North Koreans are said by Chinese experts to want first to build ties with the United States, Japan, and others in order to strengthen their hand prior to direct negotiations with the South. Also, North Korean leaders were said to be resentful of past actions of the South Korean government of Kim Young Sam and to have viewed the Kim Young Sam government as weak on account of corruption scandals and other issues in 1997. Chinese specialists did not expect North Korea to make significant progress in relations with the South until after the election of a new South Korean president in December 1997. Beijing generally welcomed the moderate and positive tone toward North Korea adopted by President Kim Dae Jung since his inauguration in February 1998. President Jiang Zemin highlighted this theme in welcoming Kim Dae Jung during a five-day visit to China in November 1998.[8]

Chinese officials also have taken pains to emphasize that the recent improvement in China's relations with South Korea has not been directed in any way at the United States or the U.S.-South Korean alliance relationship. Chinese officials have acknowledged that while Sino-South Korean relations, especially economic relations, will continue to grow, the U.S.-South

Korean relationship remains very broad and multifaceted and has a critical security dimension involving a defense treaty and U.S. troop presence in South Korea. As one Chinese official put it in mid-1997, "for South Korea, the U.S. is much more important than China."[9] South Korean officials have echoed this sentiment. They have noted that Seoul needs China's "understanding" and "constructive role" in seeking reunification, but that relations with China cannot in any way substitute for South Korea's relations with the United States.[10]

Beijing's stated intention to supplement rather than substitute for U.S.-South Korean relations has affected China's attitude toward the U.S. role in South Korea after reunification. Despite the fact that the Chinese government has officially encouraged the eventual U.S. military withdrawal from East Asia and has strongly criticized the recent strengthening of the U.S.-Japan alliance relationship,[11] Beijing officials have been moderate in response to recent calls in the United States and South Korea for a continued U.S. military presence in Korea even after Korean reunification. Chinese officials have adopted a wait-and-see attitude. They have advised that Korean unification could be a long way off. They have noted that some in South Korea want a continued U.S. military presence, but have added that the situation could change in the future.

Foreign Policy Concerns

South Korean officials have viewed better relations with China as a useful way to preclude possible Chinese expansion or pressure against South Korea as China grows in wealth and power during the twenty-first century. They also have seen good relations with China as providing protection against possible pressure from Japan against South Korea in the future. (Such continued South Korean suspicion of Japan has notably complicated U.S. policy in the region, which has relied on U.S. alliance relations with both Japan and South Korea. President Kim Dae Jung helped to ease this suspicion with a landmark visit to Tokyo in late 1998.)[12]

Officials in Seoul are careful to add that relations with China also broaden South Korean foreign policy options, allowing South Korea to appear to break out of the constraints imposed by what they see as a U.S.-centered foreign policy since the 1950s. Some South Korean opinion leaders judge that with better relations with China, Seoul can afford to be more assertive and less accommodating in relations with the United States, although South Korean officials and knowledgeable scholars are often quick to assert that relations with China or other foreign policy options provide no substitute for the essential South Korean alliance relationship with the United States.[13]

Meanwhile, given continued difficulties in U.S.-China relations, South Korean officials sometimes express an interest in boosting South Korea's international stature as a "mediator" between these two powers, both of which have friendly ties with Seoul. South Korean officials also assert that South Korea wants to avoid a situation where it might have to choose between Washington and Beijing if U.S.-Chinese tensions in Asia were to rise sharply. They say that they urge Beijing as well as Washington to try harder to maintain good relations with one another, and claim that PRC officials "appreciate" what the Republic of Korea (ROK) has to say.

According to South Korean experts, China also views good relations with Seoul as a possible hedge against Japanese power, although Chinese officials emphasize that their interests focus on regional peace and stability and on setting a good example in relations with a smaller neighbor, South Korea, in order to reassure China's other neighbors about Beijing's foreign policy intentions. More broadly, Chinese intentions are said by some South Korean experts to reflect a desire to use better relations with South Korea against perceived U.S. efforts to "contain" or hold back China's growing power and influence in Asian and world affairs. In particular, Chinese specialists and officials have voiced concern from time to time that the United States might use its alliance relationships with Japan and South Korea in order to check or build a barrier against the allegedly expanding "China threat" in northeast Asia. Closer China-South Korean relations would complicate any such U.S. strategic scheme.[14]

Symptomatic of the prevailing balance in Chinese relations with North and South Korea were the Chinese efforts, largely thwarted, to improve relations with North Korea once Kim Jong Il assumed the post of general secretary of the Korean Workers' Party in October 1997, and the cordial Chinese relationship established expeditiously with the newly installed Kim Dae Jung administration in South Korea. Chinese party chief Jiang Zemin on October 8, 1997, sent Kim Jong Il a friendly personal message of congratulations on his accession to the position of general secretary of the Korean Workers' Party, and the Chinese Foreign Ministry spokesman also "heartily congratulated" Kim.[15] But despite repeated speculation about a Chinese-North Korean summit, Jiang Zemin told Japanese visitors in February 1998 that no high-level contacts were in the offing. Jiang said that before former North Korean President Kim Il Sung died in 1994, Beijing and Pyongyang had regular state visits, but since Kim's son, Kim Jong Il, has taken over the reins of the country, such exchanges have not resumed. "After Kim Il Sung passed away, Kim Jong Il [observed] the three-year custom . . . of mourning . . . now that the three years have passed he has therefore become general secretary of the Workers' Party, but it appears he has not made any plans to visit," he said. Jiang said that as China and North Korea maintain good-neighborly ties of friendship, mutual visits are normal, but "at present we have not had the opportunity."[16]

In contrast with his oblique references to Chinese frustration with North Korea's leadership, Jiang in the same interview extended a warm welcome to South Korea's new president. "We were very happy to see that Kim Dae Jung won the South Korean elections and will be the next president. We welcome him to come to China for a visit after assuming his presidential duties."[17]

Beijing significantly made high-level approaches to the new South Korean leadership. Chinese Vice President Hu Jintao, selected by the Ninth National People's Congress in March 1998, made his first trip abroad to Japan and South Korea in April 1998. In meetings with South Korean President Kim Dae Jung, acting Prime Minister Kim Jong Il, and Foreign and Trade Minister Park Chung Soo, Hu highlighted the progress in Sino-Korean ties since relations were normalized in 1992 and emphasized the importance of a stable Korean peninsula for the entire Asia-Pacific region. The PRC vice president also assured his hosts that China's currency would not succumb to the financial pressures buffeting those of other East Asian countries. Opportunities for closer cooperation were discussed in the areas of fisheries, visa-free tourism, and nuclear energy projects. Hu also sought reaffirmation of Seoul's commitment to a one-China policy, though Taiwan-South Korea business contacts continued to thrive. Further solidifying relations, South Korean President Kim Dae Jung was warmly received by President Jiang Zemin and other senior leaders during an official visit to Beijing in November 1998.[18]

Meanwhile, military ties between Seoul and Beijing grew more slowly than political and economic relations, presumably because China wanted to maintain ties to the North Korean armed forces. Seoul continued pushing for strengthened military exchanges, but Beijing sought to limit the scope and pace of their military relationship. Military ties grew concurrently with political and economic relations, but at a slower pace. The South Korean vice defense minister visited China for the first time in November 1997, the highest-level military exchange to date. Higher-level contacts gradually developed but Beijing was slow to respond to repeated South Korean overtures to establish regular exchanges between their defense ministers and other senior military officials.[19]

Meanwhile, presumably in deference to North Korean sensitivities, Beijing delayed, in the face of repeated South Korean efforts, establishing a consulate in Shenyang, in northeastern China, closer than Beijing to the

North Korean border. There are millions of ethnic Koreans in this part of China, many of whom have knowledge about developments in North Korea. Media reports said the South Korean consulate would open in 1999.[20]

In sum, China's policy in the late 1990s continued to balance often conflicting imperatives regarding North and South Korea as it dealt with the delicate and potentially volatile situation on the peninsula. Beijing did not appear to seek big changes in the political or military status quo; it appeared intent on promoting as much stability as possible, while benefitting economically and in other ways by improving its relations with South Korea. As economic conditions in North Korea deteriorated, and as the North Korean regime persisted with provocative military and political actions, Beijing officials privately worried about possible adverse consequences for China. Nonetheless, Chinese officials still saw their basic interests as well served with a policy of continued, albeit guarded, support for the North, along with improved relations with the South and close consultations with the United States over Korean peninsula issues.

Taiwan

China's search for a stable and peaceful international environment prompts Chinese efforts to smooth over differences and emphasize common ground, especially with China's neighbors and major trading partners. While broadly successful with most major powers and regional countries, the Chinese approach has not worked with Taiwan. In part this is because the Taiwan government is not prepared to accept the PRC terms for establishing improved relations, especially demands that Taipei adhere to a "one-China" policy as defined by Beijing. And in part this is because Beijing is not nearly as accommodating with Taiwan as it is with other entities with which it has disputes.

The so-called Taiwan issue enjoyed a unique status in Chinese foreign policy priorities in the late 1990s.[21] Chinese leaders were unprepared for the rising sentiment in favor of greater separation from the mainland and a more prominent and distinctive role for Taiwan in world affairs that emerged with greater democracy on the island after the end of martial law in 1987. At first, Chinese leaders judged that the concurrent growth in cross-strait trade and other exchanges would hold these Taiwanese sentiments in check; but gradually they became deeply concerned about a perceived movement toward political independence, and deeply suspicious not only of avowed pro-independence activists in the opposition Democratic Progressive Party but also of the president and chairman of the ruling Nationalist Party, Lee Teng-hui. China's concern reached fever pitch after Lee developed his successful flexible diplomacy in visiting countries that maintained official relations with the PRC and notably gained entry to the United States, ostensibly to visit his alma mater.[22]

Beijing saw the Clinton administration's reversal of policy—first denying Lee a visa and then granting him one amid broad media and congressional pressure—as a major setback in Chinese foreign policy. President Jiang Zemin, Foreign Minister Qian Qichen, and others had to defend their handling of the issue in the face of strong criticism from other leaders. Not surprisingly, PRC policy hardened. On the one hand, China resorted to provocative military exercises designed to intimidate the people of Taiwan and their international supporters prior to important legislative and presidential elections on the island in December 1995 and March 1996, respectively. The military actions cowed Taiwan for a time, though the United States eventually sent two carrier battle groups to observe the PRC exercises—a sign that boosted Taiwan's morale and underlined for Beijing the potentially dangerous consequences of provocative military action against Taiwan. On the other hand, Beijing further intensified its foreign policy efforts to isolate Taiwan, striving by this means to push Taiwan away from pursuing its independent posture in world affairs and, over the longer term, to prompt Taiwan to accept cross-strait talks on reunification on terms acceptable to Beijing. As the United States and other powers sought improved relations with China in the mid-1990s, Chinese officials had a freer hand to devote to pressuring Taiwan in international affairs. As a result, it was fair to say that by the late 1990s, reducing Taiwan's diplomatic stature was the most important issue of immediate concern to Chinese foreign policy makers.[23]

Well aware that Beijing's continued difficult domestic priorities meant that mainland China was unlikely to take rash assertive action against Taiwan, unless provoked, Taiwan leaders gave tit-for-tat in international competition with Beijing. Mainland Chinese leaders had expected that President Jiang Zemin's summit meeting with President Clinton in Washington in October 1997 would provide a springboard for Chinese public relations and international efforts to underscore Taiwan's vulnerability and isolation. Though Taiwan reacted to the summit with a calm visage, Taiwan was concerned that improved U.S.-PRC relations could come at Taiwan's expense. The Taiwan officials also had seen mainland China win away South Africa from recognizing Taiwan; South Africa was the last major state to maintain official diplomatic relations with Taiwan. Beijing was using aid, diplomatic pressure, and other means to whittle away Taiwan's shrinking band of diplomatic allies. Thus, China used its veto power to bar UN peacekeepers from Haiti until the government there modified its tradition-ally strong support for Taiwan.[24]

the scope of the crisis began to affect a wide range of Southeast Asian states, the Taiwan government jumped into action to improve its diplomatic profile with high-level official interchanges with Southeast Asian officials. Senior Singaporean, Malaysian, and other officials stopped briefly in Taipei for talks with senior Taiwan leaders. Taiwan loomed large in their economic calculus given its relatively strong economy, its large investment role in Southeast Asia, and its entrepreneurial middle class with many billions of dollars of foreign exchange reserves. Early in 1998, Taiwanese delegations led by the vice president, the premier, senior economic ministers, and even President Lee Teng-hui's wife traveled to Singapore, the Philippines, Thailand, and Japan for discussions on the Asian crisis. Taiwan officials from Lee Teng-hui on down also repeatedly warned of the danger of a possible devaluation of China's currency, urging Taiwanese investors to seek trade and investment opportunities in "safer" areas than mainland China.[25]

Not wishing to upset relations with Asian countries seeking financial help, the PRC at first adopted a low-key response to Taiwan's maneuvers, but senior leaders leveled increasingly tough warnings later in 1998. They harshly criticized Taiwan's motives; they castigated Taiwan for deliberately exacerbating the crisis by devaluing its currency in 1997 and spreading "rumors" about a Chinese devaluation in an effort to destabilize the Hong Kong and PRC economies and provide an opening for Taiwan diplomacy. Alluding to possible U.S. support for a prominent Taiwan role in international efforts to relieve the Asian crisis, they reminded the United States of the primacy of the Taiwan issue in U.S.-China relations, calling for vigilance against Taiwan's efforts to make political gains during a period of financial turmoil.[26]

Beijing continued its pressure to isolate Taiwan further following South Africa's January 1, 1998, switch of official recognition from Taipei to Beijing. Despite preoccupation with the financial crisis, Beijing sent its Foreign Trade and Economics minister to Fiji on January 15, 1998. Fiji had official relations with Beijing but maintained cordial unofficial ties with Taiwan. Fiji was a leader of the Pacific Island countries, four of which maintained official relations with Taiwan and supported Taiwan's role as a "special dialogue partner" with the South Pacific Forum, the main regional organization. The day before the Chinese minister arrived, Fiji Television reported that Fiji's president had invited Lee Teng-hui to travel to the island the next week.[27] The visit, however, was postponed, presumably in deference to PRC sensibilities.

While the diplomatic guerrilla war continued, neither side wanted to be seen, especially in Washington, as recalcitrant on cross-strait issues. The United States was anxious to see a reduction of tensions in the Taiwan Strait by reviving the cross-strait talks that had been suspended as a result of Lee

Teng-hui's visit to the United States in 1995. PRC and Taiwan leaders sought to improve cross-strait relations but on their own terms; they were also constrained by internal disagreements. Both sides viewed their competition in zero-sum terms, particularly with respect to U.S. support. Taiwan's effort to score political gains from the Asian financial crisis also soured the atmosphere. Little real progress was expected as formal high-level exchanges resumed in October 1998.[28]

Public statements during Chinese New Year in 1998 in Beijing and Taipei suggested that cross-strait shadowboxing was intended by both sides to prevent slippage rather than create a breakthrough. Former U.S. Defense Secretary William Perry reported to Taipei that Beijing was ready to resume talks between leaders of the respective cross-strait offices (Taiwan's Straits Exchange Foundation, SEF, and China's Association for Relations Across the Taiwan Strait, ARATS) from the point where they left off in 1995; Taipei indicated its receptivity. On the "one-China" sovereignty issue, both Taipei and Beijing were edging back toward the mid-1990s approach of setting aside differing interpretations to be dealt with later. Similarly, the issue of equality between parties—a Taiwan demand—could be bypassed for the time being by again using the quasi-official ARATS/SEF forum. China had insisted the next round be formal political negotiations on reunification; Taiwan wanted unofficial technical talks. Now both were saying unofficial talks could cover all issues: economic, administrative, and political.[29]

The give on both sides was minimal, however, and intended mainly to gain time. A *People's Daily* editorial during the Chinese New Year period of 1998 repackaged old positions to project a leadership consensus on a peaceful settlement, but insisted Taipei must agree to eventual formal political negotiations, not merely to unofficial "preparatory" consultations. Similarly, Taiwan President Lee Teng-hui in a *Der Spiegel* interview at the time reiterated his willingness to visit Beijing, but only as Republic of China (ROC) president. Beijing hoped that already planned low-level exchanges would build positive momentum. Not wanting to appear obstructionist, Taiwan went along but dragged its feet until it was in a strong position.[30]

In the early 1990s, PRC leaders had appeared relatively confident of U.S. nonintervention and concentrated on building confidence among Taiwan political and economic leaders. This approach was based on Deng Xiaoping's premise that growing economic and cultural interdependence within a "greater China" (including Hong Kong) would provide a solid basis for staged reunification, beginning with unofficial technical talks and moving eventually to formal political negotiations. Beijing retained the option of using force as a hedge against independence. Lee Teng-hui's visit to the United States in 1995 undermined the PRC policy consensus and produced a more activist approach, using first military posturing and then diplomacy aimed at checking separatist trends. The United States was again viewed as a major factor in the equation.

China's policy was to seek a negotiated agreement to end the civil war in accordance with the "one-China" principle. This assumed an activist strategy of confidence building with parallel pressure to end the U.S. commitment to Taiwan's security. In Beijing's thinking, U.S. distancing from Taiwan would weaken Taiwan's resistance to talks. This strategy did not allow for politically risky concessions to Taiwan's desire for an enhanced international stature. It did, however, include opening channels to other key constituencies on the island—in business, the military, and the political opposition—as well as continued planning and preparation for military contingencies.

Lee Teng-hui's policy balanced efforts to upgrade Taiwan's international stature and defense capabilities with a go-slow approach to enhancing relations with the mainland.[31] It began with confidence-building contacts by unofficial organizations and pointed vaguely toward closer, more official relations in the future. This gradualist approach reflected the strong popular desire in Taiwan to avoid early reunification without antagonizing China. In accordance with this strategy, Taiwan initiated the SEF/ARATS channel, which had conducted talks on and off since 1992. The principals held formal talks in Singapore in 1993 and negotiated several practical cooperation measures. This was followed by staff negotiations and preparations for the next formal round of talks, scheduled for 1995 in Taipei. These talks were canceled by Beijing after Lee's U.S. visit. SEF/ARATS cultural exchanges continued, however, and Taiwanese investments in mainland enterprises grew.

U.S. initiatives to encourage both sides to resume talks were the main source of momentum in the late 1990s.[32] China wanted to take advantage of the high-profile U.S.-PRC summits of 1997 and 1998 to portray a common PRC-U.S. front. Taiwan feared lost leverage and realized the need to appear at least somewhat accommodating. Both sides focused on preventing a U.S. "tilt" toward the other; both worked hard to appear the more reasonable and aggrieved party. Beijing sought stronger U.S. pledges on Taiwan relations and arms sales. Taipei urged the United States to improve its relations with Taiwan in parallel with the warming of U.S.-PRC relations and emphasized the potential for instability in China as a strong rationale for caution.

Prior to President Clinton's trip to China in June 1998, agreement was reached to resume top-level ARATS/SEF contacts, albeit not formal negotiations. Beijing endeavored to turn to its advantage the U.S. president's affirmation in Shanghai on June 30, 1998, of the "three no's"—no support for two Chinas, one-China/one Taiwan; no support for Taiwanese independence; no support for Taiwanese representation in international organizations where statehood is required. SEF/ARATS high-level contacts resumed with SEF leader Koo Chen-fu's October 1998 visit to Shanghai and Beijing, where, notably, he met with President Jiang. There was little substantive progress in cross-strait relations, however.[33] Meanwhile, diplomatic skirmishing continued. The Taiwan prime minister visited Fiji and met with the Fijian prime minister in July 1998. In June 1998, the Taiwan foreign minister made a surprise visit to the Organization of African Unity meeting in western Africa, spoiling the first visit to the region by China's newly appointed foreign minister. In July 1998, Vice Premier Qian Qichen, who reportedly remained in charge of coordinating Chinese decision-making on foreign affairs and Taiwan, led a delegation to five Caribbean countries with the aim of undercutting Taiwan. Qian retired as foreign minister in March 1998, but the Caribbean trip, the first he led abroad after his retirement, demonstrated the high priority the Beijing leadership gave to combating Taiwan's flexible diplomacy, even among relatively small nations. Beijing succeeded in wooing Tonga away from Taiwan and established diplomatic relations with the Pacific Island State in November 1998. Taiwan wooed the Marshall Islands away from Beijing around the same time, and in early 1999 achieved diplomatic relations with Macedonia.[34]

In sum, the Taiwan issue remained a top priority and a major headache for China's leadership. Diplomatic pressure, continued cross-strait economic exchanges, a PRC military buildup opposite Taiwan, and other actions had not lessened Taiwan's determination to remain separate and distinct from the PRC; successful elections in Taiwan in December 1998 underlined the island government's favorable democratic image in the United States and the West precisely when PRC leaders began cracking down on dissidents. Under pressure from Congress, the Clinton administration was boosting contacts with and military support for Taiwan, including possibly considering providing Taiwan with a means to counter the PRC ballistic missile threat. Beijing remained very sensitive about overt Taiwan moves to declare independence or U.S. moves to notably upgrade military sales to Taiwan by possibly providing a "theater missile defense" for the island. It hoped that its longer-term strategy of positive and negative incentives would eventually create conditions that would persuade Taiwan to seek reunification with the mainland on terms acceptable to the PRC.[35]

Notes

1. For background, see Chae-Jin Lee, *China and Korea: Dynamic Relations*, Stanford: Hoover Institution, 1996; Fei-Ling Wang, *Tacit Acceptance and Watchful Eyes: Beijing's Views about the U.S.-ROK Alliance*, Carlisle, Pa.: U.S. Army War

College, 1997; and Bonnie Glaser and Ronald Montaperto, "Northeast Asia Interviews with Chinese Defense Officials, Washington, D.C.," in *Strategic Trends in China*, ed. Hans Binnendijk and Ronald Montaperto, Washington, D.C.: National Defense University, 1998, pp. 111-122.

2. The episode is reviewed in *Korea: Improved South Korean-Chinese Relations—Motives and Implications*, Washington, D.C.: Library of Congress, Congressional Research Service (CRS) Report 97-681F, July 1997, p. 1.

3. Economic relations are reviewed in *Korea: Improved South Korean-Chinese Relations*, p. 2.

4. See, among others, "ROK Exports to PRC Decline," Seoul, *Yonhap* in English, March 2, 1998 (internet version).

5. Reviewed in *Korea: Improved South Korean-Chinese Relations*, p. 2.

6. For background see, among others, *Korea: U.S.-South Korean Relations*, Washington, D.C.: Library of Congress, CRS Issue Brief 98045 (updated regularly).

7. Chinese, South Korean, and U.S. opinions noted here are based on consultations with over a hundred Chinese, South Korean, and U.S. specialists in Beijing, Seoul, and Washington during 1997 and 1998. For a written assessment, see, among others, *Korea: Improved South Korean-Chinese Relations*. See also assessment in Glaser and Montaperto, "Northeast Asia."

8. See *China Daily*, November 13, 1998.

9. Recounted in *Korea: Improved South Korean-Chinese Relations*, p. 4.

10. Ibid.

11. For background, see Glaser and Montaperto, "Northeast Asia."

12. Reviewed in *Korea: U.S.-South Korean Relations*, CRS Issue Brief.

13. Interviews, Seoul and Beijing, 1997; interviews, Washington, D.C., 1998, reported in *Korea Improved South Korean-Chinese Relations*.

14. For background, see Wang, *Tacit Acceptance*.

15. *Xinhua*, October 8, 1997, carried by Foreign Broadcast Information Service (FBIS) (internet version).

16. "Jiang Invites Kim Dae Jung to Visit PRC," *Kyodo*, February 24, 1998 (internet version).

17. Ibid.

18. See *China Daily*'s coverage of these two visits, in April and November 1998.

19. Interviews with Chinese defense officials, Washington, D.C., December 1997.

20. *The Korean Herald* (internet version), January 18, 1999.

21. See Charles Freeman, "Preventing War in the Taiwan Strait," *Foreign Affairs*, July-August 1998; and Steven Goldstein, *Taiwan Faces the Twenty-First Century*, New York: Foreign Policy Association, 1997.

22. See Ralph Clough and Scott Snyder, "Taiwan and the South China Sea," in Binnendijk and Montaperto, *Strategic Trends in China*, pp. 91-100. See also Nancy Bernkopf Tucker, "China-Taiwan: U.S. Debates and Policy Choices," *Survival* 40, 4 (winter 1998-1999): 150-167.

23. See reviews in, among others, Robert Ross, ed. *After the Cold War: Domestic Factors and U.S.-China Relations*, Armonk, N.Y.: M. E. Sharpe, 1998, pp. 80-97; Harvey Feldman, "Cross Strait Relations with Taiwan," in *Between Diplomacy and Deterrence*, ed. Kim Holmes and James Przystup, Washington, D.C.: Heritage Foundation, 1998, pp. 141-162; John W. Garver, *Face-Off*, Seattle: University of Washington Press, 1997.

24. Reviewed in *Taiwan: Recent Developments and U.S. Policy Choices*, Washington, D.C.: Library of Congress, CRS Issue Brief 98034 (updated regularly).

25. See review in Ralph Clough, *Cooperation or Conflict in the Taiwan Strait?* Boulder, Colo.: Rowman & Littlefield, 1999.

26. Ibid.

27. Fiji Television, January 14, 1998, carried by FBIS (internet version).

28. See *Taiwan-Mainland China Talks*, Washington, D.C.: Library of Congress, CRS Report No. 98-887.

29. Reviewed in, among others, Clough, *Cooperation or Conflict.*

30. Reviewed in, among others, *Taiwan: Recent Developments.*

31. The PRC and Taiwan strategies and motives are assessed in *Taiwan-Mainland China Talks*, pp. 2-5.

32. See the comprehensive assessment in Nancy Bernkopf Tucker, "China-Taiwan," pp. 150-167.

33. See *Taiwan-Mainland Talks.*

34. See *Taiwan: Recent Developments.*

35. Ibid.

Chapter 7

China-Southeast Asia-Pacific Relations

The rise of China as an economic and regional power is an important development affecting Southeast Asia in the 1990s. China's rapidly growing economic and political interaction with the members of ASEAN (the Association of Southeast Asian Nations, which includes Brunei, Indonesia, Laos, Malaysia, Myanmar [Burma], the Philippines, Singapore, Thailand, and Vietnam) presents important opportunities and challenges for these countries, who make up the bulk of Southeast Asian states. China's past assertive policies toward Southeast Asia, and its more recent rising military power and occasional resort to forceful rhetoric or military action concerning regional territorial disputes, produce continued wariness about China's intentions among many Southeast Asian leaders.

Chinese trade with and investment in Southeast Asian countries grew in the 1990s at an annual rate double the impressive rate of growth of the ASEAN and Chinese economies. This has been accompanied by an ever-widening array of high-level official contacts. In 1997, ASEAN and China set up an umbrella organization, the ASEAN-China Joint Cooperation Committee, to oversee already established ASEAN-Chinese political, economic, security, and science-technology exchanges. Chinese President Jiang Zemin led a delegation to ASEAN's thirtieth anniversary celebration and informal summit, and signed the first Chinese-ASEAN joint statement in December 1997.[1]

Both China and ASEAN are preoccupied currently with efforts to deal with the consequences of the Asian economic crisis. Thus far, Beijing's careful responses to the crisis, including its pledges to maintain economic growth, eschew devaluation of the Chinese currency, support IMF rescue efforts, and provide supplementary support of $1 billion to Thailand and a reported several billion dollars to Indonesia, have been well received in the region. Of course, it is widely known that the first two Chinese measures are mainly for Chinese domestic purposes; that Chinese support for IMF funding actually costs Beijing little; and that extra funding and support for Thailand and Indonesia have been slow in coming as Beijing has become more concerned with its own financial health and is particularly wary of deep involvement in Indonesia without significant economic and political reform there.[2]

Beijing has been generally discreet in reaction to anti-Chinese violence in Indonesia. It has been sharply critical of Taiwan's efforts to use offers of economic aid to foster high-level government contacts in the region, but has stopped well short of taking significant retaliatory measures against the Southeast Asian governments involved.[3]

The underlying issues in recent Chinese relations with Southeast Asia focus on economic competition for markets and foreign investment, territorial disputes in the South China Sea, and concerns over regional security, especially the implications of China's military modernization. Many in ASEAN have cooperated with China against U.S.-backed efforts to foster greater support for international human rights, but they are privately concerned about China's support for the repressive regime in Burma and its involvement with the Hun Sen regime in Cambodia. ASEAN leaders also continue to support the U.S.-Japan alliance and the U.S. military presence in Asia, despite China's criticism of these.[4]

Recent Chinese-ASEAN Cooperation

The best evidence of Chinese and ASEAN cooperation in the 1990s is the rapid growth of trade and other economic interchanges. By 1992, Sino-ASEAN trade had already increased fifteen times over the volume in 1975. In 1993, Sino-ASEAN trade amounted to 5.4 percent of China's foreign trade, making ASEAN China's fifth largest trading partner after Japan, Hong Kong, the United States, and the European Community.[5] Trade increased by about 30 percent in 1994, and by 40 percent in 1995, reaching a level of $20 billion annually that was sustained in 1996 and 1997. ASEAN in the mid-1990s accounted for about 7 percent of China's foreign trade, and China accounted for just under 5 percent of total ASEAN trade. In general, imports and exports in China-ASEAN trade were in balance.[6]

Investment also has grown rapidly. By the end of 1991, the ASEAN states had committed $1.41 billion in 1,042 projects approved by Beijing.

Singapore leads the ASEAN states in trade and investment in China. By mid-1994, Singapore became China's fifth largest overseas investor after Hong Kong, Taiwan, the United States, and Japan. By that time, Singapore had invested in 3,834 projects in China with a promised investment of $6.8 billion. Most notable was the agreement to jointly develop a multi-billion dollar project at the Fuzhou Industrial Park in China's Jiangsu Province.[7] By early 1996, the Chinese government had approved 10,926 ASEAN country-invested projects with agreed investments of $26.4 billion, of which $6.2 billion was already paid.[8] By the end of the year, there were 12,342 approved investment projects valued at $34.3 billion, of which $9.4 billion was already paid. Five hundred ninety-six were added in the first half of 1997.

Chinese investment in ASEAN is much smaller in scale (less than $1 billion). Beijing is considering collaborating with ASEAN in the development of the Mekong River region; a large number of Chinese companies have set up operations in ASEAN countries, notably in Singapore, as a base from which to penetrate global markets, and Chinese companies have won labor contracts (that is, deals involving large groups of Chinese laborers working under contract in foreign countries) in the ASEAN region (in 1993 Beijing completed 609 labor contracts valued at $250 million).[9]

ASEAN-Chinese accords to manage the economic interchange include the Joint Committee on Economic and Trade Cooperation, agreed to in 1994 in order to facilitate Sino-ASEAN economic cooperation. This committee, along with bilateral agreements between China and some of the individual ASEAN states on investment protection and avoidance of some double taxation, helps to facilitate Sino-ASEAN economic cooperation.

Meanwhile, some ASEAN states are interested in promoting scientific and technological cooperation with an eye toward furthering each side's competitiveness. China is said to have a relatively strong scientific and technological research base, while it has difficulty applying the results to the production process and marketing the resulting products abroad. For their part, some of the ASEAN states have experience in commercialization of science and technology, application of scientific and advanced technological findings to the production process, and marketing. As a result, some of the ASEAN states have signed agreements on joint scientific and technological cooperation with China, and ASEAN as a whole signed an agreement with China to set up a Joint Committee on Scientific and Technological Cooperation in 1994.[10]

To reinforce economic cooperation and enhance high-level political cooperation, Chinese and ASEAN leaders in recent years have undertaken a wide range of senior-level political contacts and exchanges. Top-level Chinese leaders like President Jiang Zemin, Premier Li Peng, Vice Premier Zhu Rongji, and the Chinese foreign and defense ministers have traveled to the ASEAN region and have reciprocated with warm welcomes for their visiting counterparts from ASEAN countries.[11] Notably, China set a new pattern in its close relations with Thailand by releasing, on February 5, 1999, an elaborate joint statement to guide the two countries' close cooperation in the twenty-first century.[12]

China and the ASEAN countries have established bilateral mechanisms for regular high-level political dialogue, and such dialogue between China and ASEAN has developed markedly. Since 1991, the Chinese foreign minister has attended, by invitation, the annual ASEAN foreign ministers' conference. In 1995, China asked to become a "full dialogue partner" of ASEAN at the annual ASEAN foreign ministers' meeting, and this was accepted. Meanwhile, China was invited by ASEAN in 1994 to become a consultative partner in the regional security dialogue carried on by the ASEAN Regional Forum (ARF).[13] China has recently become more actively involved in the ARF, notably hosting, along with the Philippines, an ARF meeting on regional confidence-building measures in March 1997. In December 1997, President Jiang Zemin attended the informal ASEAN summit in Kuala Lumpur, and China and ASEAN issued their first joint statement.[14]

China and several of the more politically authoritarian ASEAN states have also found common ground in opposition to U.S. and Western criticisms of human rights conditions in those countries.[15] The Chinese government is also a strong supporter of the Malaysian prime minister's call for the establishment of an East Asian Economic Caucus (EAEC). The proposed EAEC is viewed warily by the United States, which would be excluded, along with Australia, Canada, and other Pacific-rim countries, from membership in the group. The United States strongly supports the more inclusive Asian Pacific Economic Cooperation (APEC) forum, which has been actively dealing with regional economic issues for several years.[16]

As noted below, security issues, especially China's rising military power and its occasionally assertive stance over disputed territorial claims in the South China Sea, complicate ASEAN-Chinese relations. The two sides use a variety of consultative mechanisms to deal with these questions. In general, China has preferred to deal with the issues bilaterally, as was evidenced in the Sino-Philippines agreements reached in 1996 on a military code of conduct, military exchanges, and the establishment of some communications between military detachments in disputed areas in the South China Sea. China and the Philippines also agreed on joint maritime scientific research, fishing, control of piracy, and other endeavors.[17] This convergence did not prevent continued friction, however. In 1999, the Philippines were particularly upset with Chinese military-backed construction on Mischief Reef—a set of islets close to the Philippines and claimed by them. Media speculation said Chinese forces were taking advantage of ASEAN's preoccupation with the Asian economic crisis to assert Chinese territorial claims in disputed parts of the South China Sea.[18] ASEAN has often favored a multilateral approach in dealing with security issues involving China. Thus, Indonesia succeeded in gaining China's participation in an annual multilateral workshop on "managing potential conflicts in the South China Sea," where participants exchanged ideas on dealing with the disputed territories. ASEAN officials also discussed the territorial issues in ASEAN-PRC meetings of senior working-level officials.[19]

ASEAN and China in February 1997 set up an umbrella panel, called the ASEAN-China Joint Cooperation Committee (JCC), to oversee ASEAN-China relations. The JCC will identify projects to be undertaken by ASEAN and China and will coordinate four other parallel mechanisms, namely the following:

- The ASEAN-China senior officials' political consultations;
- The ASEAN-Chinese Joint Committee on Economic and Trade Cooperation;
- The ASEAN-China Joint Committee on Science and Technology;
- The ASEAN Committee in Beijing.

Together, these represent the overall structure of the ASEAN-China dialogue.[20]

Issues in Chinese-ASEAN Relations

Chinese and ASEAN leaders have endeavored in the 1990s to foster mutually beneficial economic relations and improve political-military relations, but they have faced difficulties caused by the negative historical record of Sino-Southeast Asian relations and contemporary economic and security problems. The net effect of these difficulties is to serve as an overall drag on meaningful forward movement in Sino-ASEAN relations and to perpetuate an underlying sense of wariness by both sides about future relations.

Lessons of History

The PRC's relations with most of the countries of Southeast Asia were volatile, contentious, and often violent until recent years. China saw many of these states as aligned at one time or another with its major adversaries (the United States in the 1950s and 1960s, the USSR in the 1970s and 1980s) and pursuing policies designed to pressure China or "contain" the expansion of Chinese influence. Beijing often adopted truculent and confrontational policies, short of all-out war directly involving China, in order to intimidate the Southeast Asian states and fend off their great-power backers. Examples included strong support for the Viet Minh's all-out assault against the French forces in Indochina in the 1950s; support of Hanoi's militant stance against the United States in the 1960s; and widespread support for antigovernment guerrilla movements in most non-communist Southeast Asian countries in the 1960s and 1970s. This was complemented by close Chinese involvement with the large Indonesian Communist Party prior to the crushing of the movement in 1965, and the use of links with the economically influential overseas Chinese communities in Southeast Asia in order to exert influence there.[21]

Relations between China and the non-communist Southeast Asian countries gradually normalized beginning in the mid-1970s. Malaysia, Thailand, and the Philippines improved their official relations with China following the end of the Vietnam War and the decline of the U.S.-backed military presence in the region. Indeed, these and other states in the region saw common ground with China, along with the United States, in resisting the danger in the late 1970s of a militarily strong Vietnam, backed by the Soviet Union, occupying Cambodia by military force. To persuade Vietnam to pull out of Cambodia and no longer serve as a base for Soviet military operations, China launched a month-long border war against Vietnam in 1979. It kept up military pressure along the border for ten years and remained the main supporter of the Cambodian resistance to the Vietnamese military occupation.[22]

The Cambodian quagmire, declining Soviet support, and deteriorating internal conditions made Vietnam change course and seek reconciliation with China in the early 1990s. By that time, the ASEAN states most wary of China's intentions, notably Indonesia, had normalized their diplomatic relations with China. Beijing had cut its ties with indigenous guerrilla groups in Southeast Asia, which no longer posed a substantial security problem to the governments there. China also endeavored to clarify its policies toward overseas Chinese, notably passing a nationality law in 1989 that appeared to end Chinese government claims to authority over overseas Chinese who had taken citizenship in foreign countries and advised Chinese citizens residing abroad to adhere to local laws.[23]

By the 1990s, the importance of the largely negative historical record in China-Southeast Asian relations was gradually declining. Nevertheless, mutual suspicions based on the past rose up from time to time as China occasionally strongly asserted its claim to disputed territories in the South

China Sea, continued to modernize its naval and air power capabilities, and took strong military action in nearby areas, notably near Taiwan in 1995-1996. Against this backdrop, many in ASEAN welcomed, either publicly or privately, U.S., Japanese, Australian, and other statements and actions showing concern over Chinese assertiveness.[24] This in turn aroused Chinese suspicions that at least some in the region may be interested in reviving previous practice, which it perceived as working with outside powers in order to hold back China's rising power and influence in the region.[25]

Recent Issues

Economic Competition

Officials and entrepreneurs in Southeast Asia have seen the rapidly rising Chinese economy as a major competitive challenge as well as an economic opportunity. For example, of the $100 billion in direct foreign investment flowing into developing countries in 1994, about 40 percent went to China. By contrast, the total going to ASEAN was about 15 percent. As the rapidly developing Chinese economy attracted the attention of Japanese, Korean, Taiwanese, U.S., and Western investors, who might otherwise have been inclined to invest in Southeast Asia, ASEAN leaders felt pressured to take steps to liberalize their economies. They also discussed further liberalizing the investment opportunities in ASEAN and endeavored to establish special economic zones along the lines of those in China.[26] The Asian economic crisis led to redoubled ASEAN efforts to attract outside investment.

At least some ASEAN officials have been concerned about the net imbalance in ASEAN-Chinese investment, with ASEAN investment in China being many times greater than Chinese investment in ASEAN. Most ASEAN investment in China is carried out by overseas Chinese business people. Some nonethnic Chinese observers in countries like Indonesia and Malaysia argue that such investment is made at the expense of domestic development and reflects PRC efforts to work with overseas Chinese communities for China's benefit. Periodic discussion of the concept of a possible "greater China economic circle" involving ethnic Chinese business people on the China mainland, Hong Kong, Taiwan, Singapore, and elsewhere in Southeast Asia concerns some Southeast Asian officials. Thus, the Malaysian deputy finance minister said in 1996 that it was Malaysia's view that "overzealousness on the part of Malaysian businessmen of Chinese origin could have adverse repercussions racially in their own country."[27]

Also, ASEAN and Chinese exporters are often at similar levels of economic development. They compete for market shares in light manufactured products such as textiles, shoes, leather wares, electric appliances, toys, and electronics. This competition is expected to intensify as ASEAN economies seek to export more as they try to recover from the Asian financial crisis.

Territorial Claims

Conflicting claims in the South China Sea represent the most salient security issue in Sino-ASEAN relations. ASEAN has followed an approach emphasizing establishing confidence-building measures first, through a series of technical and scientific cooperation efforts, and solving problems of sovereignty later. ASEAN seeks to promote a peaceful atmosphere and maintain the territorial status quo.[28]

China says it is in general agreement with this approach, but it occasionally takes military actions, or actions involving oil exploration or fisheries, that seem to challenge the status quo. China has been wary about discussing military matters involving the disputed territories at the Indonesian-sponsored workshops on the South China Sea; it prefers to deal with claimants bilaterally rather than multilaterally; and it bristles in response to statements by outside parties, notably the United States, about their concern that conflicting territorial claims should not disrupt sea lines of communication and broader regional stability.[29]

Some in ASEAN are cautiously optimistic that they are making headway in persuading China that its broader interests in the region are best served by an approach that works closely with ASEAN's incremental effort to reduce tensions, develop common ground, and preserve the territorial status quo. Others point to periodic Chinese assertiveness over the territorial disputes, the increased capability of Chinese air and naval forces in the region, and the strong sense of nationalism among Chinese elites and common people, to warn of an alleged Chinese dual track approach. That is, while Chinese diplomats conciliate their ASEAN counterparts in various fora about the South China Sea, the Chinese military is preparing to expand its hold in the region whenever the benefits of such a move would outweigh the costs.

China's Military Policies

ASEAN and Chinese observers alike recognize that China's growing defense capabilities and possible intentions to use these forces represent a serious problem in ASEAN-Chinese relations. In general, the immediate problem is the lack of transparency in China's military policies and practices. ASEAN observers know China's economic growth means that China is more and more capable of building up its military power and that China is increasing its defense expenditures; but they have little sound idea as to what this means for regional stability. As a result, they urge China to participate more actively in regional security fora, notably the ARF, and to take unilateral steps in order to make Chinese defense policies and practices more transparent. Some in ASEAN are optimistic that China's recently more active participation in ARF fora (for example, Beijing in March 1997 co-hosted with the Philippines an ARF session devoted to regional confidence-building measures) will lead to a convergence of ASEAN-Chinese approaches to regional stability. They also take solace in the increased Chinese military diplomacy with ASEAN, often involving high-level military exchanges and discussions that help to clarify mutual intentions. Others judge that China's purchase of advanced Russian jet fighters, surface naval combat vessels, and submarines presages a PRC-military-backed effort to intimidate Southeast Asian countries and become the dominant power in the region.[30]

Other Issues

Burma: Many in ASEAN are concerned by instability in Burma since the uprising of 1988 and the ascendancy of the repressive military regime that has been in power since that time. Part of the concern involves China. Despite deteriorating economic conditions in the country, the Burmese regime maintains a half million-person armed force backed by a stockpile of weapons—over one billion dollars worth, primarily from China. China has reportedly supplied helicopters, armored vehicles, field guns, assault rifles, and patrol boats. There are recurrent though unsubstantiated reports of China establishing listening posts or disguised bases of operation along the Burmese coast.[31]

Meanwhile, Chinese-made manufactured goods are pervasive in Burma. China may also have an interest in opening its isolated southern provinces via the Irawaddy corridor in Burma and other river/overland routes. Rich entrepreneurs from China's southern rim are buying up real estate in traditional residential areas of prominent Burmese cities. Some people worry about a replay of the vicious anti-Chinese bloodletting that occurred in Burma in the mid-1960s, due largely to perceived economic disparities.[32] Meanwhile, Beijing is particularly wary of cross-border drug-trafficking affecting stability in China.

For these and other reasons, ASEAN leaders have moved to integrate Burma into ASEAN. China does not oppose the move. Chinese involvement in Burma is openly criticized by some U.S. and other Western officials who object strongly to the Burma regime's human rights violations. Unlike the leaders of ASEAN, these Westerners have often opposed ASEAN's moves to welcome the Burmese regime into ASEAN.

Cambodia: Following the 1991 Paris peace accords, Beijing ended support for its former ally, the Khmer Rouge, and began efforts to normalize relations with the Phnom Penh leadership. More recently, Cambodia's stormy internal politics—in particular the incessant sparring between Hun Sen's Cambodian People's Party (CPP) and Prince Ranariddh's royalist National United Front for an Independent, Neutral, Peaceful, and Cooperative Cambodia (FUNCINPEC) party—have presented Beijing with a dilemma. China has wanted to work with ASEAN in finding a resolution to the turmoil but also sees Hun Sen as the strongest force in Phnom Penh at present. Fostering good relations with Hun Sen serves broader PRC interests in securing a stable southeastern perimeter and balancing the influence of other major countries, including the United States and Japan, in the region. China has also exploited the relationship to cramp Taiwan's efforts to establish strong ties with Cambodia.[33]

As Beijing sensed that Hun Sen was gaining the upper hand in his rivalry with Ranariddh, it consented to meetings in 1996 with Jiang Zemin and Li Peng without FUNCINPEC participation. The Hun Sen visit signaled increased trade, investment, and PRC-CPP relations. China was, notably, the first foreign power to provide substantial military equipment—heavy trucks—to Hun Sen's regime following the violent July 1997 conflict between Hun Sen and Ranariddh forces. It welcomed Hun Sen's decision in 1997 to break existing relations with Taiwan.[34] The close China-Hun Sen relationship strengthened during the Cambodian leader's February 1999 trip to China where he signed five new agreements with the PRC. The two sides also worked together to fend off international calls for trials of Khmer Rouge leaders for crimes against humanity.[35]

Despite its obvious tilt to Hun Sen, Beijing maintains an ostensibly hands-off policy toward Cambodia and urges other powers to do the same. China has accepted ASEAN's mediating role in the Cambodia dispute, viewing the organization as an increasingly important counterbalance to U.S. and Japanese influence in Southeast Asia. Beijing was reluctant to support the "Friends of Cambodia" initiative in part because it perceived the group as aligned with Western interest in intervening in Cambodia. Beijing's stance has eased anxieties among most in ASEAN over China's ultimate objectives in Cambodia, though Vietnam can be expected to look warily at any close China-Cambodia relations.[36]

Taiwan: Taiwan President Lee Teng-hui first practiced his controversial "pragmatic diplomacy," making visits to states that recognize the PRC, by going to ASEAN states in the late 1980s and early 1990s. Beijing reacted fairly mildly to the trips. Following Lee's successful private visit to the United States in 1995, however, Beijing reacted with force, launching repeated military exercises in the Taiwan Strait. Eventually, the PRC actions prompted a strong U.S. show of force in the region.[37]

ASEAN officials derived mixed lessons from the developments. On the one hand, they were unwilling to provoke PRC ire by again allowing Lee or other senior leaders to make similar visits to the region. On the other hand, some have been concerned that the forceful PRC treatment of Taiwan could presage PRC action against ASEAN if the issues are seen as of sufficient importance to the PRC. Territorial disputes over the South China Sea are seen to represent a possible cause for forceful PRC action.[38]

Taipei was quick to exploit the diplomatic opportunities flowing from the Asian financial crisis. Possible aid from Taiwan entrepreneurs, including the businesses owned by the ruling Nationalist Party, was likely to come to Southeast Asia a lot faster than government programs promised by interested countries and international organizations. Thus, senior-level leaders in Indonesia, Malaysia, Singapore, and the Philippines met with their Taiwan counterparts to discuss the crisis. Unwilling to match Taiwan's aid offers, and recognizing that a harsh response to the Southeast Asians could be counterproductive, Beijing focused its invective against Taiwan and took little substantive action against the ASEAN states.

Indonesia: Beijing's cautious approach to the Asian economic crisis in Southeast Asia was graphically illustrated in China's relations with Indonesia—the most seriously affected and most unstable of the ASEAN states impacted by the crisis. China waited until April 11, 1998, before sending a senior official to Indonesia to discuss the situation. Newly appointed Foreign Minister Tang Jiaxuan, a regional expert, met with President Suharto and explicitly endorsed his "leadership," pledged $3 million in Chinese medicine, $200 million in export credits, and greater use of barter in Sino-Indonesian trade, and recognized without complaint that anti-Chinese violence in Indonesia was an Indonesian "internal affair."[39]

The timing and scope of the visit did not appear to be accidental. China was reluctant to commit aid to Indonesia until Jakarta worked out relief arrangements with the IMF. And Chinese aid was largely tied to exchanges that would have little or no net cost to the Chinese economy.

The subsequent collapse of the Suharto regime amid widespread anti-Chinese violence tested China's policy of noninterference and prompted acute Chinese concern that China's one-party regime could follow the Indonesian example if it did not manage the Chinese economy more effectively. While eschewing any change in its policy stance against meddling in other countries' "internal affairs," Chinese officials in August 1998 began publicly to strongly urge Indonesian authorities to protect ethnic Chinese in Indonesia. This came in the wake of a groundswell of pressure for public condemnation of widely reported rapes of ethnic Chinese in Indonesia. The pressure came from Chinese communities throughout the world and also prompted the Taiwan and Hong Kong authorities to publicly condemn the rapes and demand protection for ethnic Chinese. The Chinese media also drew lessons from the Suharto regime's collapse, seeing the cause primarily as economic mismanagement, not the absence of political democracy and government accountability as seen by a number of Western officials and media commentators.[40]

U.S. Military Presence: The ASEAN countries, including the two U.S. military allies, Thailand and the Philippines, have generally supported a continued U.S. military presence in Asia and a continued U.S.-Japan alliance.[41] Thus far, they have generally avoided taking sides in the nascent dispute between China on the one hand and the United States and Japan on the other about the strategic framework for post-cold war East Asia. The United States and Japan say that strengthening their alliance is in accordance with their own and with broader regional interests. By contrast, China argues that such cold war alliances should not govern the future order of the region. China has said that U.S. forces should be withdrawn, allowing Asian countries to manage their own security.[42]

In sum, Chinese relations with Southeast Asia in the 1990s present a mixed picture of substantial gains for Chinese influence but continued signs of regional differences and wariness of the growing Chinese power. There was little sign that Beijing intended to change its generally pragmatic and moderate approach to regional developments, though it continued to look for opportunities to expand its control of contested territory in the South China Sea and its bilateral relations with controversial regimes in Burma and Cambodia. The Asian economic crisis and the resulting political instability, especially in Indonesia, worried Chinese officials but prompted no fundamental shift in Chinese policy toward the region.

Australia, New Zealand, and the Pacific Islands

Beijing's relations with countries farther to the south and east —Australia, New Zealand, and the Pacific Islands—are generally much less important for recent Chinese foreign policy than relations with states closer to China's borders. During the mid-1990s, Chinese officials worried considerably about the strengthening of U.S. alliance relations with the newly installed conservative government of Prime Minister John Howard in Canberra. One of Howard's first foreign policy acts was to firmly endorse the U.S. naval show of force at the time of provocative Chinese military exercises in the Taiwan area during March 1996. The Australian stance reinforced a Chinese tendency to view Australian policy in the region as the same as that of the United States; taken together with concurrent U.S. efforts to strengthen the U.S. alliance relationship with Japan, the Australian position added to a deep-seated Chinese official paranoia over alleged U.S. efforts, supported by allies and associates, to "contain" Chinese regional influence.[43]

Meanwhile, because China gave such a high priority to thwarting Taiwan's search for greater international recognition, especially after it failed to block Lee Teng-hui's 1995 visit to the United States, Beijing gave considerable attention to the smaller states, even some with only a few thousand people, in the South Pacific. Taiwan had close ties with several of these small states. Chinese officials and media also played up growing economic interchanges, especially trade ties with Australia and New Zealand.

Sensing that it needed to strike a less pro-U.S. stance in relations with Beijing in order to preserve important Australian economic and other interests with respect to China, the Howard government took steps in 1997 to adjust its policy toward China in ways that put some distance between the U.S. and Australian positions. Relations with China had deteriorated after the U.S.-China Taiwan Strait face-off in March 1996, as the Howard government strongly endorsed the U.S.-Japan alliance revitalization plan announced in April 1996, took steps to reinforce its own military relations with Japan as well as with Washington, and welcomed the Dalai Lama to Australia. But in 1997 Canberra split from the United States and some other Western countries in refusing to stand with them in sponsoring the annual resolution on Chinese human rights considered by the UN Human Rights Commission. Senior Chinese Vice Premier Zhu Rongji traveled to Australia on an official visit in 1997. Australia and New Zealand also gained favor with Beijing by attending, without reservation, ceremonies marking the handover of Hong Kong to Chinese rule on July 1, 1997. The United States and some other Western countries had noted their reservations about antidemocratic developments in Hong Kong and did not attend all the ceremonies.[44]

At the end of 1997, Australian Foreign Minister Alexander Downer traveled to Beijing to advance relations. He announced a deal giving $3.7 million to China as part of a project to help China to prepare for membership in the WTO, and a second deal worth $2 million to improve health care and drinking water in Tibet. He also said Australia would spend about $20 million over the next five years to help China deal with environmental degradation. By this time, the Howard government had named China as one of Australia's four priority relationships. Trade had grown to over $5 billion a year, and overall Australian development assistance was about $36 million annually.[45]

In their talks with Downer and concurrent year-end media reviews, Chinese officials duly noted their satisfaction with trends in Chinese relations with Australia and the entire region. In addition to Zhu Rongji, the chairman of the Chinese People's Political Consultative Conference, Li Ruihuan, also a member of the party Politburo's Standing Committee, traveled to the region in 1997. Senior officials from Australia, New Zealand, and several Pacific Island countries traveled to China. China established diplomatic relations with the Cook Islands on July 25, 1997, thereby raising the number of the region's nations having diplomatic ties with China to ten. In October 1998, Beijing established diplomatic relations with Tonga, a previously long-standing diplomatic supporter of Taiwan.[46]

In addition to being Australia's fifth largest trading partner, China was New Zealand's seventh largest trading partner and was carrying out mining, logging, and other investment activities in these countries. China had signed bilateral trade agreements with seven Pacific Island nations, had civil aviation agreements with several states in the region, and saw large numbers of Chinese citizens travel to the countries of the region (over sixty thousand went to Australia in 1997). China actively supported efforts by the main regional body, the South Pacific Forum, to protect the environment, promote economic development, and maintain stability. The South Pacific Forum also decided to establish an economic and trade representative office in China.[47]

China's diplomatic presence and assistance effort in the Pacific Islands countries remained large and expensive relative to its economic interests. A driving motive for this effort was the continuing rivalry with Taiwan for political influence. Four regional states—the Solomon Islands, Nauru, Tuvalu, and Tonga—had long maintained diplomatic relations with Taiwan. Tonga switched to Beijing in October 1998. Others, including such regional leaders as Papua New Guinea and Fiji, recognized the PRC but had long-standing high-level unofficial relations with Taiwan, which the PRC protested but was forced to tolerate. Taiwan has been able to act as an unofficial "special dialogue" partner with the South Pacific Forum and to maintain unofficial but cordial links with other regional organizations such as the Forum Fisheries Agency and the South Pacific Commission.[48]

In addition to the rivalry with Taiwan, Chinese efforts in the Pacific were driven by the desire to assert the PRC's position as a global power, and to legitimate the leadership at home by maintaining constant news of international exchanges.[49] China initiated strong efforts to woo smaller developing countries when it found itself relatively isolated after Tiananmen. Although the PRC greatly improved its international standing in the 1990s, it continued to invest a great deal of time and money, including personal effort by the leadership, in maintaining friendly relations with as wide a variety of countries as possible. In this context, the island states of the South

Pacific Forum constituted a significant presence in the UN, in which eight were full members, and other international forums. China apparently considered its diplomatic and assistance effort a reasonable price to pay for the two objectives of countering Taiwan and enhancing its own international prestige. The Chinese effort also helped head off criticism: for example, China would be embarrassed if the Pacific Island countries, uniquely vulnerable to and active on the threat of global warning, should turn from pressuring the developed countries to criticizing the PRC, the fastest-growing producer of carbon emissions. The PRC's commercial interests in the region were growing—for example fishing, textile factories, and other enterprises—but still modest relative to the scope of diplomatic activity.

In Kiribati, located along the equator and well positioned in the middle of the Pacific Ocean, a large new PRC embassy and an adjacent commercial building were inaugurated on July 4, 1997, and a Chinese satellite-tracking station was formally opened on Tarawa on October 7, 1997. In reporting the official opening, the New China News Agency described the facility as "equipped with advanced remote sensing and receiving apparatus, equipment for measuring satellite orbits . . . it will expand the coverage of China's space observation and control network." The station appeared to be well located for its stated purpose of monitoring Chinese satellite launches beyond the range of mainland observation facilities; proximity to the equator is an advantage. Some observers also suspect that the station will be able to monitor activities at the U.S. missile test facility at Kwajalein Atoll in the nearby Marshall Islands.[50]

Taiwan, meanwhile, continues to compete actively for influence in the region. Taiwan's aid to the region—possibly exceeding the PRC's in value—has gone primarily to those states with which Taiwan has formal diplomatic relations. Taiwan's regional economic presence is significant. Taiwan has one of the largest fishing fleets in the region. In the past this has often been a source of tension as Taiwanese boats have had a reputation for illegal fishing and avoidance of payments to host governments, but the Taiwan authorities have sought to improve their supervision of the fleet. In the absence of formal diplomatic relations, fishing agreements have been negotiated by the Taiwan Fishery Association with host waters countries. Taiwanese fishing interests have been making increasing use of lower-cost PRC fishing crews and boats in exploiting Pacific fisheries, making this an area where cooperation rather than competition reigns between Taiwanese and PRC interests.

A good example of PRC-Taiwan competition is seen in those newly independent states of the Pacific Islands that remain in "free association" with the United States—the Republic of the Marshall Islands (RMI), the Federated States of Micronesia (FSM), and Palau.[51] PRC embassies were established soon after independence in the RMI and FSM, and in both Majuro and Kolonia the PRC remained one of only three countries to maintain resident embassies. The RMI reciprocated with an embassy in Beijing (Papua New Guinea is the only other Pacific Island nation to maintain a Beijing embassy). Beijing granted economic assistance to the Marshall Islands and Papua New Guinea, although details and statistics are lacking. Taiwan managed to get the RMI to establish formal diplomatic relations in November 1998, and Beijing broke its ties accordingly.[52]

Palau to date has not formally recognized either the PRC or Taiwan. The PRC hosted and presumably financed a visit to Beijing and other Chinese cities by a delegation led by President Nakamura in May 1997. The participants met with President Jiang Zemin, Foreign Minister Qian Qichen, and NPC Standing Committee Chairman Qiao Shi. Nakamura's reception may have been in part an attempt by Beijing to regain the diplomatic initiative from Taiwan. The PRC's representative (the PRC ambassador to the FSM) to Nakamura's January 26, 1997, inauguration had walked out in protest over the high-profile reception of a Taiwan delegation. That delegation included a Taiwan minister of state and a vice minister of Foreign Affairs. Taiwan's interests have been heavily involved in development of Palau's tourist industry and other sectors of the economy, and Palau and Taiwan have maintained reciprocal trade and friendship offices. Taiwan and Palau on November 3, 1997, signed an aviation agreement that gives Taiwan "fifth freedom" rights to carry passengers through Koror to tourist destinations such as Saipan and Guam. As a result, Taiwan expects to increase its flights to Palau, a contribution to the capacity of Palau's small but developing tourism industry.[53]

As Pacific Island countries endeavor to seek advantages in relations with the PRC and Taiwan, they sometimes find themselves in embarrassing situations. In January 1998, for example, the Fijian government had to postpone plans to receive a visit from Taiwan's president. A senior Chinese economic delegation, headed by the Chinese foreign trade minister, was coming to Fiji at the same time, and officials realized belatedly that the country, though among the largest Pacific Island states, was not big enough for both of them. In an unusual demonstration of back-to-back high-level visits, Beijing followed up by sending its defense minister to Fiji in February 1998 for official meetings. The military delegation also went to Australia and New Zealand, marking the most senior Chinese military exchanges with these governments.[54]

In sum, Beijing's foreign policy attention to this region grew in the 1990s as Chinese leaders sought to ease differences and to step up their worldwide diplomatic competition with Taiwan. Chinese military contacts with the countries of this region grew significantly. Beijing's other interests were relatively small, though trade with Australia and New Zealand was important, and China's satellite tracking station in Kiribati revealed broader Chinese strategic interests in this part of the world.

Notes

1. See Jiang Zemin, speech at East Asian Summit, *Xinhua*, December 15, 1997, carried by Foreign Broadcast Information Service (FBIS) (internet version).

2. See "China Says Actively Funding IMF Indonesia Plan," *Reuters*, March 17, 1998 (internet version); "News Analysis Views ASEAN Challenges," *Xinhua*, July 21, 1998, carried by FBIS (internet version); "Kyodo Reports on PRC Media Coverage of Indonesia Crisis," *Kyodo*, May 22, 1998, carried by FBIS (internet version).

3. "China Assails Habibie over Persecution of Chinese," *Financial Times*, September 5, 1998, p. 3.

4. See review in *China-Southeast Asia Relations: Trends, Issues, and Implications for the United* States, Washington, D.C.: Library of Congress, Congressional Research Service (CRS) Report 97-553F, May 20, 1997.

5. Lai To Lee, "The China Factor in ASEAN Security," conference paper, Ost-West Koelleg, Bruhl, Germany, March 6, 1997, p. 5. See Rosemary Foote, "China in the ASEAN Regional Forum," *Asian Survey*, May 1998, pp. 425-440.

6. Songlu Chen, "China and ASEAN," conference paper, Keio University, December 6, 1996, p. 3. See also *China-Southeast Asia Relations*, pp. 3-6.

7. Lee, "China Factor," p. 6.

8. Chen, "China and ASEAN," p. 3.

9. Lee, "China Factor," p. 6.

10. Ibid., p. 7.

11. See, among others, Jusuf Wanandi, *Southeast Asia-China Relations*, Taipei: Chinese Council of Advanced Policy Studies, December 1996. See also *China-Southeast Asia Relations*.

12. "Text of Sino-Thai Joint Statement," *Xinhua*, February 5, 1999 (internet version).

13. Chen, "China and ASEAN," p. 2.

14. "PRC Expands Cooperation with ASEAN," *Xinhua*, January 4, 1998, carried by FBIS (internet version).

15. See Richard Cronin, *"Asian Values" and Asian Assertiveness: Implications for U.S. Interests*, Washington, D.C., Library of Congress, CRS Report 96-610F, July 9, 1996.

16. See, among others, "Trip Report on Visit to Kuala Lumpur," CRS General Distribution memorandum, Library of Congress, Washington, D.C., May 4, 1993.

17. Vietnam, the PRC, and Taiwan claim most of the territories (mainly small islands) in the South China Sea; Malaysia, the Philippines, and Brunei have claims to some of the territories. Disputes over offshore oil and gas sometimes involve

Indonesia. See, among others, *East Asia: Disputed Islands and Offshore Claims—Issues for U.S. Policy*, Washington, D.C., Library of Congress, CRS Report 92-614S, July 28, 1992, and *The South China Sea Dispute*, Washington, D.C., Library of Congress, CRS Report 95-634F, August 29, 1995.

18. "Chinese Moves Roil Region," *Defense News*, February 8, 1999, p. 1.

19. Wanandi, *Southeast Asia-China Relations*, pp. 11-14.

20. Lee, "China Factor," p. 12.

21. Discussed in Wanandi, *Southeast Asia-China Relations*, pp. 6-10.

22. See review in *Southeast Asian Security*, Washington, D.C., Library of Congress, CRS Report 95-927S, August 1, 1995, pp. 2-3.

23. Discussed in Wanandi, *Southeast Asia-China Relations*, pp. 7-8.

24. ASEAN states also steadily modernized their own military forces and promoted military interaction with other powers, including New Zealand and Great Britain. See *Far Eastern Economic Review*, April 24, 1997. See also *China as Security Concern in Asia*, Washington, D.C.: Library of Congress, CRS Report 95-46S, December 22, 1994. See Foote, "China in the ASEAN Regional Forum."

25. *China's Sinister View of U.S. Policy: Origins, Implications and Options*, Washington, D.C.: Library of Congress, CRS Report 95-750S, June 26, 1995.

26. See Umar Juoro, "China's Emergence as a Regional Economic Power: Implications for Southeast Asia and China-Indonesia Relations," conference paper, Ost-West Koelleg, Bruhl, Germany, March 6, 1997, p. 2.

27. Cited in Lee, "China Factor," p. 8. See also discussion in works of Umar Juoro and Jusuf Wanandi, cited above.

28. *The South China Sea Dispute*. See also Wanandi, *Southeast Asia-China Relations*, pp. 10-13.

29. Reviewed in *China-Southeast Asia Relations*, pp. 8-9.

30. See "Text of Defense White Paper on China's National Defense," *Xinhua*, July 27, 1998, carried by FBIS (internet version). See also discussion in *China-Southeast Asia Relations*, pp. 9-10, and in works cited above by Jusuf Wanandi, Umar Juoro, Songlu Chen, and Lai To Lee.

31. See, among others, William Carpenter et. al., *Asian Security Handbook*, New York: M. E., Sharpe, 1996, pp. 118-120.

32. Ibid.

33. See review in *Cambodia Crisis*, Washington, D.C.: Library of Congress, CRS Issue Brief 98036 (updated regularly).

34. Ibid.

35. "PRC, Cambodia Sign 5 Agreements," *Xinhua*, February 9, 1999 (internet version); *New York Times*, March 2, 1999, p. 1.

36. See, among others, "Cambodian Election Ends," *Xinhua*, July 26, 1998, carried by FBIS (internet version); "News Analysis Views Cambodia Election," *Xinhua*, July 27, 1998, carried by FBIS (internet version).

37. See *Taiwan: Recent Developments and U.S. Policy Choices*, Washington, D.C.: Library of Congress, CRS Issue Brief 98034 (updated regularly).

38. Discussed in Wanandi, *Southeast Asia-China Relations*, pp. 20-21.

39. "China Says Indonesia's Ethnic Riots Internal Issue," *Reuters*, April 13, 1998; "China Pledges to Help Indonesia Overcome Financial Crisis, *Associated Press*, April 12, 1998; "Suharto Meets PRC Foreign Minister," Jakarta Radio, April 13, 1998, carried by FBIS (internet version).

40. "Chinese Media Asked to Play down Indonesia Riots," *Ming Pao*, May 16, 1998, p. A15.

41. Some U.S.-based experts argue that ASEAN officials worry about Japanese expansion, along with their concerns about Chinese expansion. Accordingly, the U.S.-Japan alliance is seen as a useful way to curb any potential Japanese military assertiveness in the region (interview, April 28, 1997).

42. See *Asian-Pacific Security Arrangements: The U.S.-Japanese Alliance and China's Strategic View*, Washington, D.C.: Library of Congress, CRS Report 97375F, March 21, 1997.

43. See, among others, *Asian Pacific Security Arrangements*; Greg Austin, ed., *Missile Diplomacy and Taiwan's Future*, Canberra, Australia: Australian National University, Canbina Papers on Strategy and Defense, no. 122, 1997.

44. See notably "Australian Foreign Minister Announces China WTO, Tibet Deal," *Reuters*, December 9, 1997; "PRC, South Pacific Nations Strengthen Ties," *Xinhua*, December 31, 1997, carried by FBIS (internet version).

45. "Australian Foreign Minister."

46. "Taiwan Reviews Policy on China," *Financial Times*, November 3, 1998, p. 8.

47. "PRC, South Pacific Nations Strengthen Ties."

48. See "Fiji Premier Rejects PRC Request Not to Meet Taiwan Premier," Radio Australia, July 3, 1998, carried by FBIS (internet version).

49. See "Chi Haotian Discusses Ties with Fiji Officials," *Xinhua*, February 9, 1998, carried by FBIS (internet version); "Fiji President Meets Chinese Defense Minister," *Xinhua*, February 10, 1998, carried by FBIS (internet version); "China Eyes U.S. Military in South Pacific," *Christian Science Monitor*, October 30, 1997; "Pacific Outpost," *Far Eastern Economic Review*, April 30, 1998.

50. Beijing *Keji Ribao*, October 7, 1997, p. 1, carried by FBIS (internet version).

51. For up-to-date coverage of this issue, see, among others, *The Washington Pacific Report*, a bimonthly newsletter covering Pacific Island events published in Alexandria, Va.

52. *Free China Journal* (Taipei), November 27, 1998, p. 1.

53. Reviewed in relevant issues of *The Washington Pacific Report*.

54. See, among others, "Chi Haotian Discusses Ties with Fiji Officials," *Xinhua*, February 20, 1998; "Fiji Officials Welcome Siew Despite PRC Protest," *Central News Agency* (Taiwan), July 5, 1998, carried by FBIS (internet version).

Chapter 8

Relations with South and Central Asia

China's leadership has worked assiduously in recent years to ease tensions and incrementally advance Chinese influence with countries along China's border with South and Central Asia. The end of the cold war and collapse of the Soviet Union opened opportunities for spreading Chinese interests in both areas. Beijing made considerable progress in improving relations with India, now devoid of a close strategic alignment with Moscow and more open to international economic and political exchange. The progress was made to some degree at the expense of traditionally close Sino-Pakistani relations, though Chinese leaders did their best to persuade Islamabad that Pakistan's interests were well served by a Sino-Indian rapprochement. China reportedly also continued its close support for Pakistan's nuclear weapons, ballistic missile, and other defense programs, at least until the Pakistanis had the ability to advance these sophisticated programs on their own. And Beijing continued its economic support for the sometimes crisis-prone Pakistani economy.[1]

Indian nuclear tests carried out in May 1998 by a newly installed nationalistic government in New Delhi posed the most serious challenge to China's strategy in the region since the end of the cold war. Subsequently, Chinese officials demonstrated a carefully calculated reaction that endeavored to preserve Chinese interests in avoiding debilitating entanglements in South Asia while checking Indian nationalistic aspirations for greater regional and international prominence and preserving the close Chinese relationship with Pakistan. Beijing sought to work closely with the United States in the process, hoping to capitalize on their common interests and to avoid international publicity regarding China's role as a key supporter of nuclear weapons proliferation in Pakistan.[2]

In Central Asia, the collapse of the USSR resulted in a power vacuum that posed problems for Chinese security. Generally preoccupied with affairs at home, Chinese officials showed an interest in improving relations with newly independent Central Asian states as much for defensive reasons as for reasons of expanding Chinese influence and interests. Thus, Chinese comment was supportive of Russia's residual influence in the region and Moscow's efforts to preserve a strong position in the face of perceived encroachment from the West. Beijing reportedly was keenly interested in getting Central Asian governments to take stronger actions against pan-Turkic and other radicals who were linked to bombings, insurrections, and other disturbances among Turkic minorities in Xinjiang Autonomous Region and other parts of China. At the same time, China wished to benefit from economic, military, and political exchanges, and took several notable steps to advance cooperation in joint ventures to exploit Central Asian oil resources.[3]

South Asia

Recent Chinese policy toward South Asia has generally been in line with broader efforts by China to reduce tensions around its periphery in order to stabilize the "peaceful international environment" needed for China's ambitious agenda of economic and other domestic changes and reforms. Using "dialogues," high-level visits, and other diplomatic measures, Beijing has publicly emphasized the positive and endeavored to minimize the negative with all its South Asian neighbors, including India. In this tactical process, the Chinese authorities have avoided compromising core Chinese territorial, economic, political, and other interests, while they have sought to benefit through methodical and generally constructive interaction with the South Asian countries.[4]

China faced a difficult task in influencing India, the dominant regional power. India has long been at odds with China over territorial issues and over long-standing Chinese support for India's rival, Pakistan. Notably, China and India fought a border war in 1962; India was humiliated. But incremental efforts to ease tensions and improve relations moved forward in the 1980s and appeared to receive an added boost from the collapse of the Soviet Union. For many years, the latter had fostered a close strategic relationship with India based in part on their mutual suspicion of China. Prime Minister Rajiv Gandhi visited China in 1988; Premier Li Peng visited India in 1990; and President Jiang Zemin traveled there in 1996.[5]

As India and China improved relations, China modified its long-standing support for Pakistan. It was already evident in the 1970s that China was unwilling to take significant military action against India in the event of an Indo-Pakistani war. During the 1965 Indo-Pakistani war, Chinese forces did take assertive actions along the Indian border in order to divert Indian forces and weaken their assault against Pakistan. But when India defeated Pakistan in the 1972 war, which saw the dismemberment of Pakistan and the creation of an independent Bangladesh, China took no significant military action.

In the 1980s and 1990s, China further modified its public stance in support of Pakistani claims against India over territorial and other issues. Beijing notably adhered to an increasingly even-handed approach over the sensitive Indo-Pakistani dispute over Kashmir. China continued its close military and economic support for Pakistan. There have continued to be numerous reports and there is some evidence that China played a major role for many years in assisting Pakistan's development of nuclear weapons and related ballistic missile delivery systems, though Chinese officials deny this. President Jiang Zemin was asked in an interview published on June 3, 1998, "Has China helped Pakistan to make its nuclear bomb?" He replied, "No, China has not helped Pakistan. . . ."[6]

Continuing to benefit from Chinese military, economic, and political support, Pakistan has chosen to emphasize the positive in Sino-Pakistani relations and has deemed counterproductive any significant show of irritation with Beijing's shift toward a more even-handed public posture in the subcontinent. Sino-Indian relations also improved, although both powers recognized significant areas of disagreement,[7] notably the following:

- Border issues. Large expanses of territory along India's northwestern and northeastern frontier remain in dispute. Despite eighteen rounds of border talks since 1981, the two sides have made no significant progress in their putative effort to delineate the so-called Line of Actual Control and other lingering problems. During Jiang Zemin's 1996 visit to India, the two sides codified many of the ad hoc confidence-building measures that had evolved over the years along the mostly quiet frontiers.
- Chinese ties with Pakistan, Burma. Long-standing close Chinese military ties with Pakistan and more recently with Burma are viewed by some Indian officials as a Chinese "pincer movement" to contain India. Some also see the United States playing a supporting role through its engagement policy toward China.
- Tibet. Beijing gives high priority to countering the efforts by the Dalai Lama and his supporters to seek a greater international profile for

Tibet, and remains at odds with New Delhi over the issue of India's continued hosting of the spiritual leader and his government in exile.
* Trade. Recent Indian efforts to open the economy and increase exports have led to nascent economic competition with Chinese exports.

Chinese Reaction to the South Asian Crisis, 1998

Chinese officials were apparently surprised by the Indian tests and by New Delhi's emphasis on the so-called "Chinese threat" as a major rationale for its development of nuclear weapons. At first, Chinese officials had hoped that a strong international response to the Indian government might show the action to have been counterproductive for Indian interests, and might also have the effect of persuading Pakistan not to test. China reacted with strong rhetoric against the Indian tests. Chinese media also positively highlighted the U.S. response, including the imposition of sanctions, though Chinese officials made clear that Beijing would not impose sanctions of its own. (Having been subject to massive sanctions during the cold war and more recently to milder sanctions after the 1989 Tiananmen incident, Beijing opposes international sanctions as, in principle, contrary to Chinese interests.)[8]

Privately concerned that other major powers (for example, Russia, France) were less than forceful in their reaction to the Indian tests, Chinese officials were uncertain whether the international reaction would be sufficient to dissuade Pakistan from testing. Chinese leaders were asked by the United States and others to help persuade Pakistan not to test and they may have done so, but it is not publicly known how much emphasis they put on this effort. (It is probably true that without Chinese help, Pakistan would not yet have had a bomb to test.) Chinese officials voiced their sympathy with Pakistan's situation, gave no indication of decreasing their ongoing economic and military assistance to Pakistan, and placed the full blame on India for starting the crisis. Meanwhile, Pakistan sought added assurances from China during high-level official exchanges, though there was no indication from either side of any significant increase in support for Pakistan in the face of the newly apparent Indian threat.[9]

Typical of China's public response to the crisis were Foreign Ministry, authoritative *People's Daily,* and other commentaries critical of the Indian tests. Beijing followed its strong condemnation of India, in a rare Foreign Ministry statement of May 13, with a harsh, authoritative party response in the *People's Daily* (*Renmin Ribao*). A new wave of criticism appeared in two "commentator articles" in *Renmin Ribao* on May 15 and 19, and in a series of signed articles carried in the military daily *Jiefangjun Bao* on May 19. The commentator articles reiterated China's earlier call for international censure of New Delhi, but focused primarily on Beijing's ire over bilateral issues, especially New Delhi's charge that China remained a threat to Indian security and Beijing's claim that the tests had exposed India's drive to dominate South Asia. The articles also contained uncommonly strong personal criticism of India's leaders.[10]

Asserting that the weapons tests "aroused strong condemnation all over the world" and constituted a "serious situation," the May 15 commentator article reiterated China's call for the international community to "strongly demand" that "necessary measures" be taken against India, and that New Delhi "immediately" abandon its nuclear weapons program. Sharpening this criticism after Indian Prime Minister Vajapyee declared India a nuclear power, the May 19 commentator article denounced him as "brazen" for saying India would not sign the comprehensive test ban treaty and attacked the "perverse" deeds of Indian authorities who, it said, "have no intention whatsoever to show restraint." As a result, it claimed, India had fallen into a state of unprecedented isolation.

Despite this attack on India for snubbing international opinion, the commentator articles made it clear that New Delhi's use of the "China threat theory" to justify its nuclear weapons program touched a very sensitive nerve in Beijing. Both articles, as well as the articles in the military paper, directed the bulk of their criticism to refuting this charge and amplifying Beijing's countercharge that the root cause of India's actions was a desire to bolster its alleged quest for hegemony in the region. The May 15 commentator article, for example, declared that the reason the Indian government had "disregarded the fundamental interests of the vast number of its people" and caused "serious unease among its neighbors" was "nothing less than a desire to threaten" those neighbors and "dominate South Asia." The article went on to attack the "even more disgusting" ploy of the Indian government of blaming Chinese military power for its actions, a tactic it said was "not at all clever" and "grossly underestimated the ability of people to judge things correctly." It also launched into a personal criticism of Indian Defense Minister George Fernandes, characterizing his allegations of China's military threat as "spouting nonsense" and sarcastically dismissing his recent "smiling" assurances to PLA Chief of Staff Fu Quanyou regarding the "peaceful and stable" Sino-Indian border as duplicitous. Fu had visited India prior to the Indian tests.

The May 19 commentator article attacked a letter reportedly sent by Prime Minister Vajapyee to U.S. President Bill Clinton tracing the Chinese threat to Chinese aggression in the 1962 Sino-Indian border war. Declaring that "nobody believes such preposterous logic" and "lies," the article went on to add a new charge against India for its "extremely ignominious role in the Tibet issue" in allowing the Dalai Lama to conduct "separatist activity" from Indian soil. The article concluded that "the Indian authorities owe the Chinese people an apology."

China's military leadership was not observed to take an official stance in PRC media on the Indian problem in May 1998. However, according to a Beijing press agency directed at overseas Chinese, the PLA's authoritative daily, *Jiefangjun Bao,* on May 19 devoted a full page to signed articles that "assailed" New Delhi's "military expansionism" and "ambition of seeking regional hegemony."[11] The articles, which detailed India's military spending and weapons program, warned that these military developments warranted "more attention and vigilance." The press agency account called attention to a lengthy analytical piece in *Jiefangjun Bao,* claiming that since the end of the cold war, India had "intensified" efforts to "make war preparation," rather than focusing on economic development. This effort, the article claimed, was a means of attaining New Delhi's strategic goal of "dominating South Asia, containing China, controlling the Indian Ocean, and becoming a major military power." The article also noted that India possessed intermediate-range nuclear-capable missiles that could reach the southern half of China.

Another commentary in the paper reportedly exposed Indian "double-dealing" as having "seriously damaged the security structure and political atmosphere in South Asia." Repeating a metaphor used by Beijing in the past to warn potential adversaries to change their ways, the article said that a country which "vainly hopes to dominate . . . a region," will "end up lifting a rock only to drop it on its own toes."[12]

Despite these acerbic attacks on the Indian government and its top leaders, the May 19 *Renmin Ribao* commentator article stopped short of threatening specific action and called on New Delhi to avoid further damage to bilateral ties—suggesting that Beijing still hoped to avoid a rupture in Sino-Indian ties. Following the pattern of China's earlier official protest, the articles called only for a strong international demand that India discontinue its nuclear weapons program. The commentator article of May 15, for example, noted the steady improvement in relations in recent years and went on to "advise" the Indian side to "treasure the fruit of bilateral relations—which is not easy to come by—and refrain from saying anymore" that will "damage" relations. Repeating this admonition, the May 19 article stated that the common interests of the two countries are "far greater than their differences" and advised Indian authorities to "look to the future" and "not become the stumbling block obstructing" improvement in ties. It called the tests "an unwise move" by "a small number of Indian power-holders" acting against the people's wishes and disregarding the overall interests of "Sino-Indian friendship."

The Chinese commentary in May presaged the balanced Chinese approach to the crisis that emerged in mid-1998 and appeared to be aimed at maximizing Chinese advantages while avoiding complicating entanglements and costly involvements. Consultations with twenty Chinese and foreign officials as well as a careful review of China's statements on South Asian issues in 1998 helped to clarify the Chinese government's assessments and goals in the new situation.[13] The Chinese goals inclined Chinese leaders to continue close cooperation with the United States in the crisis, notably by issuing a joint statement on South Asia during President Clinton's June 1998 visit to Beijing.[14] In general, the Chinese goals could be reduced to the following points:

1. The situation was not yet a threat to China; therefore, avoid entanglements. The South Asian situation was not yet a threat to China and therefore did not warrant substantial increases in military or other resources to deal with the problem. Chinese leaders' priorities remained focused on domestic issues. Beijing would revise its assessment if a major conflict broke out or India deployed nuclear weapons. For the present, Beijing intended to keep its lines open to New Delhi; it sent its new ambassador there after the Indian tests, and the Chinese media highlighted calls for improved relations by Indian politicians. Beijing registered strong concern for the future of international efforts to curb nuclear proliferation, with Chinese and foreign experts saying, unsurprisingly, that China's interests are best served by capping the number of members in the nuclear club at five.

2. Work with the Perm-Five, especially the United States. The United States was in the lead among world powers and the five permanent members of the UN Security Council (the Perm-Five) in taking strong action against India. China strongly supported U.S. action,[15] while avoiding sanctions or other substantial commitments of its own. The two governments worked closely together to come up with a unified Perm-Five position at a meeting of the five powers in Geneva on June 4, 1998. China was much less enthusiastic about broader international efforts to deal with the crisis such as that of the G-8 industrial powers who met on the issue on June 12, 1998. Beijing thought these might dilute the international pressure on India and diminish China's prominent international role.

3. Press India, support Pakistan. Though the Perm-Five statement of June 4, 1998, was critical of both India and Pakistan, Chinese leaders continued to focus their criticism on India for "triggering" the crisis. They stressed strongly that India's perceived great power aspirations should in no

way be rewarded by special consideration in joining the Nuclear Nonproliferation Treaty, the Comprehensive Test Ban Treaty, or the UN Security
Council as a permanent member. For Pakistan, Beijing expressed understanding and continued active military and economic support. On Kashmir,
Beijing was supportive of Pakistani-backed calls for greater international
efforts to ease tensions, though it stuck to the long-standing Chinese position
that the dispute should be settled by the parties concerned (Beijing opposes
international involvement in its own territorial disputes with bordering
countries, as well as with Taiwan).

4. Highlight China's international role and avoid negative publicity on
Chinese proliferation. The Chinese media were replete with references to
China's positive and constructive role in the Perm-Five meeting and other
fora in dealing with the crisis. Beijing officials dismissed as "groundless"
accusations by Indian officials and some in the West about China's
reportedly deep involvement in Pakistan's nuclear weapons and ballistic
missile programs. They hoped to emphasize China's constructive role and
minimize its involvement in Pakistan's programs in order to create a positive
atmosphere for the Sino-U.S. summit in late June.

Kashmir

China demonstrated its careful balance on South Asian issues after the
Indian and Pakistani tests by adhering to a nuanced and evenhanded public
posture on the sensitive issue of Kashmir. Many analysts judged that Indian-
Pakistani tensions and the confrontation of their respective military forces
in Kashmir would provide the spark for an escalating military conflict in the
region.[16]

To calm the situation, Beijing urged moderation on both sides. During
deliberations leading to a UN Security Council resolution on the South
Asian tests, China's UN Permanent Representative called on the two sides
to seek a "mutually acceptable solution" in accordance with "relevant UN
resolutions and the Simla Agreement."[17] The latter was an accord on
differences between India and Pakistan reached in 1972.

Beijing had come to this evenhanded position through a long process,
where China no longer saw the advantages of a decided tilt toward Pakistan
on this or other issues.[18] Reflecting its deep antagonism to India, and the
nascent Indian-Soviet strategic alignment, China strongly supported Pakistan
in the 1960s. Premier Zhou Enlai used a 1964 joint statement with Pakistan
to underline Beijing's position in support of the Kashmir people's right to
self-determination. This leaned toward Pakistan's preference for a UN

plebiscite as called for by 1948-1949 UN declarations on Kashmir. During the 1960s and early 1970s, Beijing also used threats of military action against India and in support of Pakistan in ultimately unsuccessful efforts to prevent Indian-backed dismemberment of Pakistan. New Delhi, backed by the USSR, called China's bluff in supporting Bangladeshi independence, facilitating Pakistan's dismemberment in 1971-1972.

As Beijing sought to reduce tensions with New Delhi in the late 1970s, China grew sensitive to criticism by India's leaders that China's stance on Kashmir was complicating Sino-Indian relations. China's foreign minister in 1980 called for a just settlement in accordance with relevant UN resolutions and the 1972 Simla Agreement. The latter accord followed Islamabad's defeat in the third India-Pakistan war and (at India's insistence) called for bilateral negotiations to resolve the dispute. In further deference to India, China largely dropped public reference to Kashmir's self-determination, even during the late 1980s-early 1990s when rapprochement was severely threatened first by escalating military tension along the Sino-Indian border and then by friction between Islamabad and New Delhi after the outbreak of the Kashmir insurgency. China has moved further away from uncritical support for Pakistan during the 1990s by refusing to back Islamabad on Kashmir in the UN Human Rights Commission.

The balanced Chinese stance on Kashmir notified India of China's continued interest in improved relations despite sometimes heated Chinese commentary directed at the nationalistic Indian government. Indian policy makers, of course, had historic grievances regarding China and the Kashmir dispute. The Sino-Indian border war of 1962 confirmed Beijing's control of sixteen thousand square miles of disputed territory in Kashmir, which contains a strategic road connecting China's Xinjiang Autonomous Region with Tibet.

The altered Chinese stance on Kashmir was one of the disappointments Pakistan faced in watching its Chinese ally pursue its advantage in the new situation. Pakistani and Chinese officials alike emphasized the positive features of their relationship while soft pedaling the reality that Pakistan, as the weaker party, needed to continue to cater to China and rely on Chinese support, even when Beijing's backing was notably less strong than in the past.

In sum, China's moderate and pragmatic approach to South Asia in the 1990s faced a major challenge as a result of India's nuclear tests and anti-China posture in 1998. Chinese leaders reacted calmly, hoping to encourage strong international pressure, led by the United States, to curb Indian ambitions. Beijing remained sensitive to perceived backsliding by the United States and especially Russia. Beijing refused Russian Prime Minister Yevgeni Primakov's suggestion in December 1998 that Russia, India, and China join forces to influence world politics.[19] Meanwhile, it solidified its relations with Pakistan, notably sending the Chinese defense minister there in February 1999.[20]

Central Asia

The broad outlines of China's policy toward Central Asia in the post-cold war period remain fairly clear. China has expanded its ties across Central Asia to stabilize its western frontier, gain access to the region's energy resources, and balance Western influence in an area Beijing has traditionally viewed as Russia's reserve. Beijing has calculated that improved ties with Central Asian states, which are also concerned about problems arising from the linkage of religion and politics, can shield Xinjiang Province and its ethnically Turkic population from outside Muslim and pan-Turkic influence. Central Asian leaders assure Beijing they will not tolerate separatist groups targeting the province, though China suspects its neighbors may lack sufficient resolve to eradicate the threat.[21]

China's Central Asian energy projects reflect PRC efforts to obtain secure supply lines and avoid overdependence on a few sources of energy. Beijing has an agreement to develop two major Kazakhstan oil and gas fields and construct pipelines to Xinjiang, and reportedly is exploring gas and other pipeline links with Turkmenistan and others. But the projects are expensive, logistically difficult, and complicated by inadequate energy-processing and transport systems in western China.

China and Kazakhstan on September 24, 1997, signed two agreements worth $9.5 billion for the development of two major oil and gas fields and the construction of two pipelines in Kazakhstan, according to press reports.[22] One pipeline was to cover three thousand kilometers from Kazakhstan into western China and take an estimated five years to build; the other would extend two hundred fifty kilometers to the Turkmen border and be connected to a pipeline into Iran.

Political and economic factors may have tilted Almaty toward China rather than toward competing U.S. companies. President Nazarbayev is presumably sensitive to Chinese political concerns, including pressure to clamp down on Uighur exiles who provide support to dissidents in Xinjiang and complaints about Almaty's increasing cooperation with the United States, including cooperation on NATO expansion.[23]

Kazakhstani officials are also aware that Beijing's large foreign exchange reserves could help it win any bid it wanted. Moreover, China's proposal to build a pipeline eastward—and thereby link the eastern

Kazakhstani cities with its oil resources, before joining a planned trans-China pipeline—also favored the PRC.

However, even under the best of circumstances these projects are fraught with difficulties. The China National Petroleum Corporation is regarded within the industry as lacking world-class technology and experience in managing such complex international construction projects. Moreover, regional politics—including energy politics—remain complicated.[24]

China carefully monitors the growing Western commercial presence in Central Asia and views expanding NATO activities as indicative of U.S. efforts to extend its influence to the region, squeeze out Russia, and, with the U.S.-Japan military alliance, contain China. Beijing sharply criticized a September 1997 Partnership for Peace (PFP)-sponsored exercise in Kazakhstan and Uzbekistan, which involved the Central Asian Peacekeeping Battalion and contingents from four other countries, including Russia. The exercise featured the record-setting long-distance air transport of five hundred U.S. troops to Kazakhstan. Despite its participation, Russia was at best ambivalent about the exercise and its NATO connection.[25]

China's expanding influence in Central Asia has prompted little adverse reaction from Moscow, which heretofore jealously guarded the region's resources. Beijing regards a Central Asian power balance favoring Russia as advantageous to its own interests, but believes the Russian leadership may be too weak to guarantee security in the former Soviet territories. China nonetheless pursues its interests in Central Asia cautiously, presumably in part to avoid provoking its strategic partner into discontinuing the steady supply of Russian arms to China and possibly risking a strong nationalist backlash from President Yeltsin's successor.[26]

The complex range of factors influencing Chinese policy in the region is revealed in the Chinese relationship with Turkey, an influential actor in Central Asian diplomacy. The visit to Beijing by the Turkish deputy prime minister in June 1998 reflected these factors as it marked ongoing efforts to strengthen economic ties and play down differences, especially over the treatment of Turkic Uighurs in Xinjiang.

Relations had remained somewhat chilled between these two generally low-key competitors for Central Asian markets and political influence since the PRC crackdown against Xinjiang's assertive Uighurs following a violent post-Ramadan uprising in early 1997. The Turkish Foreign Ministry at that time issued a statement deploring the "bloody developments" while respecting China's territorial integrity and stating that the people of Xinjiang should be a "bridge of friendship" between the two countries.[27]

In Beijing in June 1998, Turkish Deputy Prime Minister Ecevit again acknowledged PRC sovereignty over Xinjiang but suggested that Ankara was limited in its ability to prevent demonstrations in Turkey by Uighur separatist elements, according to Turkish press reports.[28] Turkey, unlike the Central Asian states, has resisted Chinese pressure to issue public assurances that separatist activities will not be tolerated or otherwise crack down on such groups.

Turkey's NATO ties are also, presumably, problematic for PRC hardliners, who perceive Turkey as a U.S. bridgehead for expanding NATO into Central Asia to squeeze out Russia and contain China. Beijing also closely monitors U.S.-Turkish collaboration on negotiations for a Central Asian pipeline, owing to concerns that China's own energy security might be affected if Central Asian oil flows predominantly westward. Chinese leaders view two additional developments—Turkey's growing military ties with Israel and Turkish incursions into Northern Iraq in pursuit of Kurdish insurgents—as threats to regional stability with serious implications for China's friends in the Arab world and Iran.

Both countries see increased trade and economic ties as one means of smoothing over their differences. This is consistent with China's emphasis on this approach in its foreign relations to secure a stable environment for its domestic reform program. Turkey in recent years has sought stronger ties with Central and East Asia, and has shown particular interest in gaining access to the Caspian region's energy resources.

A Turkish state minister during an April 1998 visit to Beijing underscored the need for more balanced trade and announced an agreement with Chinese officials to increase the annual bilateral trade volume to more than $1.2 billion, according to press reports.[29] Turkish imports from China, primarily manufactured goods, totaled about $560 million in 1997; exports to China amounted to just over $64 million.

Typical of China's frequent diplomatic and high-level exchanges with Central Asian states was President Jiang Zemin's hosting of Kyrgyzstan President Askar Akayevich Akayev in April 1998.[30] Chinese media recalled that Jiang and Akayev had signed, along with Russian and other Central Asian leaders, a 1997 agreement on trust-strengthening measures and on cutting military forces in border areas. Jiang explicitly thanked Akayev for his government's opposition to "national separatism"—a presumed allusion to radical movements in Xinjiang. Akayev said that the Kyrgyz Republic opposes separatism and religious extremism, and "has learned from Chinese experiences on handling relations among ethnic groups." After pledging to improve trade and promote regional prosperity and peace, the two presidents witnessed the signing of four documents providing for the following:

- An agreement on economic cooperation and trade;
- A framework for providing loans with reduced interest to the Kyrgyz Republic by China;
- Exchanges of the ratification certificates of a Chinese-Kyrgyz boundary agreement; and
- An agreement on extradition.

Meanwhile, Beijing adopts a typically evenhanded public stance on the most contentious political issue in Central Asian politics—the continuing civil war in Afghanistan. In China's view, all the warring parties should stop fighting, and the factions should discuss their problems among themselves without any outside interference. China is willing to support international proposals for peace, but typically supports a major role for the UN, where China has a permanent seat on the Security Council. The Chinese were also reported to suspect the Taliban faction in Afghanistan of being supportive of radicals in Xinjiang.[31] The Chinese Foreign Ministry sent a delegation to the Taliban regime in early 1999, reportedly seeking to build relations.[32]

Mongolia

Closer proximity to Chinese population centers and long-standing experience in dealing with its massive neighbor to the south have made Mongolia much more wary than states in Central Asia in dealing with China. Having lost its Soviet ally and being determined to make its own way with a vibrant and sometimes confusing drive toward a market economy and democratic system, the Mongolian government watches carefully for signs of Chinese dominance while seeking reassurances from other powers, especially the United States. Thus far, Beijing has demonstrated little concern over trends in Mongolia, well aware that Ulan Bator and other regional capitals are sensitive to possible adverse Chinese reactions if they are seen to align themselves in ways contrary to basic Chinese interests.[33]

Mongolia seeks to become more economically and politically integrated into East Asia. A larger regional role for Mongolia enables it to balance its relations with China and Russia, without depending too heavily on the United States. Mongolia has publicly stated that enhanced cooperation with the United States is a major pillar of its foreign policy and a means of preserving its independence and security.

Mongolia supports the U.S. role in Asian security, in particular in northeast Asia. The government works hard to maintain good relations with other regional actors—Russia, China, both Koreas, Japan—but Mongolian officials have expressed concern privately about potential Russian and Chinese rivalry over Mongolia. As part of its regional security strategy, Mongolia also seeks deeper trade and economic links with East Asian countries.

The Mongolian government looks to expand its international contacts beyond its two neighbors. Mongolia does not see itself as a part of Central Asia for cultural, religious, and political reasons, and clearly identifies itself as part of northeast Asia. It aspires to participation in the ASEAN Regional Forum, seeks to join APEC, and wants to join northeast Asian regional fora (for example, a Track Two group on security issues, which includes both Koreas, Russia, China, and Japan).

Historic animosity and distrust of China's intentions toward Mongolia continue to be factors in Mongolia's relations with its southern neighbor. The cornerstone of the Mongolian-Chinese relationship is a 1994 Treaty of Friendship and Cooperation, which codifies mutual respect for the independence and territorial integrity of both sides. Mongolian leaders in private say they continue to fear political forces in China that question Mongolian independence.

Despite their concerns, Mongolian leaders recognize that a return to economic prosperity in their country depends upon maintaining and improving Mongolia's economic ties with China and Russia. Mongolia is encouraged that both Russia and China are moving rapidly to integrate with the world politically and economically. Mongolia beat both its neighbors into the WTO with its January 1997 accession.

The issue of Tibet is one of some sensitivity in Mongolian-Chinese relations. Mongolia shares with Tibet its brand of Buddhism and in recent years has received visits from the Dalai Lama, despite Chinese protests. Mongolians sympathize with the plight of Tibet, recognizing that but for the backing of the Soviet Union they might have suffered a similar fate. Realistically, however, they know there is little they can do for Tibet.

In sum, Chinese government pragmatism in the 1990s has spread Chinese influence throughout the countries along its northern and western borders. Chinese leaders are well aware of the limits of Chinese influence, given the fluid political situation in many of these states. They are especially concerned about the inability to curb cross-border dissidents and terrorists bent on causing incidents in China for the sake of greater freedom and autonomy for Islamic peoples in China. They favor residual Russian power over increases in U.S.-backed NATO influence in the region. And they seek oil resources in order to keep a healthy diversity of international suppliers for the Chinese economy.

Notes

1. See, among others, John Garver, "China and South Asia," *Annals of the American Academy of Political and Social Science* 519 (January 1992): 67-85; J. Mohan Malik, "Chinese-Indian Relations in the Post-Soviet Era," *China Quarterly*, no. 142 (June 1995), 317-355.

2. See assessment in "South Asian Crisis: China's Assessments and Goals," Congressional Research Service (CRS) memorandum, Library of Congress, Washington, D.C., June 6, 1998. This memo was based especially on twenty interviews conducted with Chinese and other official experts following the Indian nuclear tests.

3. See, among others, Guang Wan, "The U.S. New Central Asia Strategy," Beijing *Xiandai Guoji Guanxi* (*Contemporary International Relations*) in Chinese, November 27, 1997, no. 11, pp. 13-16; "Text of Jiang Zemin Speech at the Five-Nation meeting of China, Kazakhstan, Kyrgyzstan, Russia and Tajikistan," *Xinhua*, July 3, 1998, carried by Foreign Broadcast Information Service (FBIS), internet version.

4. Abu Taher Salahuddin Ahmed, "India-China Relations in the 1990s," *Journal of Contemporary Asia* 26, 1 (1996): 100-115.

5. Denny Roy, *China's Foreign Relations*, Boulder, Colo.: Rowman & Littlefield, 1998, pp. 170-174.

6. Hong Kong *AFP* in English, June 3, 1998, carried by FBIS (internet version). On China's reported proliferation to Pakistan, Washington, D.C.: Library of Congress, CRS Report 97-850F, updated January 16, 1998.

7. Reviewed in, among others, Malik, "Chinese-Indian Relations," and Ahmed, "India-China Relations."

8. See, among others, "PRC on India Tests," FBIS *Trends*, May 19, 1998 (internet version).

9. See review in "South Asian Crisis: China's Assessments and Goals," p. 3.

10. This is taken from the review in "PRC on India Tests." The *Peoples' Daily* (*Renmin Ribao*) and *Jiefangjung Bao* articles were published promptly by *Xinhua* and carried by FBIS (internet version).

11. Cited in "PRC on India Tests."

12. Ibid.

13. See review of these consultations in "South Asian Crisis: China's Assessments and Goals," pp. 3-4.

14. See "Sino-U.S. Joint Statement on South Asia," *Xinhua*, June 27, 1998, carried by FBIS (internet version).

15. Some Chinese officials privately encouraged the United States to take stronger action against India by asserting that such action was needed to counter Pakistani charges, echoed by some in China, that one of the reasons India carried out tests in the first place was that the United States tacitly "supported" India's rising power, partly as a check against China. The U.S. "failure" to detect and prevent the initial Indian test was seen as evidence of this alleged U.S. strategic plan for the region. Interviews, May-June 1998. See "South Asian Crisis."

16. "Beijing Radio Comments on India's Foreign Policy," Beijing Radio, May 28, 1998, carried by FBIS (internet version).

17. See, among others, "Tang Jiaxuan on UNSC Meeting, South Asian Situation," *Xinhua*, June 4, 1998, carried by FBIS (internet version).

18. Garver, "China and South Asia."

19. "Primakov Seeks 'Strategic Triangle,'" *International Herald Tribune*, December 22, 1998.

20. "Chi Haotian-Led Chinese Delegation to Visit Pakistan, Islamabad," *The Nation*, February 7, 1999, p. 16.

21. Lillian Craig Harris, "Xinjiang, Central Asia and the Implications for China's Policy in the Islamic World," *China Quarterly*, vol. 133 (March 1993): 111-129; Peter Ferdinand, "The New Central Asia and China," in *The New States of Central Asia and Their Neighbors*, ed. Peter Ferdinand, New York: Council on Foreign Relations, 1994; "China's Muslim Rebels: The Uighurs," *Economist*, July 13, 1996, vol. 340, p. 33; "The Ethnic Tinderbox inside China," *Business Week*, March 31, 1997, p. 57; Li Peng, "China's Basic Policy toward Central Asia," *Beijing Review*, vol. 39, July 22, 1996, pp. 8-9; Ross Munro, "Central Asia and China," in *Central Asia and the World*, ed. Michael Mandelbaum, New York: Council on Foreign Relations, 1994.

22. Carried by FBIS (internet version). See also Chinese and other press coverage, carried by FBIS, during Jiang Zemin's visit to Kazakhstan on July 3-4, 1998.

23. See Wan, "The U.S. New Central Asia Strategy."

24. See, among others, Shireen T. Hunter, *Central Asia since Independence*, New York: Praeger, 1996; Martha Brill Olcott, *Central Asia's New States*, Washington, D.C.: U.S. Institute of Peace, 1996.

25. Wan, "The U.S. New Central Asia Strategy."

26. See "Text of Jiang Speech at 5 Nation Meeting," *Xinhua*, July 3, 1998, carried by FBIS (internet version); "Text of 5 Nation Meeting Joint Statement," *Xinhua*, July 3, 1998, carried by FBIS (internet version).

27. Dru Gladney, "Rumblings from the Uighur," *Current History*, September 1997, pp. 287-290; "Ecevit Comments on Demonstrations in Xinjiang Province," Ankara TRT Television, June 1, 1998, carried by FBIS (internet version).

28. "Turkey Willing to Expand Ties with China," *Xinhua*, May 29, 1998, carried by FBIS (internet version).

29. These were carried at the time by FBIS (internet version).

30. See "Roundup on Chinese-Kyrgyz Ties," *Xinhua*, April 25, 1998, carried by FBIS (internet version). "Jiang Zemin Holds Talks with Kyrgyz Counterpart," China Daily, April 28, 1998; "China, Kyrgyzstan Sign Joint Statement," *Xinhua*, April 28, 1998, carried by FBIS (internet version).

31. "Year Ender on Peace in Afghanistan," *Xinhua*, December 8, 1997, carried by FBIS (internet version).

32. "Chinese Foreign Ministry Delegation Arrives in Afghanistan," Kabul Radio, January 31, 1999, carried by FBIS (internet version).

33. See the review in Michael Mitchell, "Mongolia," in *Asian Security Handbook*, ed. William Carpenter, Armonk, N.Y.: M. E. Sharpe, 1996, pp. 184-191.

Chapter 9

Europe, the Middle East, Africa, and Latin America

Europe

Relations with Europe remain secondary in Chinese foreign policy priorities after the cold war. Relations with the United States, Japan, and powers along China's periphery continue to receive primary attention. But burgeoning economic contacts, along with political and security concerns related to Chinese and others' interest in creating a more "multipolar" world order, have undergirded rapidly developing relations in the 1990s. By early 1998, Chinese leaders were traveling to Europe one after another, and senior European officials were visiting China, discussing a variety of issues centered largely on the disturbing economic trends in East Asia and China's proposed entry into the World Trade Organization.[1]

Reflecting in large part the European desire to become more closely linked with China's rising market within the East Asian economies in the 1990s, the sixteen-member European Union (EU) was unusually active in the 1990s in building ties with Beijing. The highlights included major policy pronouncements, high-level exchanges, and limited assistance programs, backed by EU-China trade flows that more than tripled during the ten years before 1996. The prospects for continued trade and economic interchange appeared reasonably good, although the Asian economic crisis dampened EU enthusiasm for Asian investments. Broader political and security

149

interaction remained constrained by the relatively low priority Beijing assigned to relations with Europe, by organizational and institutional limitations in the EU and among its members, and by the divergence in EU-Chinese views on the importance of conformity to internationally accepted norms regarding trade practices, human rights, weapons proliferation, the use of military force, and other matters.[2]

Representing sixteen nations, including the large majority of the countries of Western Europe, the EU was unusually active in the 1990s in building ties with East Asia, and particularly China. The efforts saw several exchanges of high-level visits, cultural exchanges, and the use of development assistance and training aid. Highlights included the European Union's 1994 statement "Towards a New Asia Strategy," the summit meeting between European Union leaders and those of East Asian countries at the so-called Asia-Europe Meeting (ASEM) in Bangkok on March 1-2, 1996, the European Union's July 1995 statement on a "Long-Term Policy for Europe-China Relations," the ASEM summit of April 1998, the EU-China summit of April 1998, and the March 1998 EU document, "The Establishment of Full Partnership with China."

Chinese leaders appeared anxious to reciprocate the heightened European interest, with senior leaders including President Jiang Zemin, past premier Li Peng, and current premier Zhu Rongji making highly publicized visits to major EU countries in recent years. Those visits were accompanied by reports of major sales by EU countries of sophisticated transportation and other equipment to China.[3]

Impressive statistics, especially in the area of trade, rested behind the European Union's first formal declaration of policy toward and growing interaction with China. Members of the union saw their trade with China triple in ten years, from $14.3 billion in 1985 to $45.6 billion in 1994. The pace of growth was accelerating, with trade levels in 1993 seeing a 65 percent increase over the previous year. China became the fourth largest supplier and the fourth largest market for EU members. This trend came within a broader wave of European-East Asian trade, which saw the two sides' trade with each other become roughly equal to their trade with the United States. The upswing stabilized by 1997, when EU-China trade was $43 billion.[4] The trade level increased by about 15 percent in 1998.[5]

U.S. policy reactions to emerging European-Chinese relations were mixed. On the one hand, improved relations provided a number of benefits, including exposing China more to Western ideas and institutions that over time might encourage the type of change in China favored by the United States, and providing greater European experience in dealing with China, which would help to achieve improved U.S.-EU communication on China-related questions. On the other hand, U.S. officials and other observers sometimes complained that greater European involvement with China complicated U.S. efforts to prompt the Chinese government to conform more closely to internationally accepted norms. Thus, EU representatives were seen to be less stringent in dealing with China on sensitive issues like human rights, market access, intellectual property rights, and other questions. Assistant Secretary of State Winston Lord told the House Ways and Means Committee hearing on the issue of U.S. most favored nation (MFN) tariff treatment for China on June 11, 1996, that European traders, among others, were poised to take commercial advantage of U.S. efforts to impose sanctions on China over human rights and other questions.[6]

The incentives for increased contacts in the 1990s came mainly from the Europeans. The moves by the European Union toward China came in the context of a general sense among European leaders that the union and its members needed to take more decisive action in order to continue to be seen as important actors in East Asian affairs. This was deemed particularly important as it became evident in Europe in the early 1990s that East Asia's economic growth would surpass that of other major markets, and that Europe's future economic health would be determined by how well EU members adjusted to and profited from the opportunities in the region. The Europeans were said to be concerned that they had missed an opportunity to be included in the Asian Pacific Economic Cooperation (APEC) forum uniting the economic powers of the Pacific rim. The Europeans also judged that China's rising power and influence were central in determining East Asia's prosperity and that the European Union needed to focus special efforts on building a closer relationship with China.

The European statements on China also made it clear that union members placed an emphasis on China's importance to broader European interests regarding such issues as the world trading system, the proliferation of weapons of mass destruction and related technology, environmental concerns, and others. China was seen as particularly important in determining the future importance of the World Trade Organization (WTO), which was a top priority to the Europeans; and in influencing the future stability on the Korean peninsula (EU members were concerned about nuclear proliferation and stability there).[7] EU members Britain and Portugal had special concerns with China because of the reversion of their respective colonial possessions, Hong Kong and Macau, to Chinese control in 1997 and 1999, respectively.

Nonetheless, amid the rhetoric of European determination to build closer ties with China were several realities limiting European-Chinese relations, according to European and Chinese experts:

- China's view of Europe. Beijing was anxious to gain economically from improved relations with Europe. Over time, Beijing was also anxious to foster greater European political and strategic independence from the United States as part of broader PRC efforts to foster a multipolar world more advantageous to China than the current international system. For the present, Beijing was seen to chafe under an international order that viewed the United States as the dominant power, often pressing the PRC hard on a variety of international and domestic questions. Thus, for China, Europe was said to represent a kind of "card" that could be played in the more important game of U.S.-Chinese relations.[8]

- China notably opposed NATO expansion and tried from time to time to play up intra-alliance rivalries, especially between the U.S. and French governments. But this effort was largely in vain given strong alliance support for NATO expansion.

- This kind of thinking underlined some of the limits of Chinese interests in and attention to Europe. It reflected the fact that in the order of PRC foreign policy, first priority was given to the United States; next came Japan and the important countries in the East Asian area; Europe and other areas came a distant third.

- Meanwhile, Chinese understanding of the European Union was said to be weak and confused, with many Chinese officials thinking of the union as, at bottom, a protectionist trading bloc designed to keep PRC products out of Europe.

- European limitations. These focused heavily on organizational and institutional weaknesses, according to European and Chinese experts.[9] Thus, several experts mentioned that Europe's interest in China was mainly economic and that the European Union was most effective when dealing with a country like China on the basis of economic issues.

- As a diplomatic actor or as a force on security issues, the union was said to be less well suited to take actions vis-à-vis China, especially as EU members were reluctant to allow the union very much leeway to deal with important defense or security issues. As an example, the union was very slow to come out in support of the American show of force off the Taiwan Strait in the face of provocative PRC military exercises in early 1996, while some member governments were prompt in supporting the move.

- Some European specialists also suggested that the European Union's emphasis on China was in part to compensate for the union's alleged inability to arrive at effective and decisive policies on more critical issues requiring European cooperation, such as Atlantic relations, European security, and the Middle East. The European Union was also unsuccessful in meeting the 1993 Maastricht Treaty's call for a common foreign and defense policy.

Recent Developments

China began the year 1998 with significant policy advances in Europe. After back-to-back visits by the British and French foreign ministers in January, Beijing sent a senior vice premier to the World Economic Summit in Davos, Switzerland, and to several EU capitals, outgoing premier Li Peng visited the Netherlands in February, and newly appointed premier Zhu Rongji capped off the effort with a masterful performance at the ASEAN-EU meeting (ASEM) and EU-China summits in London in April, along with official state visits to Great Britain and France.[10]

Highlighting China's role as an influential economic actor and anchor of stability in the Asian economic crisis, the Beijing envoys concluded economic deals that were advantageous both to China and to Europe and argued that China's responsible international stance should be rewarded with expeditious entry into the World Trade Organization (WTO). Beijing diplomatically outflanked those in the West still interested in pursuing a China resolution at the UN Human Rights Commission (UNHRC) meeting in April—a top Chinese priority. It welcomed clear signs of heightened EU interest in cooperating pragmatically with China, notably the March 25 European Commission document, "The Establishment of Full Partnership with China."[11]

Senior Chinese economic leaders, headed by Vice Premier Li Lanqing and China's chief WTO negotiator, participated actively in the World Economic Forum at Davos in early February 1998, and held side meetings with WTO Director General Ruggiero and EU Trade Commissioner Brittan, the EU's point man on China/WTO. The delegation visited Switzerland, Spain, Belgium, the EU headquarters in Brussels, and Denmark over the next two weeks before returning home via Russia.[12] Premier Li Peng traveled to the Netherlands in February and also visited Russia.[13]

At Davos, Vice Premier Li repeatedly portrayed China as an anchor in the Asian economic storm, holding the line against currency devaluation in China and Hong Kong while promoting China's continued opening and growth for the benefit of the region and the world. Beijing's line at Davos was that it deserved "positive" consideration for its WTO application because China was adhering to an internationally responsible stance despite the risk of negative consequences, such as a drop in export growth, as it sought to foster regional economic stability.[14]

When hosting the British and French officials in January 1998, Beijing had argued that progress in Chinese human rights practices and growing interest in mutually advantageous economic and political relations should reduce Western support for the UNHRC resolution. Subsequent Chinese delegations to Europe amplified Beijing's message. In January, Beijing invited UN Human Rights Commissioner Mary Robinson to China, welcomed an International Committee of the Red Cross delegation to visit in February 1998, invited an EU human rights delegation to visit Tibet, and pressed ahead with ongoing human rights dialogues with the European Union, the United Kingdom, and France. Beijing also agreed to the first-ever EU-China summit, where human rights issues would be discussed, to be held concurrently with the EU-Asia summit in London in early April; the timing appeared to have the effect of further dampening the already declining Western European enthusiasm for sponsoring a resolution critical of China in March. Beijing also took special steps to improve relations with the Netherlands and Denmark, which appeared to back away from their active roles in sponsoring the human rights resolution in 1997 that had led to a downturn in their relations with China. The Danish foreign minister played down publicly the possibility of sponsoring the resolution in 1998, while the Netherlands government seemed more focused on the high-level trade delegation due to travel to Beijing immediately after Li Peng's visit.[15]

At its General Affairs Council meeting on February 23, the European Union agreed to support the United States should it seek to have China's human rights abuses condemned at the mid-March UNHRC meeting, according to press reports.[16] EU ministers cited as progress the encouraging results of the EU-China human rights dialogue, China's signature in 1997 of the UN International Covenant on Economic, Social, and Cultural Rights, and Beijing's invitation to UN Commissioner for Human Rights Robinson to visit China.

The EU-China summit on April 2, 1998, in London met both sides' expectations in upgrading and intensifying Europe's political and economic dialogue with China. While providing a big publicity splash, the summit provided few significant new developments; it was mainly of symbolic importance. The summit saw a Chinese delegation headed by Premier Zhu Rongji, Foreign Minister Tang Jiaxuan, and Trade Minister Shi Guangshang on their maiden foreign trip after receiving their new positions at the Ninth National People's Congress in March 1998. Agenda items included trade issues and China's WTO membership, human rights conditions in China, and the Asian economic crisis.[17]

Following their April 2 summit meeting, EU and Chinese officials released a joint press statement that noted a shared commitment to China's entry into the WTO at an early date on terms that reinforce the world trading system. The European Union and China agreed to strengthen their exchanges and cooperation in the international financial and monetary field. The European Union praised China's announcement of its intention to sign the international covenant on civil and political rights, and both sides agreed on the need to achieve more progress through the EU-China human rights dialogue.[18]

Meanwhile, as Europeans increased their interaction with China, experts judged that several other areas bore watching in addition to the burgeoning bilateral trade relationship:[19]

- Europe's weak profile in China. Would the European Union or its members increase educational and other exchanges in order to improve Europe's image in China and improve Chinese understanding of the union and its members? In the 1990s, for example, the number of EU students studying in China and Chinese students studying in EU countries was only a small fraction of the numbers of U.S. students in China and Chinese students in the United States.

- How would the European Union handle the intense competition among member states that saw them foster trade benefits and other forms of subsidized economic competition in order to land trade deals for companies in their particular country? The competition for sales in China not only complicated EU-U.S. relations there but also worked against unity among the EU members.

- How active were the union and its members prepared to be on issues like security questions, human rights, Hong Kong's reversion, Taiwan, and others that were important to segments of European opinion but thus far had been dealt with discreetly or not at all by the European Union in its new, mainly economically focused initiatives toward China?

- Would the European Union allow itself to be played as a "card" in China's dealings with the United States, in effect complicating or undermining U.S. efforts to press the Chinese government to conform to internationally accepted norms? (Chinese leaders have a long history of playing off one outside power against another and have been anxious to exploit perceived splits among the Western countries over human rights, WTO entry, and other issues.)

In sum, the Chinese government leaders in the 1990s found considerable common ground in developing economic relations with the countries of the European Union. Political and security cooperation was more difficult to achieve on account of differences over issues like human rights and NATO's expanded membership. Nonetheless, Beijing was anxious to work closely with the growing European interest in cooperation with China. It devoted a substantial high-level leadership effort to that cause, seeing such cooperation as significantly strengthening China's rising international political profile and global influences.

The Middle East

Chinese officials for decades viewed the Middle East as a key arena of East-West competition for world dominance, and of resistance by third-world states and liberation movements against outside powers and their local allies. Beijing lined up on the side of the "progressive" forces resisting U.S. and/or Soviet dominance, and provided some military aid and training and other support to some resistance movements. In general, however, Chinese leaders saw the Middle East as distant from primary Chinese foreign policy concerns.[20]

The end of the cold war and the collapse of the Soviet Union did not change this basic calculus. Because of its isolation from Western and other governments as a result of the Tiananmen incident of 1989, Chinese officials endeavored to build closer ties with the many authoritarian governments in the Middle East region. President Yang Shangkun, Premier Li Peng, and Foreign Minister Qian Qichen traveled widely in the area, as well as in other third-world locales in an apparent effort to persuade audiences at home and abroad that the Chinese regime could not be effectively isolated. Beijing continued to gain both economically and politically from active arms sales to the region, notably during the Iran-Iraq war. And it followed the establishment of diplomatic relations with Saudi Arabia in 1990 with the multi-billion dollar sale of older Chinese intermediate-range ballistic missiles. China also improved its relations with Israel, establishing formal diplomatic ties in 1992.[21]

Its economic and global strategy seemed to lead China toward policies that would avoid offending any major Middle Eastern country and open opportunities for trade and for imports of oil to China's burgeoning industrial economy. In addition to arms sales and Chinese-Middle Eastern trade valued at $3 billion a year by the early 1990s, Beijing had earned on average over half a billion dollars annually from labor contracts in the region since the late 1970s.[22]

The Persian Gulf War in 1990-1991 added to regional economic difficulties, including Western sanctions, crimped regional economic development, and curbed opportunities for Chinese economic interchange and arms sales. Meanwhile, the U.S.-led victory in the Persian Gulf War came at China's political expense in the sense that Beijing's efforts to keep on good terms with all sides in the conflict counted for little as U.S.-backed power moved to dominate the region. Coming on top of U.S.-backed efforts to isolate China and pressure it to change in accordance with international standards supported by the United States, this development prompted Beijing to react by seeking opportunities to undercut U.S. world influence while building Chinese ties with countries in the region. It was at this juncture that Chinese officials moved forward in relations with many Arab governments and with Iran.[23]

In general terms, the Middle East in the mid-1990s was also seen as important to China because of its close relationship to China's unstable western areas, especially Xinjiang. Beijing worried about support from the region to Islamic separatists or other radicals in China. As China became a net importer of oil in 1993, Beijing worked hard to diversify its international supplies, and the Middle East loomed large with its abundant oil reserves. The Chinese also sought to develop trade in military items and technologies with countries that were on poor terms with the United States (for example, Iran), in part to use those ties as leverage in dealing with suspected U.S. plots to contain or pressure China. Meanwhile, Chinese officials, though victorious over Taiwan in establishing relations with the conservative Saudi Arabian government, devoted strong efforts to curbing any Taiwan inroads in the Middle East, as well as elsewhere.[24]

Continuing past Chinese efforts to build productive ties with all Middle Eastern countries, Beijing's relationship with Israel flourished in trade, political exchanges, and defense ties. Chinese officials continued to lean toward the Arab position on Middle East peace issues but duly acknowledged the legitimacy of Israeli concerns.[25] Chinese officials disapproved of U.S. or Western-backed pressure against so-called "rouge" states like Iraq, Iran, Libya, and Syria, though Chinese policy usually followed the international consensus in the United Nations when it dealt with Iraqi recalcitrance or other issues.[26]

The improvement in U.S.-Chinese relations after 1996, and especially the summit meetings of 1997 and 1998, had an indirect impact on Chinese policy in the Middle East. On the one hand, it reinforced the judgment by some in China that Beijing had more to gain by working more or less cooperatively with the United States than by lining up with states strongly hostile to the United States. And it encouraged China to be more active on regional issues that heretofore had been the prime domain of other powers, and to do so in ways that at least outwardly seemed supportive of U.S. goals in stability and peace. Thus, for example, Chinese leaders during 1997 and 1998 summit meetings with the United States promised to stop cooperation with Iran on nuclear matters, to halt sales of antiship cruise missiles to Iran, and to halt support for Iran ballistic missile development.[27] Beijing also strove to work in support of U.S.-led efforts to revitalize the stalled Middle East peace process, notably through the visit of Vice Premier and Foreign

Minister Qian Qichen to frontline states in December 1997 and his subsequent interchanges with U.S. officials on Middle East peace issues.[28]

The transition toward a Middle East posture more in line with U.S. interests remained muddled, however. Beijing at times still saw its interest as well served by staking out tough anti-U.S. stances on sensitive regional questions. For instance, in commenting on a crisis in late 1997 between the U.S. on one side and Iraq on the other over whether UN weapons inspectors would have free access to Iraqi sites, *Xinhua* on November 20, 1997, stated that even though UN inspectors were returned to Iraq, as the United States had demanded, "in reality the United States was the loser and Iraq the winner" in the face-off. As evidence, *Xinhua* cited Iraq's "correct assessment" of regional and international impatience with the prolonged sanctions and widespread reluctance to go along with U.S. military pressure against Iraq.[29]

Xinhua and a PRC-controlled Hong Kong paper on November 23 hailed Russia as "the biggest winner of all," judging that Moscow's mediation in the crisis had enhanced its stature in the region and "made it possible for Russia to show its influence as a superpower again." Other comments noted that Russia and China had added balance to a recent critical UN report on Iraq with references to Iraqi "sovereignty, territorial integrity, and security concerns."[30]

The official Chinese press commentary had ended three weeks of Chinese public circumspection and ostensible neutrality during the crisis. Partly to avoid serous difficulties with the United States and other concerned powers, Chinese officials were prudent in their exchanges and generally cooperative with UN-backed restrictions on Iraq. Nonetheless, Beijing signaled that its long-term interests in developing a more multipolar power configuration in the region were well served by the outcome of diminishing U.S. power. Media comment also highlighted disagreements with U.S. policy by its Western allies, Russia, U.S. associates in the Middle East region, and regional opponents such as Iraq and Iran.[31]

Meanwhile, the stalled U.S.-led peace talks on the Middle East gave the Chinese an opening to play a greater regional role, though in this case Beijing endeavored to strike a pose at least ostensibly supportive of U.S. goals and reasonably balanced in dealing with Arab-Israeli issues. Beijing announced in early December 1998 that Chinese Foreign Minister Qian would visit Lebanon, Syria, Israel, Egypt, and the Palestinian Authority (PA) from December 18 to 26. This marked the highest-level Chinese visit to either Israel or the PA, and the first simultaneous visit to nearly all the frontline states. Chinese commentary made clear that "all parties" in the Middle East peace process wanted China to play a more active role, mentioning specific requests for greater Chinese involvement from the countries Qian would visit, including the PA. Chinese comment also claimed "common points" with Washington over the peace process, gave a positive assessment of recent U.S. efforts to move the process forward, and sought ministerial and working-level U.S.-China consultations as well as summit-level discussion on Middle East issues.[32]

Concurrent adjustments in Chinese policy toward Iran and Iraq at the end of the year had mixed import for Israel, the United States, and others. Beijing reassured Tehran of its friendship but curbed nuclear and other sales for the sake of reaching a nuclear cooperation agreement with the United States. The policy shift reportedly came partly in response to Israeli concerns over Chinese weapons cooperation with Iran, as well as frustration over Iran's negotiating tactics and disappointment with its slow pace in paying for assistance.[33] With regard to Iraq, Beijing continued to harbor reservations about U.S. policy toward Saddam Hussein's regime and repeatedly joined Russia and others in trying to moderate U.S.-backed pressure on Baghdad over the weapons inspection impasse, urging diplomatic negotiations over the use of force and reiterating calls for the eventual easing of sanctions.[34]

While working to maintain good relations with all parties in the region, Beijing saw an opportunity in the stalled peace process to broaden its influence and bolster its image as a responsible major power. Its long-term goals included expanding trade and securing access to needed oil imports. (China's oil consumption grew at 7 percent a year in the mid-1990s; its import bill was about $5 billion in 1997, with half coming from the Middle East.) Beijing also benefited from sales of materiel to the region and from purchases of military technology from Israel. In the context of poor relations with Washington earlier in the 1990s, China had withdrawn from the Bush administration-backed Middle East peace conference while strengthening ties with regional powers, such as Iran, that would resist U.S. "hegemony" and "power politics." Chinese policy continued to affirm a longer-term interest of encouraging a "multipolar" regional balance less dominated by Washington, but Beijing appeared somewhat more sanguine about general U.S. foreign policy following the U.S.-China summit of October 1997, and it apparently expected U.S. regional policy to bend in the face of allied and regional opposition. *Xinhua* on December 9, 1997, highlighted U.S. calls for dialogue with Iran as a shift made because the United States was feeling "left out in the cold," while its closest Arab allies attended the Organization of the Islamic Conference summit in Tehran.

During his visit to the frontline states, Vice Premier and Foreign Minister Qian Qichen boosted China's pro-Arab profile on the peace process and took the opportunity to register Beijing's growing impatience with international sanctions against Libya and Iraq. Reflecting increased Chinese ties with Israel since the establishment of diplomatic relations in 1992, Qian was moderate in his talks with Israeli leaders. He said China understood their security concerns and strongly opposed terrorism. At other stops, however, Qian blamed Israeli Prime Minister Netanyahu's government for the impasse, charging that it had failed to live up to the previous government's commitments to the land-for-peace principle.[35] Concurrent Chinese media comment was tougher on Israel and criticized U.S. policy—a topic Qian avoided. *Xinhua* on December 18 attacked the "Likud clique's" stubborn stance, backed by the "unprincipled protection" of U.S. policy.

Qian, who returned to Beijing on January 2, 1998, was typically circumspect in addressing China's role in the Middle East peace process, an issue of secondary importance in Chinese foreign policy. He said China would introduce no major policy initiatives and would not serve as a formal mediator, but it would use its permanent seat on the UN Security Council and other means to facilitate the process. In Cairo, Qian voiced heightened Chinese impatience with the protracted international sanctions against Libya and Iraq, and he noted that China was prepared to buy Iraqi oil once sanctions were lifted.[36]

In early 1998, the Beijing press and PRC-owned Hong Kong papers focused on increasing U.S. frustration as the Arab states and big powers, particularly European powers and Russia, continued to distance themselves from the United States. Typically, in January, the *People's Daily* depicted the United States as "arrogant" in threatening force against Iraq despite Arab opposition and observed that multipolarization was "violently pounding" U.S. unipolarization; it also noted a U.S. "sense of urgency" in moving the Middle East peace talks forward and a sense that "time was running out" to broker an agreement in a region always viewed as an important link in the U.S.'s "global strategy."[37]

In February, Chinese media observed that Arab states were in "vociferous opposition" to U.S. pressure on Iraq, its "do-nothing attitude" in the Middle East peace talks, and its forceful efforts to protect U.S. economic interests. They described the Middle East failure of the United States in attempting to monopolize the Arab-Israeli peace talks, losing Arab confidence, and generally running counter to global multipolar trends. And they linked U.S. efforts to dominate the Persian Gulf with NATO expansion into Central Asia and an overall strategy to control "two major oil depots" and ensure U.S. global hegemony.[38]

In March 1998, Chinese media criticized the United States for imposing its will on the United Nations Special Commission deliberations on Iraq, playing the role of world policeman, and damaging the Middle East peace process and U.S.-Arab relations. They linked the Iraq crisis to developed-developing country competition and hailed Europe's increasing distance from the United States on regional issues. They replayed remarks by Middle East specialists from PRC think tanks who credited rising powers other than the United States with resolving the Gulf crisis, highlighted Russian, European, and Arab challenges to U.S. dominance, and linked the "long-frustrated Middle East policy" of the United States with the super-power's declining influence.[39]

Mirroring what Chinese officials saw as the "two-handed" U.S. policy of engagement and containment toward China, the Chinese government came up with a two-pronged policy of its own with regard to U.S. interests in the Middle East. Thus, China continued to employ strategic partnerships, such as those forged with France and Russia, and historical affinity with the region's developing countries to weaken U.S. dominance; at the same time, it continued to promote cooperation and avoided direct confrontation in the ongoing dialogue with the United States on key regional issues. Beijing probably calculated that discreetly keeping the United States off balance in the Middle East and other global hot spots diverted U.S. energies from containing China's expanding influence internationally. Another calculation driving China's newly assertive policy toward the Middle East was the need—as the UN Perm-Five's only developing country—for China to demonstrate increased responsibility and activism in addressing global problems on behalf of its developing country counterparts. As China continued to mold its multipolar foreign policy, it presumably anticipated occasional friction in big power relationships—in the Middle East and elsewhere—as rivals, not enemies, competed to advance national interests. With the United States in particular, China envisioned relations character-ized by alternating competition and cooperation.[40]

The Chinese government welcomed Israeli Prime Minister Netanyahu for a visit on May 25-28, 1998.[41] The Chinese side told the Israeli leader of their great concern about the stalemate in the peace process; they blamed Israel's failure to commit to signed agreements with Arab parties concerned; and they voiced Chinese support for the Palestinian people in particular and the Arab people in general. China supported the land-for-peace principle as the basis of a just, comprehensive settlement. At the same time, Chinese officials acknowledged Israel's security concerns. They insisted that China was not playing the role of a "middleman" in the peace process, but was trying to work together with the United States and others in the interna-tional community to bring about a peaceful solution. Press reports also indicated that the two sides discussed ways to boost the $300 million annual bilateral trade relationship as well as ways to increase a reported several hundred million dollars in annual secret military trade. According to Israeli Radio, Premier Zhu Rongji told Netanyahu that China would not sell nuclear and missile technology to Iran.[42]

After the second U.S.-China summit in mid-1998, Beijing appeared to further moderate its anti-U.S. stance in the Middle East. Seeing Chinese interests as best served by close ties with a powerful United States in matters sensitive to China, like the Asian economic crisis and the nuclear crisis in South Asia, Beijing at least for a time decided to play down past emphasis on multipolarity and friction with the United States. It tended to try to advance Chinese power and influence by working closely with and supporting U.S. power and influence. In the Middle East, this led China to further cut back missile development cooperation with Iran, to treat U.S.-Iraqi disputes in an evenhanded way in the Chinese media, and to portray the United States and Iran in more or less positive ways as they groped toward a means to ease bilateral tensions and to open the door to improved relations. The moderate Chinese approach was evident during Chinese leaders' meetings with Yasir Arafat during his summit meeting in Beijing during July 1998.[43]

In sum, China in the 1990s made significant gains in pursuing multifaceted political, economic, and strategic interests in the Middle East. In particular, it boosted Beijing's role as an interested party in the Middle East peace process and the international confrontation with Iraq. Chinese policy aimed at keeping on good terms with all sides in the often contentious politics of the region, thereby serving the Chinese economic interests of ensuring diverse supplies of oil and access to regional markets. Beijing sometimes chafed under U.S. strategic dominance in the Persian Gulf and elsewhere in the region, but it generally did not allow its anti-U.S. rhetoric to spoil its more important effort to stabilize U.S.-China relations.

Africa

In many respects, relations with most African countries are not of major importance to China's leadership.[44] African states are of little help in China's primary efforts focused on economic modernization. Chinese-African trade and investment remains small. Most African countries require extensive foreign assistance, which Beijing is loath to give, especially in light of its own status as a major recipient of international financial institution loans and other support. China is interested in tapping Africa's oil supplies for the growing Chinese industrial economy.

Africa remains an important arena of diplomatic competition with Taiwan—a top Chinese foreign policy priority. Beijing also nurtures good relations with African governments to win their support in the United Nations and in other international fora where China is sometimes at odds with other world powers, notably the United States. Unlike the cold war period, when China viewed Africa as an important region in the global East-West and Sino-Soviet competition for influence, nowadays Beijing only occasionally sees manifestations of competition in Africa that warrant

Chinese attention. In general, Beijing comment tends to welcome trends in the region that work against the perceived objectives of the United States, though this approach has moderated as Chinese relations have improved with the United States during the summit meetings of 1997 and 1998.

The history of Chinese relations with Africa is full of often visionary and sometimes quixotic efforts to throw off outside influence and foster rapid development and social progress. Chinese officials to this day continue a long-standing practice of comparing Africa's suffering under the European colonialists with China's hundred years of humiliation. Chinese aid efforts have waxed and waned according to the urgency of changing Chinese priorities. At times during the cold war, Beijing was an important supplier of basic military equipment and training to a number of liberation groups and newly emerged governments. Chinese leaders proclaimed Africa ripe for revolution in the 1960s and provided a range of assistance to groups ranging from providing help to dissident factions opposed to the UN-backed regime in Congo-Leopoldville to providing backing for Mobutu's Zaire to check Soviet-backed incursions from Angola in the 1970s. The Chinese were key backers of liberation fighters against the Portuguese in Angola and Mozambique; they supported Robert Mugabe in his struggle against white-ruled Rhodesia; and they backed other radical groups in South Africa and elsewhere.[45]

Chinese efforts to rally third-world support to remove Taiwan from the UN in 1971 relied heavily on support from African countries. Competition for diplomatic recognition continued, and intensified when Beijing gave higher priority to checking Taiwan's flexible diplomacy, especially following Taiwan President Lee Teng-hui's visit to the United States in 1995.

Large-scale demonstration projects also characterized Chinese policy in Africa. The Tan-Zam Railway, linking Zambia's copper fields and the Tanzanian coast, was undertaken by Chinese engineers even though it was previously judged ill-advised by Western and other international experts. Despite great obstacles, Chinese government workers completed the project after many years of effort, the loss of many lives, and great expense.

Post-Mao Chinese leaders were much less interested in spending money overseas, especially when their political standing at home rested heavily on their ability to improve economic conditions for the Chinese people. Thus, by the late 1970s, the overriding focus on domestic modernization led to a reduction in Chinese enthusiasm for funding expansive African assistance programs. Chinese officials also recognized that past efforts to roll back superpower influence in the region had not worked well. Aid levels dropped markedly in the late 1970s and remained around $100 million annually. Chinese assistance increasingly took the form of training, export credits for Chinese goods, or joint financing plans. As the Chinese export economy grew, so did Chinese trade, from about $300 million in 1976 to $2.2

billion in 1988. However, this still was only a small fraction of overall Chinese trade.

Post-Mao China was willing and anxious to receive foreign aid from the World Bank, the IMF, and other international bodies and donor countries. This put China in direct competition with African states seeking aid. The newly open Chinese economy was also seen by some as taking foreign investment that might have gone to African ventures. African grumbling over these trends grew. Even some long-time African friends sensed increasing ambiguity in their ties with China. With mixed results, Chinese officials used diplomacy, propaganda, and exchanges to preserve Beijing's self-described position as an intimate supporter of struggling African states. While acknowledging China's political support, African governments recognized that they had to follow China's example in cultivating ties with the developed economies, including the United States, Europe, and Japan, if they expected to markedly boost their modernization efforts. Meanwhile, long-standing Chinese efforts to offer university and other training for African students were clouded by several incidents showing apparent Chinese social bias against Africans in the late 1980s.

Chinese incentives to improve relations with African countries increased after the Tiananmen incident of 1989.[46] Officials anxiously sought African and other third-world support to offset Beijing's isolation and to reduce international pressure against China. The period also saw Taiwan launch its pragmatic or flexible diplomacy. Taipei used offers of aid or other means to woo aid-dependent African countries and to have them establish relations with Taiwan even though they had diplomatic relations with Beijing. Whenever this occurred, mainland China broke ties with the African state concerned, providing a net diplomatic gain for Taipei.

Chinese leaders shortly after the Tiananmen incident directed PRC diplomats to focus on "resuming and developing relations with old friends," including African states, that remained supportive of Beijing. Foreign Minister Qian Qichen visited eleven African countries one month after Tiananmen.[47] African states, which had been marginalized when major Western and Asian investors turned their attention to Russia and the newly independent states after the demise of the USSR in the early 1990s, generally welcomed China's renewed emphasis on strengthening ties.

High-level Sino-African exchanges in the post-Tiananmen era resumed in full force in July 1992 when President Yang Shangkun, Foreign Minister Qian Qichen, and a PRC trade delegation visited Morocco, Tunisia, and the Ivory Coast. The Chinese press played up the visit as a major event in Sino-African relations, noted China's sensitivity to the widening political and economic gap between the developed countries and Africa, and hailed Yang's reaffirmation of cooperation with the third world as a basic tenet of

China's foreign policy. An active travel schedule continued in the mid-to-late 1990s:[48]

- Vice-Premier Zhu Rongji during a seven-country trip in July-August 1995 laid out a four-point formula for joint ventures and limited direct assistance for public projects;
- President Jiang Zemin during a six-country swing in May 1996 declared China and Africa to be "all-weather friends," signed twenty-three economic and technical agreements, and promised that China would always stand firmly alongside Africa;
- Foreign Minister Qian Qichen in January 1997 visited six countries, noted overall improvements in PRC-Africa relations, and hammered Taiwan for allegedly attempting to buy diplomatic relations with African states;
- Premier Li Peng during a seven-country visit in spring 1997 praised African states for supporting China on the human rights and Taiwan issues, and stressed that, unlike Western countries, China provided assistance to Africa without political conditions;
- Foreign Minister Qian Qichen in December 1997 visited South Africa to sign a joint communiqué normalizing relations and officially switching South African diplomatic recognition from Taipei to Beijing;
- Vice President Hu Jintao visited four African countries in January-February 1999.

The Chinese military was also active in Africa, in exchanges, training, and a variety of small arms sales. The deputy chief of the PLA's General Staff, Xiong Guangkai, offered a perceptive view of Chinese assessments of African conditions during a speech at the Zimbabwe Defense Staff College in 1997.[49] He realistically assessed Africa's many problems stemming from "internal wars" and "sustained economic difficulties," "the old irrational institutional economic order" that provided low profits for producers of most primary products and raw materials, and interference in African affairs by "hegemonism and power politics."

Xiong strongly reaffirmed ties between China, "the largest developing country in the world," and Africa, "the largest developing continent in the world." China supported African efforts to determine their own political and economic systems without outside interference. It pledged to continue "model" Sino-African ties for "sincere, equal, friendly and cooperative relations." Citing Chinese support for the reelection of African Boutros Ghali as UN secretary-general—a stance enjoying wide support in Africa but opposed by the United States—Xiong strove to portray broad common ground in Sino-African political relations. He capped his talk with reference to Jiang Zemin's May 1996 visit to Africa, during which Jiang set forth five points that were to continue to govern Sino-African relations into the twenty-first century. These were to be sincere and friendly and be each other's reliable all-weather friends; to stand on an equal footing, respect each other's sovereignty, and not interfere into each other's internal affairs; to be equal and mutually beneficial and seek for common development; to strengthen consultation and cooperate closely in international affairs; and to create a better world with an eye toward the future.

By 1998, against the backdrop of the long-standing Chinese emphasis on strengthened ties with developing countries in Africa and elsewhere, PRC leaders typically characterized PRC-third world solidarity as essential for promoting China's multipolar worldview, defending PRC positions in international fora such as the UN, and standing firm against U.S. global dominance. Aspiring to more equal status with the world's great powers, China also viewed positive relations with African states and other developing countries as important for pressing forward on their national priorities of securing vital energy and mineral resources, expanding exports, including conventional arms, and pressing for eventual Taiwan-mainland reunification.

A heightened PRC focus on these priorities was on display across Africa as China pursued oil deals (Nigeria, the Sudan, Angola), and mineral extractions rights (Congo-Kinshasa, Zambia),[50] exports of textiles, machinery, electronic equipment, and other manufactured goods to multiple countries and notably a multi-million trade/investment package deal with South Africa, arms sales to several African states, and a one-China policy. Taiwan's diplomatic ties in Africa fell to eight mostly small countries following Beijing's success in winning over South Africa and establishing formal diplomatic relations on January 1, 1998. In early 1999, Taiwan had official diplomatic relations with the following countries in Africa: Burkina Faso, Chad, the Gambia, Liberia, Malawi, Sao Tome and Principe, Senegal, and Swaziland.

Other nodes of recognition for Taiwan were in Latin America where it had official relations with Belize, Costa Rica, Dominica, the Dominican Republic, El Salvador, Granada, Guatemala, Haiti, Honduras, Nicaragua, Panama, Paraguay, St. Christopher and Nevis, and St. Vincent and the Grenadines; and Oceania, where it had official relations with the Marshall Islands, the Solomon Islands, Tuvalu, and Naura. It also had official relations with the Vatican and Macedonia. Taiwan continued to fight back, however. In June 1998, Taiwan's foreign minister appeared at the thirty-fourth annual conference of the Organization of African Unity (OAU) in Burkina Faso, effectively upstaging the Chinese foreign minister, who was making his first African tour to nearby West African countries.[51]

Continued Chinese success in Africa hinged on several factors, not the least of which was Beijing's drive to compete with the other large powers, especially the United States. There were signs in 1997 and 1998 that Beijing was losing interest in this effort. For one thing, Beijing found it difficult to compete with U.S. power. Unlike the proxy battles of the 1960s and 1970s, China increasingly considered that its competition in Africa with the big powers during the 1990s and beyond would be primarily economic in nature. (It was only about 2 percent of African's total trade volume, but Sino-African trade continued to rise, nearing $5.7 billion in 1997; it stayed at about the same level in 1998.)[52] To differentiate itself from Western and Japanese suitors competing for African market shares, Beijing continued to play up themes of PRC-African solidarity while criticizing its competitors for their colonial (or hegemonist) track records of plundering less-developed countries, for their offers of assistance with political strings (such as democratization and human rights) attached, and for their decisions to divert investments away from Africa after the cold war.

But as U.S.-China relations improved, Chinese commentary became less interested in carping against U.S. objectives. To be sure, the Chinese media found areas to complain about during President Clinton's landmark African trip in 1998, but their critical rhetoric was more low-keyed than that dealing with Secretary of State Madeleine Albright's visit to seven African countries in late 1997.[53] As time went on and U.S.-China relations improved, Beijing seemed to see China's interests as better served by cooperating with U.S. power in ways that would advance Chinese influence as well, rather than viewing U.S. and Chinese influence in zero-sum terms.

China also faced a major challenge in trying to continue its relationship as Africa's "all-weather friend." As most African countries developed slowly or not at all and post-Mao China averaged over 9 percent annual growth for twenty years, the gap among the developing countries became increasingly hard to bridge. Thus, China found it more difficult to appeal for African sympathy and support on the basis of their common basis as developing countries. And yet, China judged itself to be in no position to try to win African states' favor with generous foreign assistance. African leaders too were aware of the ambivalence of China's role, though they were often appreciative of whatever support they could get from whatever quarter.

In sum, China continued to devote considerable political attention to African countries in order to compete with Taiwan, show solidarity with members of the third-world bloc in the United Nations and other world organizations, facilitate some advantageous trade in oil and other commodities, and portray China's international image as that of a power of growing international stature and influence. It generally eschewed commitments that would involve substantial Chinese material resources or would antagonize disputants in the continent's many conflicts. Given the low level of U.S. or other outside powers' involvement in African affairs, Beijing devoted a low level of media and political attention to criticizing U.S. and other powers' policies that were incompatible with Chinese goals on the continent.

Latin America

China has followed a low-keyed and pragmatic effort in recent years to build better relations with Latin American countries. Beijing is well aware of China's limited standing in a region that has long been dominated by U.S. power and influence while developing improved economic and political relations with European powers, Japan, South Korea, and others. Radical movements in the region in the past looked to Moscow rather than Beijing for support and guidance. China maintains an active diplomatic presence, engages in a wide range of government-sponsored political, economic, and military contracts, and has seen its economic relations grow to a point where trade with the region, while only a small fraction of Chinese trade overall, surpasses Chinese trade with Africa.[54]

Chinese motives in Latin America are similar to its motives in Africa. Beijing seeks to nurture common bonds with Latin American countries, striving to win their support for China's positions in the United Nations and other international organizations. Latin America, especially Central America and the Caribbean, represents the main battlefront in Beijing's international competition with Taiwan. Chinese officials have gone to extraordinary lengths, even using China's veto power in the UN Security Council,[55] in order to curb the still strong support for Taiwan on the part of several regional states. Chinese commentaries have also routinely focused on criticism of U.S. policy in Latin America and have highlighted European and Japanese resistance to the U.S.'s efforts to have its way in the area. The rhetoric has fit into the broader Chinese tendency to see signs of emerging multipolarity in the world when the U.S. superpower meets resistance from other powers determined to protect their interests in an economically and politically competitive world environment. As a result of the marked improvement in U.S.-Chinese relations in 1997-1998, Chinese officials and commentary devoted less attention to these themes, suggesting that China was inclined, at least for the time being, to pursue its interests by not standing against the United States on a variety of sensitive world issues.

China historically has paid less attention to Latin America than to any other third-world region. Geographic distance and preoccupation with issues closer to home put Latin American issues low on China's list of priorities. In the time of East-West and Sino-Soviet competition for global influence during the cold war, Beijing at times tried to make headway among radical

Latin American groups. In general, there was little to show for this effort as U.S. power and influence remained very strong among established governments while leftists in Cuba, Chile, Nicaragua, and elsewhere tended to look to the Soviet bloc for tangible assistance, rather than to seek the political advice and rhetorical support offered by Maoist China.[56]

Post-Mao leaders pursued pragmatic approaches in order to build conventional political, economic, and military relations with established Latin American governments. As in other parts of the third world, Chinese leaders eschewed the tendency of Maoist leaders to take sides on third-world issues, especially those having symbolic value in the East-West and Sino-Soviet competition for global influence. Instead, they sought to align China with whatever consensus was emerging among Latin American states over sensitive issues. Thus, Beijing supported the Contadora peace process for Central America and took the Latin American side on North-South economic issues. China officials also repeatedly emphasized Chinese-Latin American common ground in seeking greater South-South economic cooperation.[57]

Although Beijing had some contact with leftist anti-Soviet parties in Latin America during the radical phases of the Chinese Cultural Revolution, post-Mao leaders minimized or cut those ties. Beijing ignored the Maoist-oriented Sendero Luminiso in Peru, and its contacts with the Farabundo Marti Movement for National Liberation (FMLN) guerrilla front in El Salvador were minimal. By contrast, China markedly increased its exchanges with ruling parties and administrations in Latin America, endeavoring to improve state-to-state relations wherever possible.[58]

The economic imperative behind recent Chinese policy was illustrated in year-end commentaries in December 1997.[59] It emphasized the recent economic dynamism of Latin American economies. It said the region's overall growth had reached a seventeen-year high of 5 percent. Stressing Latin America's new openness to trade, investment, and other economic interchange with various world economic centers, the commentary emphasized a strong European challenge to the traditionally dominant U.S. role. It noted that the European Union had overtaken the United States in annual trade with Latin America, though the United States remained Latin America's largest outside investor and foreign market. As far as Latin American trade with Asia was concerned, the Chinese authors depicted burgeoning growth, especially in trade with Mexico, Brazil, and Venezuela. They noted that China's trade with the Latin American region had more than doubled since 1990, growing from $3 billion in that year to $8 billion in 1997 and $8 billion in 1998.[60]

China's economic aid to the region is minimal. In March 1998, Beijing provided $19 million in economic assistance to Cuba. Anxious to receive aid from any quarter, the Cuban media played up the grant, though they also gave attention to the much larger $300 million annual trade between China and Cuba in 1987.[61]

Political relations have seen a steady stream of generally second-level Chinese leaders travel to the region recently, and warm Chinese welcomes for Latin American dignitaries.[62] Comment during these exchanges underscores Beijing's determination to be seen as a close friend of Latin American countries, sharing common feelings and experiences in the struggle for economic development and nation-building. In May 1988, the number two leader of China's National People's Congress paid an extensive visit to Brazil, Chile, and Peru.[63] Visiting many places in each country, he promoted greater mutual understanding and cooperation, especially between China's parliament and the parliaments of Latin American states. A senior leader of China's united-front political organ, the Chinese People's Political Consultative Conference, paid a visit to Brazil to foster greater Sino-Brazilian understanding and cooperation.

Sino-Latin American relations feature a wide range of military leadership exchanges. In 1998, senior Chinese military contacts with Latin America included the visit of the chief of the Chinese Air Force to Argentina, Brazil, and Chile, and the visit of a senior general and the party's Central Military Commission to Cuba and Peru. The Chinese defense minister and other senior military leaders hosted Latin American visitors. Defense Minister Chi Haotian in March 1997 told the chairman of Venezuela's Joint Chiefs of Staff that China and Venezuela had strong similarities and common interests that allowed for the development of close and smooth bilateral relations. Minister Chi led a delegation to Mexico and Cuba in early 1999.[64] There are few major Latin American recipients of Chinese military sales or aid, though Chinese defense officials use small-scale training opportunities and military equipment transfers to establish and build up good relations with their Latin American counterparts.[65]

Beijing seeks to avoid controversy in Latin America with two major exceptions—Taiwan and U.S. policy. Chinese diplomacy and commentary have been unrelenting in their push against Taiwan's influence in the region. Reports of secret aid offers, advantageous trade deals, and other means to gain influence are common. Both Beijing and Taipei are engaged in a kind of nonviolent guerrilla war for recognition.[66] In the process, Beijing has not been reluctant to use coercive means to get what it wants. In 1997, for example, the Chinese delegation vetoed a UN resolution to support the peacekeeping effort in Haiti on account of Haiti's pro-Taiwan foreign policy. It later relented, once Haiti took steps to adjust its policy toward Taiwan and the mainland.

Criticizing U.S. dominance in Latin America has been a staple of Chinese propaganda for decades. Recent comment has highlighted the U.S. struggle to preserve its economic advantage in the face of a vigorous challenge by the European Union. And it has focused on European, Canadian, and other opposition to the sanctions imposed by the U.S. Helms-Burton Act against foreign companies in dealing with Cuban companies involving property appropriated from the United States forty years ago. A favorite target is U.S. policy toward Cuba. When President Clinton decided on March 20, 1998, to ease some restrictions on U.S. interaction with Cuba, Chinese commentary gave scant praise.[67] Rather it portrayed the move as reflecting the failure of the U.S. policy of forcing change in Cuba through an economic and diplomatic blockade. And when Secretary of State Madeleine Albright traveled to the Caribbean in April 1998, Chinese commentary highlighted the visit's alleged lack of success; the visit failed on account of reportedly deep resentment in the Caribbean countries of the overbearing U.S. attitude that provides small amounts of aid with many political, economic, and other conditions attached.[68]

The Chinese media's extensive coverage of President Clinton's visit to the summit of the Americas in Santiago in mid-April 1998 suggested that Beijing might be losing interest in criticizing U.S. power and influence in Latin America.[69] There was little of the often tendentious Chinese commentary seen in the past about alleged U.S. desires to dominate the region. Generally straightforward coverage reported an effort by all sides to reach mutually advantageous economic arrangements at the summit. It noted differences of approach between the United States and some regional actors, and noted the disappointment in the region over the U.S. failure to enact fast-track legislative authority to expedite U.S. approval of a proposed free trade area of the Americas. But it also highlighted President Clinton's commitment to obtain congressional support for the authority and to approve the free trade area agreement when it is ready. It concluded with the observation that the summit was "not a bad start" to the process of Western Hemisphere economic integration.

In sum, Latin America, like sub-Saharan Africa, remains a region receiving a relatively low priority from the Chinese leadership. Nonetheless, Chinese activities there reflect multifaceted political and economic interests focused on competition with Taiwan and a search for advantageous trade opportunities. Beijing also nurtures relations with Latin American countries to ensure their support in the UN and other world bodies.

Notes

1. Much of this activity had to do with the Asia-European (ASEM) summit and the China-EU summit held in London in April 1998. The head of the Chinese delegation, the newly selected premier, Zhu Rongji, also made official visits to England and France. See especially *"People's Daily* Hails Zhu Rongji's Europe Tour,"

Xinhua, April 8, 1998, carried by Foreign Broadcast Information Service (FBIS) (internet version).

2. For background, see Commission of the European Communities, "Towards a New Asia Strategy," July 13, 1994; Commission of the European Communities, "A Long-Term Policy for China-Europe Relations," July 5, 1995; Commission of the European Communities, Communication of the Commission to the Council and Parliament, "Regarding the Asia-Europe Meeting (ASEM) to Be Held in Bangkok on 1-2 March 1996;" Commission of the European Communities, "Building Comprehensive Partnership with China," June 29, 1998. See also "Text of China-EU Summit Statement," *Xinhua*, April 2, 1998, carried by FBIS (internet version).

3. See notably the section on Europe in the chronology of Chinese events published regularly in the *China Quarterly*. Also Donald Klein, "Japan and Europe in Chinese Foreign Relations," in Samuel Kim, ed., *China and the World*, Boulder, Colo.: Westview Press, 1998, pp. 133-137.

4. "China Posts First EU Trade Surplus in Five Years," *Reuters*, February 4, 1998 (internet version). See also Klein, "Japan and Europe"; and *Europe and China: An Emerging Relationship*, Washington, D.C.: Library of Congress, Congressional Research Service (CRS) Report 96-566F, June 21, 1996, p. 2.

5. "PRC-EU Trade Growth in 1999," *Xinhua*, January 22, 1999, (internet version).

6. *New York Times*, June 12, 1996. Lord's remarks came the day after China's premier told the *Financial Times* that "If the Europeans adopt more cooperation with China in all areas, not just in economic areas but also in political and other areas . . . I believe the Europeans can get more orders from China," *Financial Times*, June 11, 1996.

7. The size and growth of China's economy, especially in the area of trade and outside investment, is seen as particularly important in influencing the future of the WTO. Regarding security in Korea, some EU members contributed to the Korean Economic Development Organization (KEDO), which was founded as part of the U.S.-North Korean compromise on nuclear issues reached in 1994.

8. For background on Chinese policy toward Europe, see, among others, Michael Yahuda, "China and Europe: The Significance of a Secondary Relationship," in *Chinese Foreign Policy: Theory and Practice*, ed. Thomas Robinson and David Shambaugh, Oxford: Oxford University Press, 1994. See also Feng Zhongping, "EU's China Policy Analyzed," *Contemporary International Relations* (Beijing) 8, 4 (April 1998): 1-6.

9. This assessment benefited from the in-depth discussion at the Castelgandolfo Colloquium on Atlantic Affairs, Rome, Italy, June 7-8, 1996, and the international Workshop on Europe and China, Rome, Italy, June 9, 1996. See especially *Globalization in the Economy, Regionalization in Security*, Ce SPI memoranda 8, Rome: Centro Studide Politica Internazionale, 1997, pp. 96-136.

10. See sources in note 1. See also "Premier Li Peng on China's Policy toward EU," *Xinhua*, February 16, 1998, carried by FBIS (internet version); "Li Lanqing to Visit Europe," *Xinhua*, January 23, 1998, carried by FBIS (internet version); "Tang Jiaxuan's London News Conference," *Ta Kung Pao*, April 5, 1998, carried by FBIS

(internet version).

11. Commission of the European Communities, "The Establishment of Full Partnership with China," March 25, 1998.

12. "Li Lanqing to Visit Europe," *Xinhua*, January 23, 1998, carried by FBIS (internet version).

13. "Chinese Premier Li Peng Begins Five Day Visit," *Agence France Press (AFP)*, February 13, 1998, carried by FBIS (internet version).

14. Chinese officials continued this approach throughout 1998.

15. For details on this flurry of Chinese-European diplomatic activity, see sources noted in notes 1 and 9, plus "Qian Qichen, French Foreign Minister Hold Talks," *Xinhua*, January 23, 1998, carried by FBIS (internet version); Shen Yihuai, "Cross-Century European-Chinese Relations," Beijing *Liaowang*, no. 14, April 6, 1998, pp. 40-41; "Li Peng to Visit Netherlands," Rotterdam, *Algemeen Dagblad*, January 16, 1998, carried by FBIS (internet version); "ASEM Conference Seen as Successful," *China Daily*, April 6, 1998.

16. Shen, "Cross-Century."

17. "Text of China-EU Joint Statement," *Xinhua*, April 2, 1998, carried by FBIS (internet version).

18. Ibid.

19. See sources in note 8.

20. Lillian Harris, *China Considers the Middle East*, London: Tauris, 1993; Lillian Harris, "Myth and Reality in China's Relations with the Middle East," in *Chinese Foreign Policy*, ed. Robinson and Shambaugh, pp. 322-347.

21. For highlights of Chinese relations with the Middle East, see the section on the Middle East in the chronology of Chinese events published regularly in the *China Quarterly*.

22. Han Xiaoxing, "China-Middle East Links," *China Business Review*, March-April 1994, pp. 44-46.

23. Alexander Lennon, "Trading Guns, Not Butter," *China Business Review*, March-April 1994, pp. 47-49; Guang Pan, "China's Success in the Middle East," *Middle East Quarterly*, December 1997, pp. 35-40.

24. Reviewed in Guang Pan, "China's Success"; Lillian Harris, *China Considers.*

25. See "Israel's Netanyahu Kicks off Talks in China," *Reuters*, May 25, 1998 (internet version).

26. See, among others, Huai Chengbo, "Why Do Arab Nations Widen the Gap with the United States?" *Liaowang*, no. 11, March 16, 1998, p. 42.

27. "U.S. Lists Accords with China at Summit," *Reuters*, June 27, 1998 (internet version).

28. "Qian Qichen Speaks to Chinese Reporters, Concludes Trip," *Xinhua*, December 26, 1997, carried by FBIS (internet version).

29. *Xinhua*, November 20, 1997, carried by FBIS (internet version).

30. *Xinhua*, November 23, 1997; *Ta Kung Pao*, November 23, 1997, carried by FBIS (internet version).

31. Mi Ligong, "Middle East Peace, Deadlocked," *Xinhua*, January 9, 1998, carried by FBIS (internet version); Zhou Xisheng, "Military Confrontation Not Advisable," *Xinhua*, January 20, 1998, carried by FBIS (internet version); Fu Quangheng, "Use of Force Has Little Support," *Xinhua*, February 4, 1998, carried by FBIS (internet version); "Russia-China Reject Use of Force against Iraq," *Reuters* (internet version) February 17, 1998; Rong Song, "Iran's New Gulf Diplomatic Offensive," *Xinhua*, November 7, 1997, carried by FBIS (internet version); "Tomur Dawamat, Tang Jiaxuan Meet Libyan Deputy Minister," *Xinhua*, May 12, 1998, carried by FBIS (internet version).

32. Mi, "Middle East Peace"; Tang Jian, Wang Yadong and Hou Jia, "Qian Qichen's Tour of the Middle East Is a Complete Success," *Xinhua*, December 26, 1998, carried by FBIS (internet version).

33. "Jiang Urged Not to Help Iran," *South Morning China Post*, September 3, 1998.

34. "Russia-China Reject Use of Force against Iraq," *Reuters* (internet version) February 17, 1998.

35. *Xinhua*, December 9, 1997, carried by FBIS (internet version).

36. Tang et. al., "Qian Qichen's Tour," *Xinhua*, December 18, 1997, carried by FBIS (internet version).

37. Ibid.

38. *People's Daily*, January 9, 1998; January 27, 1998.

39. *Xinhua*, February 6, 1998; *Liaowang*, February 9, 1998; *Ta Kung Pao*, February 23, 1998.

40. *Wen Wei Po*, March 4, 1998; *People's Daily*, March 6, 1998; *China Daily*, March 10, 1998.

41. The visit was covered in full by *China Daily*, among others.

42. B. Rena Miller, "Israeli Source on Netanyahu Meetings," *AFP*, May 26, 1998, (internet version).

43. The visit was covered fully by *China Daily*.

44. For background, see Gerald Segal, "China and Africa," *Annals of the American Academy of Political and Social Science*, 519 (January 1992): 115-126; Philip Snow, "China and Africa: Consensus and Camouflage," in *Chinese Foreign Policy*, ed. Robinson and Shambaugh, pp. 283-321; Deborah Brautigan, *Chinese Aid and African Development*, New York: St. Martins, 1998.

45. See, among others, Philip Snow, *The Star Raft: China's Encounter with Africa*, Ithaca, N.Y.: Cornell University Press, 1988; Alaba Ogunsanwo, *China's Policy in Africa: 1958-1971*, New York: Cambridge University Press, 1979.

46. See review of these developments in Snow, "China and Africa."

47. Qian's travels were covered by *China Daily*; also see *Xinhua* coverage carried by FBIS.

48. For highlights of Chinese leaders' travel to Africa and interaction with African leaders, see the chronology of Chinese events published regularly in the *China Quarterly*.

49. Xiong Guangkai, "China's Defense Policy and Sino-African Relations—Speech at Zimbabwean Defense Staff College on June 2, 1997," Beijing, *International Strategic Studies*, no. 3, July 1997, pp. 1-5.

50. "Sudanese Minister on Growing Trends with China," *Xinhua*, February 24, 1998, carried by FBIS (internet version); "Jiang Zemin-Democratic Congo President Hold Talks," *Xinhua*, December 18, 1997, carried by FBIS (internet version); "Official Comments on Sino-African Trade Cooperation," *Xinhua*, January 14, 1998, carried by FBIS (internet version); "China to Set up Investment Promotion Center in Zambia," *Xinhua*, April 3, 1998, carried by FBIS (internet version).

51. *Conventional Arms Transfers to Developing Countries, 1990-1997*, Washington, D.C.: Library of Congress, CRS Report 98-647F, July 31, 1998.

52. "Official Comments on Sino-African Trade Cooperation," *Xinhua*, January 14, 1998; "News Analysis on Sino-African Ties," *Xinhua*, January 23, 1999, carried by FBIS (internet version).

53. Liu Yegang, "Roundup" on Criticism of New U.S. Africa Policy, *Xinhua*, March 30, 1998, carried by FBIS (internet version); Yang Rusheng, "Analysis of 'New Partnership,'" *People's Daily*, December 23, 1997, p. 6.

54. For background, see Cecil Johnson, *Communist China and Latin America*, New York: Columbia University Press, 1970; Samuel Kim, *The Third World in Chinese World Policy*, Princeton: Princeton University Press, 1989; Chien-hsun Wang, "Peking's Latin American Policy in the 1980s," *Issues and Studies* 27, 5 (May 1991): 103-118.

55. China used its veto power to hold up UN peacekeeping operations in Haiti until Haiti adjusted its pro-Taiwan policy. Reviewed in *Taiwan: Recent Developments and U.S. Policy Choices*, Washington, D.C.: Library of Congress, CRS Issue Brief 98034.

56. Peter Van Ness, *Revolution and Chinese Foreign Policy*, Berkeley: University of California Press, 1971.

57. Wang, "Peking's Latin America Policy."

58. Ibid.; see also Kim, *The Third World.*

59. "Xinhua Year-Ender on Latin American Embassy," *Xinhua*, December 19, 1997, carried by FBIS (internet version); Lin Minzhong, "Latin American Nations Vigorously Develop All-Directional Economic Cooperation and Trade," *Xinhua*, December 16, 1997, carried by FBIS (internet version).

60. "China to Boost Trade with Latin America," *Xinhua*, January 10, 1999 (internet version).

61. "Officials Sign Agreements Worth over $19 Million," Havana *Prensa Latina*, March 27, 1998, carried by FBIS (internet version).

62. "NPC's Tian Visits Brazil," *Xinhua*, May 8, 1998, carried by FBIS (internet version); "CPC Senior Official Meets Guatemalan Party Leader," *Xinhua*, February 27, 1998, carried by FBIS (internet version).

63. "NPC Delegation to Visit Latin America," *Xinhua*, April 30, 1998; "CPPCC Vice Chairman Leaves for Brazil," *Xinhua*, April 30, 1998, carried by FBIS (internet version).

64. "Chi Haotian Leaves Beijing," *Xinhua*, February 19, 1999 (internet version).

65. "Chinese Defense Minister Meets Venezuelan Visitor," *Xinhua*, March 25, 1998; "Chinese Air Force Commander Visits Brazil," *Xinhua*, March 11, 1998; "PLA Commander Leaves Beijing for Cuba, Mexico," *Xinhua*, April 28, 1998, carried by FBIS (internet version).

66. Reviewed in *Taiwan*, CRS Issue Brief 98034.

67. Li Zhiming, "Dialogue, and Not Confrontation," *People's Daily*, April 30, 1998, p. 6; Yuan Bingzhong, "Why Did the U.S. Ease Sanctions on Cuba?" *Xinhua*, March 21, 1998.

68. Yuan Bingzhong, "Albright's Caribbean Trip," *Xinhua*, April 8, 1998, carried by FBIS (internet version).

69. Zhai Jingsheng, "Roundup: FRAA Needs New Push," *Xinhua*, April 17, 1998; "Clinton Pledges to Push 'Fast Track,'" *Xinhua*, April 18, 1998.

Chapter 10

Leaders, Ideology, and Global Issues and Exchanges

Several trends of importance in China's recent policies and behavior abroad that have a substantial impact on the interests of the United States do not lend themselves to analysis focused on Chinese relations with specific countries and regions. Those trends include the following:

- The role of specific leaders and various domestic groups in Chinese foreign policy-making;
- The continuing importance of ideology in recent Chinese foreign policy;
- Trends in trade, investment, and aid exchanges, and in China's role in international environmental policies and practices;
- Other international exchanges, including nongovernmental, political party, and military exchanges;
- Recent Chinese policies and behavior toward the UN and other international organizations;
- Recent Chinese policies and practices regarding international arms control.

Those trends are treated briefly here.

Leaders and Their Influence in Foreign Policy-Making

Personalities matter in making Chinese foreign policy, though the broad outlines of policy are decided by the top-level leadership and are not subject to abrupt change on account of shifting personnel appointments. Various informal opinion groupings of policy advisors and bureaucratic actors nonetheless contend for the ear of decision makers.[1] In the year leading up to the Fifteenth Party Congress in September 1997 and the Ninth National People's Congress (NPC) in March 1998, there was some uncertainty as to who would be the most influential actors in Chinese foreign policy-making under the new leadership selected at these meetings. The following were among the particular questions included:

- What role retiring Premier Li Peng—who headed the Foreign Affairs Leading Group, China's top-level policy-making and coordinating body—would play;
- What positions and role Foreign Minister Qian Qichen would fill;
- Who would be the next foreign minister; and
- What role State Council Foreign Affairs Office Director Liu Huaqiu would play.

In the Chinese system, the "core" leader—party chief, President, and Central Military Commission Chairman Jiang Zemin—has the prerogative and duty to set the general foreign policy "line." Traditionally, he has also controlled key foreign policy accounts, including relations with the United States, potential adversaries (for example, the Soviet Union), and major regional players (North Korea and Japan). Just below the "core" leader is the Foreign Affairs Leading Group (FALG), which contains top officials from all agencies with major roles in foreign relations. Its purpose is to deliberate and recommend policy and to coordinate the strategic decisions of the top leadership within the bureaucracy. Li Peng headed the FALG for nearly a decade. This gave him significant influence over a broad range of issues, from U.S.-China relations to handling the annual UN Human Rights Commission (UNHRC) exercise.

In 1998, as expected, Li retired from the premiership to become chairman of the NPC; it was not immediately clear whether he would retain or give up his position as head of the FALG. In recent times, the premier has usually chaired the group, but not always. Executive Vice Premier Zhu Rongji replaced Li as premier. But Zhu's promotion was based on his expertise and success as an economic administrator. Moreover, the leadership planned to embark on a new wave of risky economic reforms, taking the next big step in tackling the issue of moribund state-owned enterprises. It seemed unlikely that Zhu would have the time, interest, or confidence of his peers to take over the FALG. In addition, Jiang and Li had worked as a team—privately many Chinese talked of the "Jiang-Li structure" rather than of Jiang as the "core" of the leadership—and displayed few, if any, meaningful differences on foreign policy. It was possible, therefore, that Jiang would retain Li as head of the FALG. But Li's apparent failure to engineer the promotion of his reportedly favored candidate for foreign minister, the State Council's Liu Huaqiu, indicated that his clout was limited.[2]

Another possibility was that Qian Qichen might be elevated to head the FALG. The press in 1997 reported rumors that Qian might be promoted to the top-level Politburo Standing Committee; he was already on the Politburo. Though it would have been unprecedented for a foreign policy specialist to reach this pinnacle of power, Qian was one of China's most popular and capable leaders. He received the highest vote total of all the top elected officials when he was reelected foreign minister at the last NPC, in large part because of his role in rehabilitating China's reputation after Tiananmen.[3]

Qian had served two five-year terms as foreign minister and was strongly expected to step down. Qian, however, had served only five years as vice premier and was expected to get another five-year term. His predecessor was kept on as a foreign policy advisor and vice premier after retiring as foreign minister.

Qian was increasingly involved in reunification affairs, not only overseeing Hong Kong's reversion but also taking a more central role in Taiwan policy. It was not clear whether Jiang, Li, and Qian envisioned the Qian's playing a more circumscribed, if intense, role in cross-strait relations or adding this to his broad supervisory role over foreign policy.

One reason for the uncertainty about Qian's future role in 1997 was the strong rumor that Mme. Wu Yi, China's foreign trade minister, had been selected as the new foreign minister, along with promotion to the Politburo and elevation to vice premier.[4] This would have made her Qian's equal in party and government status. During his decade at the Foreign Ministry, Qian carefully pruned out any potential challenger and any protégé of another leader, surrounding himself with competent but unexciting subordinates. Qian's territoriality was one reason State Council Foreign Affairs Office (FAO) Director Liu Huaqiu—a Li Peng partisan and reportedly Li's choice for foreign minister—left the Ministry of Foreign Affairs (MFA). Qian was reportedly pushing for the promotion of Vice Minister Tang Jiaxuan, a relatively weak candidate with experience principally as an Asianist; Tang as foreign minister would have assured Qian's continued control over the ministry. Shortly before the Beidaihe leadership conferences that began in mid-July 1997, the rumor was circulating that if the leadership was deadlocked over a replacement, Qian might stay on for two more years, another indication he hoped to retain control over the MFA—either directly or indirectly.[5]

Liu Huaqui tried hard to portray his State Council FAO as an analogue and counterpart to the U.S. National Security Council, but it was not.[6] Its role was mainly administrative, passing policy and analytical papers to foreign affairs leaders and coordinating working-level activities of foreign relations agencies. Foreign policy coordination and decision-making was carried on well above his level, in the FALG and Politburo Standing Committee. With all the other uncertainties about positions and roles in the foreign affairs apparatus, Liu's future was also murky, particularly so should Li Peng lose, or Qian Qichen gain, relative influence over foreign policy.

In the wake of the two congresses, it became clear that Qian Qichen and his protégé, Tang Jiaxuan, the new foreign minister, were ascendant. Li Peng's influence over foreign policy was in decline, and Liu Huaqiu was not as influential as before. Other actors emerged as more important spokespersons for differing points of view. Lt. General Xiong Guangkai, who had long experience as a director of Chinese military intelligence, was increasingly active representing the People's Liberation Army (PLA) on important foreign policy questions. Xiong worked in support of the PLA high command, which under Defense Minister Chi Haotian became increasingly active in international exchanges and diplomacy.[7] A more cosmopolitan view came from individuals including Jiang Zemin's mentor, Wang Daohan, the former mayor of Shanghai. Wang was sought out by visiting U.S. delegations, as he played a critical role in implementing mainland policy toward Taiwan.[8]

According to Hong Kong media analysis in mid-1998, the Foreign Affairs Leading Group was headed by Jiang Zemin with both Zhu Rongji and Qian Qichen playing key leadership roles and Liu Huaqui and the Foreign Affairs Office of the State Council being relegated to the role of secretary and secretariat general in charge of coordination and staff supervision. Li Peng's influence was much less now that he no longer served on the FALG.[9]

Several analysts saw some policy differences resulting from these shifts.[10] In particular, the opinion group headed by Qian Qichen reportedly believed that China should play a fuller role as a responsible great power on issues of global importance. In this view, China's interests are best served when China actively participates in all major international organizations and regimes, including those concerning trade and human rights. This view reflected both growing awareness of the impact of world events on China's interests and growing confidence in China's abilities to shape the world beyond its borders, with the Asian financial crisis providing a prime example of an appropriate constructive and proactive role. The unprecedented positive PRC media treatment of U.S.-China collaboration in the June 4, 1998, meeting of the Perm-Five on South Asia, which highlighted the "joint proposal" and the phone calls between U.S. and Chinese presidents and foreign ministers, was evidence of this important shift.[11]

By contrast, a more narrowly conceived view of Chinese interests was reportedly laid out by other Chinese officials, notably Li Peng and Liu Huaqui. Seeking to maximize advantage and minimize loss, this approach was characterized by tactical and confrontational geopolitical "card-playing," with a strong overlay of neo-Maoist ideological competition on behalf of developing countries against Western "hegemonism." Sino-Russian relations were an arena of conflict between the two approaches; during Li's visit to Moscow in February, 1998, for example, Li took a stance, in unity with Yeltsin and at odds with the United States, over Iraq that was notably more confrontational than the more balanced, responsible, and nuanced line followed by the Foreign Ministry and Qian Qichen at that time.[12] Li Peng's prickly guidelines on human rights diplomacy, upholding "Asian" versus U.S.-backed "Western" values, was another example. In 1996-1997, this approach was dominant, as suspicion regarding U.S. and Japan intentions toward China peaked with the Taiwan Strait crisis and the readjustment of U.S. defense guidelines as part of a new U.S. national security strategy published in May 1996. Foreign policy on many unrelated issues was colored by fear of a U.S.-Japan condominium in Asia targeted on China.

The improvement in U.S.-China relations in 1997-1998 undercut the latter school in favor of the former. It is important to note, however, that Qian Qichen and his colleagues remained committed to basic Chinese precepts involving seeking greater wealth and power, sustaining the authoritarian Chinese communist political system, and viewing with continued suspicion U.S. intentions to press for change in China's political system, to continue to support a Taiwan separate from mainland control, and to retain dominant military power in the Western Pacific and in world affairs.[13]

A third view, much less influential than the two discussed above, came from liberals and others who judged that China's future necessitated conforming to global trends in ways generally consistent with U.S. interests. Some, who apparently sought to revive debate over the values of classic Western liberalism in 1998, pointed out baldly that China had only one option in the face of escalating economic globalization—to join the Western-dominated international system and absorb Western political values and mechanisms as well. A group of Shanghai reformers clustered around former mayor and Jiang advisor Wang Daohan also challenged conventional thinking. They advocated close ties with the United States in all fields and more accommodating policies, especially toward Taiwan.[14]

Role of Ideology

The end of the cold war and the collapse of communism in the Soviet Union and other socialist states added to the crisis of ideology in China. Already disillusioned by the excesses of the Maoist era, Chinese officials and people alike were said to turn away from ideology as they went about their lives. Some observers have drawn the implication from these trends that ideology is no longer important in understanding Chinese foreign policy or policy in other areas. Typically, Chinese Foreign Ministry spokesmen played down the role of ideology in Chinese foreign policy. In an interview in December 1997 that reflected on his five years as the ministry spokesman, Shen Guofang said that China "favors the exclusion of ideology in exchange between countries."[15] In fact, closer examination shows that ideology underlines a good deal of Chinese foreign policy behavior in the post-cold war period.

Ideology in international relations often forms the underlying basis for the conduct of the foreign policy of a country. Although this does not necessarily mean that ideology is the primary factor in making foreign policy choices, it does imply that policy makers are consciously or unconsciously affected by the ideas and perceptions that make up their worldview. Chinese foreign policy from the time of Mao Zedong through the post-cold war period provides an example of both the different roles that ideology can play and the evolution of the importance of ideology to a regime. Clearly during the early Mao period, ideology was significantly more salient in policy-making than in the years following the leader's death, when emphasis was shifted more toward China's pragmatic economic development. However, some argue persuasively that a kind of "informal" ideology, in the form of historical-cultural factors, remained an important influence on China's foreign policy.[16]

It is important to understand the role played by the formal or official ideology of the Chinese government, especially during the cold war. Often referred to as Marxism-Leninism-Mao Zedong Thought, the formal ideology of the mainland Chinese state provided for its leaders "a basic orientation to foreign relations, a set of axioms to use in analyzing China's relations (and the Party's) with particular foreign actors, and a vocabulary of discourse."[17] Different from the Soviet version of socialism not only in that, for instance, resistance and revolution in China were carried out mostly by peasants, not an urban working class, and against a relatively undeveloped economic structure rather than an inadequate capitalist system, the Chinese socialist ideology also contained a strong component of anti-imperialist nationalism. As Edward Friedman notes, "the [Chinese] foreign policy makers saw themselves as engaged in a continuing struggle to free China from and defend it against imperialism in all its aspects—economic exploitation, military invasion, and cultural pollution." These goals were linked to the Marxist-Leninist aspects of the ideology with the propounded belief that "division at home made China vulnerable to foreign threats" and thus, "only the Leninist one-party dictatorship could resist imperialism by mobilizing Chinese resources against it."[18] Thus, adherence to the ideological framework of Marxism-Leninism-Mao Zedong Thought provided the basis for developing a strong China free from foreign interference.

In addition to its implications for non-socialist countries, the implementation of Marxism-Leninism-Mao Zedong Thought also held consequences for world socialism. This was probably best exemplified during the Cultural Revolution in China from 1966 to 1969. During these early years Mao tended to see the "ethos of the revolution being eroded by pragmatic policies and was determined to rekindle the fires of true faith"; consequently, China "drew sharp ideological lines and excluded from the united front anyone who did not embrace Maoist ideology."[19] Those excluded from the united front according to these sentiments were not only those within the Chinese state who disagreed with Mao, but also a majority of the international socialist actors, the most important of which was the Soviet Union. Thus, formal ideology played a significant role in determining Chinese foreign policy during the Mao era, not only toward Western capitalist democracies but also toward China's supposed socialist comrades.

After the death of the charismatic ideological leader Mao Zedong in 1976, however, and with the advent of Deng Xiaoping's new emphasis on economic development, the role played by formal ideology inevitably declined. However, Deng and other key leaders were also "unprepared to jettison Marxism-Leninism entirely or to permit the proponents of other ideologies to challenge the Party's monopoly of power."[20] Thus, despite a decreased emphasis on the importance of ideological factors in *guiding* Chinese foreign policy, ideological elements were often used to *justify* and *legitimate* policy decisions. In other words, the Chinese ideology was "transformed from a manual to something more like a catalogue from which the leadership [could] 'order' those items which suit[ed] its . . . purposes."[21]

This foreign policy link with ideology seems to have been maintained in part because leaders feared that a crisis of faith in the ideology might also lead to a crisis of power if the Chinese Communist Party were to crumble along with the ideology upon which it was based.[22] Furthermore, the link was justified by an interpretation of Marxism as a "developing science," rather than a set of principles demanding strict adherence, and one which should be integrated with reality.[23] Thus, even as formal ideology decreased vis-à-vis its direct influence on specific policies (relative to, for example, the policies of Mao's Cultural Revolution), many of the ideas that made up Marxism-Leninism-Maoism remained indirectly influential on the worldview of Deng and other Chinese leaders and the foreign policy they created.

As the influence of formal ideology on Chinese foreign policy began to wane, analysts became more cognizant of another kind of ideological influence, a more informal historical-cultural inheritance of deeply rooted attitudes and behavioral patterns that implicitly affect perceptions and actions. More specifically, one could define such an informal ideology as a "complex of cultural values, preferences, prejudices, predispositions, habits, and unstated but widely shared propositions about reality that condition the way in which political actors behave." Paradoxically, although such ideas are not usually explicit nor necessarily even conscious, they often wield greater influence than a formal, explicit ideological framework. As China scholar Michael Hunt explains, "ideologies assume formal, explicit, systematic form precisely because there is resistance to them within the culture, whereas ideology left implicit rests on a consensus and therefore exercises a greater (if more subtle) power."[24]

The beliefs and attitudes of the informal Chinese ideology tend to be similar to those of the formal ideology, especially with regard to China's sense of victimization at the hands of the imperialist powers. These concepts generally involve a sense of Chinese cultural and political superiority based upon the universal values of justice and equity, and in turn a belief that China historically has not been treated (by the imperialists, both Western and Asian) in a way worthy of its position. Such underlying aptitudes have been translated into policy in various ways. The Chinese tend to be most sensitive about issues involving national sovereignty or (what they consider to be) the interference by foreigners in Chinese domestic affairs. One good example encompassing both of these concepts is the issue of Taiwan. In brief, China considers Taiwan to be, territorially, a part of China rather than an independent entity, as well as, politically, a domestic issue rather than one that should concern the international community; moreover, Beijing normally tolerates no difference of opinion concerning this issue either within China or internationally. As this example shows, China's underlying informal ideological attitudes involving its historically inferior international position lead it to be at least highly sensitive to foreign interference in its affairs and in the policy decisions at which its government officials arrive.

Thus, it is clear that despite the decline in influence of formal ideology on Chinese foreign policy throughout the cold war and particularly following the death of Mao Zedong, ideological factors, both formal and informal, while not the primary determinants of policy, continued to be salient in Chinese foreign policy-making. Regarding the role of ideology in the current and future post-cold war China, if the past is any judge, one may argue that as China begins to focus increasingly on economic development through the growth of private enterprise and free markets, the formal Marxist-Leninist-Maoist socialist ideology will become in turn increasingly obsolete; however, the deep-seated and often unconscious attitudes, perceptions, and beliefs of the informal Chinese ideology will most likely remain in the collective conscience of the Chinese people and their leaders. Thus, foreign policy in China, though likely to be guided by explicit strategic, economic, and political concerns, will not be free from the influence of both traditional and modern Chinese ideas.

This is not to say that Chinese officials will be uniform or consistent in the informal or formal ideologies they espouse or reflect. For a time in the 1990s, the mainstream opinion of Chinese leaders appeared to support so-called Asian values in the face of the Western values of free-market economics and democracy. The authoritarian and state-directed economics of the newly industrializing countries of East Asia were held up as a paradigm for Chinese development. "Progressive" Chinese thinkers looked to the development model of Singapore to argue that China should pursue an opening to the outside world, carefully controlled by an authoritarian state, in order to ensure that resources were used for the national good and not individual gain, and that political and social order were maintained at a time of rapid economic growth.

Of course, not all Chinese thinkers saw the Asian values espoused by Singapore and others as the right path for China. Some supported the Western values of the free market and democracy as best for themselves and best for China, though their voice in Chinese policy councils was muffled.

The Asian economic crisis of the late 1990s changed this situation markedly. It became very clear to Chinese observers that the Asian development model would fail in China if China continued to rely so heavily on state-directed development. And many in China began to argue for more political reforms as needed to avoid the kinds of often corrupt vested interests that characterized government-economic relationships in several Asian states hurt by the economic crisis. Beijing did not officially shift from Asian values to new openness to the Western ideals of the free market and democracy. But Chinese leaders were aware that they would have to work hard to find ways to avoid the weaknesses of corruption, crony capitalism, and misallocation of resources that went far toward explaining the downfall of several Asian economies looked to by China in the past as models of development.[25]

In sum, leadership differences and ideology in the 1990s appeared to exert a declining influence in Chinese foreign policy. Of course, the waning of Marxism-Leninism-Mao Zedong Thought was accompanied by the waxing of a broad sense of Chinese nationalism, present throughout much of the twentieth century but emphasized strongly by Chinese leaders from time to time during the 1990s. And nationalism sometimes drove some Chinese leaders to take very tough positions on issues, like Taiwan, that had a broad impact on Chinese foreign policy and pushed Chinese foreign policy in directions contrary to the more moderate and pragmatic approaches favored by other Chinese leaders. Thus, the Taiwan crisis of 1995-1996 saw Jiang Zemin and Qian Qichen receive criticism from others for not being sufficiently nationalistic in defending PRC interests vis-à-vis the United States and Taiwan.

Trade, Investment, Aid, and Environmental Policy

A salient feature of post-Mao Chinese foreign policy has been the importance of international economic exchanges. A constant refrain of Chinese leaders in the aftermath of the cold war relates to the importance of trade, investment, and other economic matters. As China's Foreign Ministry spokesman of the previous five years summed up his tenure in December 1997 and looked ahead to the twenty-first century, he emphasized that "the economic factor has become more and more important with each passing day in state-to-state relations."[26] As if to underline this point, Chinese commentary on the Asian economic crisis of 1997-1998 clearly viewed it as the most important international development affecting China during the late 1990s. Several commentaries noted in detail the impact it had on the authoritarian government in Indonesia and drew implicit but clear parallels that China's rulers could be next if they did not manage their economic affairs well at home and abroad.[27]

In year-end reviews in late 1997 and early 1998,[28] Chinese officials and commentaries highlighted the growth and importance of Chinese foreign trade. In 1997, China ranked tenth in world trade, according to the World Trade Organization, with total trade valued at $325 billion. Prior to that, China had ranked eleventh in world trade for five consecutive years. China's trade volume grew over 12 percent from 1996 and was far above the $20.6 billion level established twenty years earlier. In 1997, exports amounted to $182.7 billion, and grew over 20 percent from the previous year, resulting in an increased Chinese trade surplus. In foreign investment, too, 1997 was a banner year. The actual use of foreign funds, excluding loans from international organizations and foreign governments, reached $51.9 billion in 1997, over 23 percent more than in 1996. By the latter part of 1997, a total of three hundred thousand foreign-invested enterprises had been licensed in China; the total contractual worth of foreign investments was $510 billion; and the amount of foreign capital actually used exceeded $210 billion. Vice Premier Wu Yi cited these and other statistics both to demonstrate the importance of outside trade and investment for the health of the Chinese economy and to show China's important role in global trade and economics. She went on to make China's case for entry into the World Trade Organization on terms compatible with China's status as a developing country requiring adjustments in the demands of the United States and others for greater Chinese trade liberalization prior to WTO entry.[29]

International labor contracts continued to be a good source of Chinese foreign-exchange earnings in 1997. Signed contracts for overseas projects and labor services were valued at $11.35 billion. This was up 10.5 percent from 1996. According to Chinese officials, the size and level of sophistication of the projects also increased. As of early 1998, there were 686 enterprises in China engaged in overseas projects and labor services.[30]

As a major recipient of foreign aid and competitor with other developing countries for assistance from international financial institutions and the donor countries among the developed nations, China adhered to a low-key posture about its own modest foreign assistance programs. *Xinhua* announced on February 10, 1998, that China provided fourteen discount-interest government soft loans abroad in 1997, involving about $299 million altogether. The report noted that since 1995 the Chinese State Council had readjusted foreign aid programs and was "vigorously promoting aid in the form of discount-interest government soft loans and joint venture cooperation between Chinese enterprises and enterprises in nations receiving aid." The report said that "after three years of hard work," the new approach on foreign aid had gained the acceptance of receiving nations. It went on to disclose that as of the end of 1997, China had signed thirty-eight framework agreements on discount-interest government soft loans involving about $500 million with thirty-one nations. It also referred to some Chinese "free" economic aid, foreign-aid joint ventures, and construction projects overseas.[31]

China has a strong and increasingly important interest in international trade in energy supplies, especially oil. By 1998, China had developed relations with a wide range of international oil suppliers, including states under U.S. or UN sanctions, to meet its burgeoning need for oil and avoid the risk of overdependence on one or two sources. Securing stable oil supplies was a key reason behind China's foreign policy efforts to develop constructive relations with all the major oil producers in the Middle East, source of one-half of China's imports.[32]

While maintaining cordial ties with conservative Arab states, Beijing in 1997 signed a $1.2 billion deal to develop an Iraqi oil field, upped its substantial purchases of oil from Iran, expressed possible interest in bidding on an oil pipeline from Kazakhstan to Iran, discussed possible energy cooperation during a vice minister's visit to Libya, and signed oil deals with Sudan. China was also seeking closer cooperation with oil exporters in Central Asia (in September 1997 it signed a multi-billion-dollar deal to develop oil and gas fields in Kazakhstan) and Africa, including reported preparations for oil exploration and production in Nigeria.

According to Chinese media and government data,[33] China's overall oil consumption rose in tandem with its rapid economic growth, while domestic oil production in 1997 increased only slightly, to about 163 million tons. Imports grew about 40 percent in 1997 to about 34 million tons. As of December 1, 1997, China's leading 1997 suppliers in descending order were Oman (7.8 million tons), Indonesia (5.9), Yemen (3.6), Angola (3.5), Iran (2.4), and Vietnam (1.2).

On the related issues of international environmental protection, China endeavored to avoid being portrayed as an international laggard, though its basic interest still centered on assuring strong economic development in China. China made clear that it had no differences "in principle" with the United States and others on environmental questions. But officials also made it clear that in implementing environmental policy, China had to pay heed realistically to its own situation. For instance, environmental measures that would negatively affect China's coal industry were seen to have a negative ripple effect on other Chinese industries.[34]

Chinese official spokesmen reiterated Beijing's interest in promoting sustainable development at such fora as the meeting of the UN Commission on Sustainable Development in late 1998. China's position on the sensitive issue of commitments regarding global climate change was that it would not undertake greenhouse gas reductions at the expense of continued economic expansion. Chinese officials were seen by outsiders as endeavoring to buy time, and in the process Beijing was strongly supporting the line of developing countries that they should not be required to adhere to global warning guidelines until the developed countries take on the major burden in dealing with the problem.[35]

Nevertheless, even more conservative Chinese leaders weighed in rhetorically and in other more substantial ways on the side of sustainable development. In his March 1, 1997, state-of-the-state address to China's legislature, Premier Li Peng called for "correctly handling" the relationship between economic growth and environmental protection, detailing a list of problems the leadership must face. In October 1997, Qiao Shi, National People's Congress chairman and third-ranking leader, said adoption of a sustainable development strategy is "not only a means of fulfilling [China's] commitment to the international community, but . . . a must for China's economic and social development."[36]

China took pride in having one of the world's fastest growing economies. According to PRC statistics, China enjoyed an average annual gross domestic product (GDP) growth rate of 11.7 percent in 1991-1995. Plans called for a 9 percent average growth rate in 1996-2000. Rapid growth led to burgeoning environmental problems. With coal still accounting for more than two-thirds of energy consumption, air pollution rapidly went from bad to worse. Water was in short supply and increasingly polluted. Until recently, incentive programs and enforcement measures were lacking, encouraging enterprises to pollute virtually unchecked.

In the early 1990s, Beijing began to look more seriously at its approaching environmental disaster. Premier Li was particularly instrumental in putting ecology on the political map. Laws were passed on air, water, solid waste, and noise pollution. Enforcement mechanisms were bolstered and funds for cleanup, inspection, education, and enforcement have been increased repeatedly.

In January 1999, a top environmental official announced that China would boost spending on "green" projects to 1.5 percent of GDP between 1997 and 2000; altogether, in 1996-2000, plans called for investing almost $60 billion in environmental programs. The agricultural bank and environmental protection agency in 1997 announced that no loans would be issued to seriously polluting firms; in 1996, some sixty thousand enterprises—mostly rural factories with no environmental safeguards—were shut down. In January 1997, Beijing set up a national center to disseminate environmentally sound technology; on March 1, 1997, the government announced the adoption of five new sets of international environmental protection standards.[37]

Despite good intentions at the top, Beijing had serious problems, especially compliance and public frustration. China had only about twenty thousand enforcement officials nationwide to inspect millions of industrial firms; enforcement authority remained weak and fragmented and penalties were anemic. Local officials judged projects more by the number of jobs they created and the revenue they generated than by the damage they did.

Local activism was also an emerging problem. Increasingly, frustrated residents and farmers were taking the "law" into their own hands. In November 1996, a Guangzhou court sentenced one village head to two years in jail for leading villagers in a protest against a polluting factory. In March 1997 hundreds of villagers in another Guangdong village trashed a factory and injured ten people out of frustration at unsettled compensation claims for their land and for pollution damage. "Green" issues could provide a fertile seedbed for the development of independent advocacy groups in China, a prospect the current leadership was well aware of and sought to forestall.[38]

International Exchanges

The Chinese government controls a wide range of government, party, military, and ostensibly unofficial channels used to promote exchanges with foreign countries advantageous to Chinese interests. Recent years have seen increasing numbers of such exchanges, ranging from visits by top-level Chinese officials to exchanges by local authorities. In general, comments during the visits and exchanges reflected the broad goals of contemporary Chinese foreign policy. Thus, through this interaction, Beijing endeavored to enlist support for China's positions on world issues important to the PRC, show Chinese attention to all countries, the small as well as the powerful, and reflect a pragmatic, nonideological, and nonthreatening Chinese image in world affairs. Specific objectives involved the following:

- Keeping relations with the United States, Japan, Russia, and other important powers on a stable course;
- Providing international prestige to China and its leaders;
- Eliciting support for China in the UN and other international agencies;
- Helping to resolve tensions over broader issues;
- Promoting advantageous economic ties;
- Offsetting the image of the "China threat" that emerged, especially following the provocative Chinese military exercises in the Taiwan Strait in 1995-1996.

Top Chinese leaders were especially active in the wake of the Fifteenth Party Congress in September 1997 in carrying out important trips abroad. President Jiang Zemin traveled to the United States, but he also held summit meetings with Russia's Boris Yeltsin and with the ASEAN leaders at the end of the year. Japan's prime minister traveled to China in September and Li Peng went to Tokyo in November. Li also visited Europe, including Russia, in February 1998. Newly appointed Premier Zhu Rongji represented China at the ASEM summit in London in April 1998 and also made separate official visits to Great Britain and France.[39]

Meanwhile, below the elite official level was a steady stream of productive Sino-foreign contacts. According to Chinese media reviews of international exchanges in 1997, the National People's Congress (NPC) had established formal relations with 140 countries and had received more than 150 delegations led by speakers or vice speakers or organized by foreign parliamentary organizations over the previous five years. Both U.S. House of Representative Speaker Newt Gingrich and U.S. Senate President Pro Tempore Strom Thurmond visited China in 1997 as guests of the NPC.[40] The Chinese People's Political Consultative Conference (CPPCC) was also active with overseas contacts. Its chairman, Li Ruihuan, visited 28 countries from 1993-1997. During that time the CPPCC organized 52 delegations to 56 countries and received 55 delegations from 34 countries. By the end of 1997, it had established formal ties with 98 organizations in 68 countries and four international organizations.[41] Similarly busy schedules for the NPC and CPPCC were reported for 1998.

The Chinese Communist Party reported at the end of 1997 that it had established formal ties with over 300 political parties and organizations from 130 countries. Party officials were particularly proud of developing relations with parties in some Latin American countries that maintained diplomatic relations with Taiwan, and they highlighted the fact that the party had rebuilt ties with West European socialist parties that had loosened their ties with China after the 1989 Tiananmen incident.[42] The number for 1998 was 340 parties in 140 countries and regions.[43]

The Chinese People's Association for Friendship with Foreign Countries, a leading, ostensibly nongovernmental, Chinese organization engaged in international exchanges, reported at the end of 1997 that it had hosted over 200 delegations from over 50 countries that year. It maintained formal contacts with over 260 organizations and social institutions in over 100 countries. In 1997, it sent Chinese delegations to more than 40 countries. The association president also pointed to its role in promoting so-called sister city relationships between Chinese cities and foreign cities. By the end of 1997 over 800 such relationships had been established.[44] Meanwhile, the Chinese Association for International Understanding said in February 1999 that it had established relations with over 200 parties, institutes, and international organizations in 90 countries.[45]

China's culture minister was endeavoring to promote China's cultural image abroad in a variety of ways, including the use of the Internet, according to Chinese media in early 1998. A plan called for introducing China's historical culture on the Internet, along with channels for promoting commercial performances and exhibitions abroad. Several Chinese cultural shows were to tour abroad, and cultural festivals were planned for sites in China.[46]

Meanwhile, growing personal wealth in China meant that Chinese people traveled abroad in unprecedented numbers. A total of 2.56 million

Chinese went abroad in 1997, an increase of 7 percent over 1996. Of that number, about a third traveled to Hong Kong, Macao, and Taiwan. Foreign visitors to China also rose. A record 57.6 million tourists came to China in 1997, up 12.6 percent from 1996. Of this number, over 80 percent were from Hong Kong and Macao, many on short trips (of a day or less).[47]

Military Diplomacy

Perhaps the most noteworthy feature of China's wide-ranging international exchange efforts was the exchange program run by the People's Liberation Army (PLA). The PLA high command has broadened and accelerated senior-level international exchanges in an effort to expand China's international influence, increase opportunities for arms sales and purchases of equipment and technology, ease concern over China's rising power, and deepen PLA leaders' international experience. Some of the top PLA officers have taken their place among the world's more widely traveled and internationally experienced military leaders.

PLA leaders expanded already active high-level strategic dialogue with U.S. and Russian defense officials as they opened new channels to important lesser powers. In 1996, China hosted more than 140 military delegations from more than 60 countries and sent military delegations to 40 countries. The 1997 pace was even more active, with a broad focus that included neighboring countries (the Kazakhstani defense minister visited China twice in the year), major powers, and a wide range of others (for example, Greece and Uruguay).[48]

In November 1997 a PLA deputy chief of staff visited France and Japan, paving the way for higher-level Chinese military visits to both countries. Germany sent its military chief of staff to China for the first time in 1998, and Australia received the Chinese defense minister in 1998. In November 1997 the PLA also welcomed its first high-level officer (a vice chief of staff) from South Korea.

Defense Minister Chi Haotian, a leading participant in and proponent of China's military diplomacy, summarized the Chinese government's approach in an article that reviewed developments in 1997.[49] He said that in 1997 China's army had invited over 150 delegations from 67 countries; 23 of the groups were headed by vice premiers or defense ministers; and 50 were headed by a commander-in-chief, chief of the general staff, vice minister of national defense, or armed services commander. In 1997, the PLA sent over 100 delegations to 70 countries. In addition, the total number of foreign embassies with accredited attachés in China reached 63 in 1997.

Chi put special stress on military exchanges with countries along

China's periphery and Sino-U.S. military exchanges. He noted how the exchanges fit in with broader Chinese foreign policy objectives, though he devoted special emphasis to countering the international argument about the so-called China threat. PLA diplomacy was long a feature of Chinese international exchanges with its allies and close friends in the third world; it was central in Beijing's efforts to reassure its neighbors following episodes of assertive Chinese military activities in the Taiwan Strait and the South China Sea in 1995 and 1996. Criticizing widespread regional concerns over an emerging "China threat," PLA leaders from the defense minister on down used in-person meetings and speeches at home and abroad to play down the threat.

In sum, Chinese leaders in the 1990s saw considerable utility in using exchanges to improve China's image and influence in world affairs. Perhaps the most important development was in military diplomacy, where the defense minister and his staff kept to an international schedule that rivaled that of the foreign minister. Focused on winning goodwill and easing concerns over the "China threat," the outreach had the added benefit of adding considerably to the PLA high command's worldliness and sophistication.

The UN and International Organizations

China has sought to maximize benefits and minimize costs in its increasing involvement with the United Nations and other international organizations in the post-cold war period. Chinese development benefits greatly from the inflow of large amounts in loans and other economic assistance from the World Bank, the Asian Development Bank, and others, even though China for several years remained the top recipient of outside investment among the third-world countries. China relied heavily on its position as a permanent member of the UN Security Council to make sure that its interests were protected on the many international issues considered by the council in the post-cold war period. The status as one of the five permanent members (the Perm-Five) also made sure that the United States and other Western powers could no longer shun China after the 1989 Tiananmen incident if they expected Chinese cooperation or at least acquiescence with their initiatives before the Security Council. Thus, despite past Chinese association with the notorious Khmer Rouge in Cambodia, Western powers sought Chinese involvement and assistance in coming up with a 1991 peace plan for Cambodia backed by the Perm-Five. And the United States and other Western governments tended to mute their recent criticism of Chinese human rights and other policies at the time of the international confrontation with Iraq following Baghdad's invasion of Kuwait in August 1990. Seeking UN Security Council endorsement for the use of force against Iraq made Washington and other Western capitals more sensitive to China's possible use of its veto power in the Security Council.[50]

Beijing's general practice was to go along with whatever broad international consensus prevailed on particular issues being considered by the United Nations. Chinese representatives especially wished to avoid choosing sides on sensitive issues dividing third-world countries, and they generally kept a low posture on those issues. Beijing was also less inclined than in the past to join the third-world bandwagon against such isolated states as Israel, especially following the normalization of Sino-Israeli diplomatic relations in 1992. At least until the marked improvement in U.S.-Chinese relations in 1997-1998, Beijing did line up with anti-U.S. forces on issues where the United States was isolated—such as its desire to use military force against Iraq in 1997-1998 because of its failure to comply with UN mandates. But even in these instances, Chinese diplomats positioned themselves behind other powers and rarely took the lead in attacking the United States. Meanwhile, China's principled opposition to international sanctions did not mean that it would work strongly to block international efforts in the UN and elsewhere to impose sanctions on perceived deviants from world norms that were broadly supported in the international organizations.

Exceptions to their low-risk strategy included, notably, efforts to block Taiwan from gaining entry into the UN or UN-affiliated organizations. To battle against efforts by Taiwan's diplomatic allies to raise the issue of Taiwan's representation in the UN, Beijing in January 1997 used its veto power for the first time in twenty-five years. It did this to block approval for UN peacekeepers in Guatemala, until Guatemala agreed to reduce its support for Taiwan's efforts to gain UN entry.[51] In 1999, it repeated the pattern in blocking the continuation of UN peacekeeping operations in Macedonia, which had just established diplomatic relations with Taiwan.[52]

Meanwhile, China's diplomats at the UN were on the front lines in endeavoring to win diplomatic relations from the few smaller states that still maintained official relations with Taiwan. China's permanent representative to the UN, Ambassador Qin Huasin, disclosed on December 30, 1997, that over the previous year he had made five visits to Central American, Caribbean, and African countries that had official relations with Taiwan, and had "made extensive contacts with leaders and social figures of those countries. This enabled them to have a deeper understanding of China's national condition and policies." Ambassador Qin concluded by noting that in the process, negotiations with the states of the Bahamas and Saint Lucia had led to their establishing official ties with Beijing and breaking official ties with Taiwan.[53]

Chinese leaders also used their Security Council seat to play a greater role on issues Beijing had been little involved with in the past. A relevant example in 1997-1998 was the Middle East peace process.

Throughout his unprecedented visit to frontline states in the Middle East peace process in December 1997, Vice Premier and Foreign Minister Qian Qichen emphasized that the Palestinian Authority and others in the region were pressing China to use its status as a member of the Perm-Five to help push the peace process forward. Meanwhile, when the nuclear tests of India and Pakistan threatened regional stability and existing proliferation regimes, China saw its interests as best served by linking up with the United States and other Perm-Five powers to establish a united front designed to press the two deviant powers, especially India, to halt testing and conform to existing international arms control regimes.[54]

China's increased involvement with high-profile issues like the Middle East peace process and the nuclear testing crisis in South Asia was accompanied by broader participation in a wide range of issues before the UN and other multilateral fora. Ambassador Qin pointed out that in 1997 China had participated in discussions of about 160 items on the agenda of the UN concerning fields such as human rights, disarmament, peacekeeping, environmental development, science and technology, and law; it had expounded its position on numerous issues; and together with numerous developing countries, it had worked hard to safeguard the legitimate rights and interests of developing countries. China's involvement came to include international peacekeeping and assistance with elections abroad. Chinese forces played peacekeeping roles in Kuwait, Western Sahara, Cambodia, and elsewhere. And China sent direct assistance to support Cambodian elections in July 1998.[55] In February 1999, China was reportedly prepared to use its veto power to block a planned UN effort to seek an international trial for Khmer Rouge leaders in Cambodia.[56]

Beijing commentary was full of discussion of budgetary, organizational, and other problems bedeviling the United Nations. When it came to concrete steps to reform the organization, however, Chinese officials were careful to avoid diluting the power and prestige that came with China's role as the sole third-world and Asian power in the Perm-Five, and to avoid incurring significantly greater financial or other expenses. In 1997, Beijing frequently attacked the United States for withholding payment of its arrears to the UN, demanding extensive UN administrative reform, and pressing for a reallocation of UN assessments whereby countries like China would pay more and the United States pay less. On November 11, 1997, the Chinese Foreign Ministry spokesman said the PRC's proportion of UN membership fees should not be determined by a single country or a few countries in private.[57] On October 27, 1997, China's UN permanent representative characterized attempts to raise China's fee scale to more than 4 percent while lowering the U.S. contribution as "someone's wishful thinking," according to *Xinhua*. He also mentioned that unilateral moves on fee adjustments that placed domestic concerns above those of the international community "will get nowhere."[58]

Commentary at the end of 1997 appeared to summarize China's interests and position in the UN. The PRC media highlighted China's role as a champion of multipolarity at the UN and criticized "unipolar" U.S. policy positions. They showed that China employed a generally low-risk strategy in 1997, effectively blunting support for Taiwan's reentry, but otherwise resisting Security Council expansion that would dilute China's privileged Perm-Five status, and seeking to safeguard its low fee assessment while presenting itself as a third-world advocate.[59]

Ambassador Qin Huasun on December 30, 1997, characterized China as actively and fully participating in key Security Council matters and "winning extensive praise" from the international community for emphasizing peaceful settlement of the Iraq issue. According to Beijing press reports, the ambassador also noted China "worked hard" to safeguard the interests of developing countries in General Assembly discussions; used its veto for the first time to discourage support for Taiwan's reentry; supported efforts to ensure that Security Council expansion reflects an appropriate developed/developing country balance; and opposed U.S.-backed fee assessment increases based on the principle of "payment according to responsibility." Late 1997 press reviews also advocated the gradual reduction of sanctions on Iran and Iraq as preferable to the alleged "dual containment," criticized the United States for talking about UN reform while pursuing "hegemonic" interests, and blasted U.S. media reports that were critical of China's position on fee increases, hinting that the United States would itself be the chief benefactor of its proposed approach to fee assessments.[60]

International Arms Control Agreements

Beijing's compliance with international arms control agreements remains subject to dispute in the United States and elsewhere. Nonetheless, the fact remains that China has seen its interests well served by joining some of these regimes, and in the process curbing some of its past practices of transferring weapons of mass destruction, delivery systems, and related technology.

Chinese compliance comes in part because of outside pressure. The united front of the United States, other nuclear powers, Japan, and much international opinion argued against a continuation of Chinese nuclear tests. As a result, China decided to join the Comprehensive Nuclear Test Ban Treaty.

Chinese compliance also comes in part because of positive incentives from abroad. Anxious to carry out productive summit meetings with President Clinton in October 1997 and June 1998, the Chinese leadership was prepared to halt all nuclear and missile cooperation with Iran, including supplying Iran with conventional cruise missiles.

In addition, Chinese compliance comes from a growing Chinese realization of the dangers to its own security as a result of the spread of nuclear weapons. Thus, Beijing reacted to the surprise Indian nuclear tests of May 1998 by lining up firmly with the United States to apply pressure on New Delhi (and on China's ally, Pakistan) to halt further tests and other provocative acts. The Chinese made clear that they were not only concerned with thwarting Indian expansionism and great power ambitions. Chinese security would be gravely jeopardized if New Delhi were to arm missiles with nuclear warheads, and if India's example were followed by other powers (for example, North Korea, Japan) with a capability and possible motivation to do so.

The mixture of positive and negative incentives goes far toward explaining the record of Chinese compliance with international arms control agreements since the end of the cold war. Of course, Chinese motives for compliance are mixed with its varied motives for proliferation of weapons of mass destruction and related technologies. In the case of nuclear and missile cooperation with Pakistan, for example, Chinese policy was driven by strategic concerns. Beijing endeavored to provide its South Asian ally with a nuclear weapons/missile delivery capability sufficient to deter Indian aggression or intimidation. China used proliferation of missile systems in the Middle East to make money and gain diplomatic advantage (for example, the sale of intermediate range ballistic missiles to Saudi Arabia was lucrative and helped solidify China's relations with this important state. China used missile and nuclear cooperation with Iran to make a profit and to undergird good relations with this major oil supplier and strategically located Persian Gulf power). But there is also ample evidence that Beijing viewed such interchanges with Iran, Libya, Syria, and others as a source of leverage against the United States. In effect, boosting the armed capability of these so-called "rouge" states hostile to the United States signaled the U.S. government that China could seriously complicate U.S. interests in critical parts of the world. The message to Washington was to turn away from its pressure tactics against Beijing and accommodate Chinese interests on issues on which the PRC was sensitive, notably U.S. arms sales to Taiwan. As it turned out, as the United States showed a willingness to end its pressure and pursue accommodation with China, Beijing curbed its relations with the states in sensitive areas.[61]

The controversy over Chinese compliance with international arms control agreements has shifted in recent years. No longer is China accused of providing completed missiles, nuclear devices, or other large components. The main arena of controversy centers on alleged Chinese provision to others of technology, components, raw materials, or expertise useful in making weapons of mass destruction or related delivery systems.

China's commitment to international arms control or nonproliferation agreements or guidelines can be summarized as follows:[62]

- The Missile Technology Control Regime (MTCR): The MTCR is not a treaty; it is a set of guidelines that calls for restraint in exports of missiles capable of delivering a 500 kg (1,100 lb) warhead to 300 km (186 mi) as well as equipment and technology for such missiles. China, in February 1992, unilaterally promised to abide by the MTCR. Also, in return for a waiver of U.S. sanctions, China committed itself, in a statement made on October 4, 1994, not to export ground-to-ground missiles "inherently capable" of delivering a 500 kg warhead to 300 km. China has not qualified to be a member of MTCR.

- The Nuclear Nonproliferation Treaty (NPT): China acceded to the NPT on March 9, 1992. The NPT is a treaty covering transfers of nuclear weapons or nuclear materials and equipment. Article 1 of the NPT states that "each nuclear-weapon State Party to the Treaty undertakes not to transfer to any recipient whatsoever nuclear weapons or other nuclear explosive devices, or control over such weapons or explosive devices." Article 3 contains a stipulation that "each State Party to the Treaty undertakes not to provide: (a) source or special fissionable material, or (b) equipment or material especially designed or prepared for the processing, use, or production of special fissionable material, to any non-nuclear-weapon State for peaceful purposes, unless the source or special fissionable material shall be subject to the safeguards required by this Article." In addition, China issued a statement on May 11, 1996, that it "will not provide assistance to unsafeguarded nuclear facilities." This statement was a result of discussions between Washington and Beijing over Chinese transfers of five thousand ring magnets to an unsafeguarded nuclear facility in Pakistan. On October 16, 1997, just before the U.S.-Chinese summit at which President Clinton agreed to issue certifications to implement the U.S.-China agreement on nuclear cooperation, China joined an international group monitoring nuclear transfers, the Zangger Committee, but did not join another such group, the Nuclear Suppliers Group.

- The Comprehensive Test Ban Treaty (CTBT): During negotiations on the CTBT, China, on July 30, 1996, became the last of the five declared nuclear powers to begin a moratorium on nuclear testing. In September 1996, China signed the treaty banning nuclear testing, but has not ratified it. The CTBT has not entered into force.
- The Biological Weapons Convention (BWC): China acceded to the BWC in 1984. The BWC bans the development, production, and stockpiling of biological agents or toxins that have no justification for peaceful purposes.
- The Chemical Weapons Convention (CWC): China signed the CWC on January 13, 1993, and deposited its instrument of ratification on April 25, 1997. The CWC bans the development, production, stockpiling, and use of chemical weapons and requires the destruction of all chemical weapons and production facilities. The convention also requires export controls on chemicals. The CWC entered into force on April 29, 1997.

China has maintained that it has not violated any international nonproliferation or arms control agreements. Press reports have suggested—and U.S. and other official statements and sanctions have sometimes confirmed—that China has violated certain international agreements, including the NPT and BWC, and may be continuing to violate its commitment to abide by the MTCR guidelines. If China's confirmed assistance to Iran's chemical weapon program continues, questions of compliance will arise.[63]

In November 1997, the U.S. secretary of defense concluded that "China's continuing and long-standing economic and security relationships provide incentives for activities that are inconsistent with some nonproliferation norms."

The MTCR

In June 1991, the Bush administration first imposed sanctions on China for transferring M-11 missile-related technology (not whole missiles) to Pakistan, since the 300 km-range M-11 short-range ballistic missile is covered by the MTCR. China promised in February 1992 to abide by the MTCR, and later, the sanctions were waived. China at a later date violated that commitment. President Clinton publicly acknowledged U.S. concerns that China may have transferred complete M-11 missiles to Pakistan. He reported to Congress on May 28, 1993, that "at present, the greatest concern involves reports that China in November 1992 transferred MTCR-class M-11 missiles or related equipment to Pakistan."

On August 24, 1993, the United States again determined that China had shipped to Pakistan equipment related to the M-11 short-range ballistic missile (not whole missiles) and imposed sanctions in accordance with Section 73(a) of the Arms Export Control Act and Section 11B(b)(1) of the Export Administration Act. Since that action, the Clinton administration has not determined that China transferred missiles or missile-related technology that contravene the MTCR guidelines. On October 4, 1994, Secretary of State Warren Christopher and Chinese Foreign Minister Qian Qichen signed a joint statement in which the United States agreed to lift the August 1993 sanctions and China agreed not to export "ground-to-ground missiles," which are "inherently capable" of delivering at least 500 kg to at least 300 km.

In January 1998, Deputy Assistant Secretary of State for Nonproliferation Robert Einhorn publicly gave assurances that China has not exported "complete ground-to-ground missiles" since the October 1994 pledge. However, he conceded that China continues to provide components and technology to both Pakistan and Iran to assist their production of missiles.

The NPT

Since China's accession to the NPT in March 1992, significant concerns have persisted about its compliance with the NPT, which, unlike the MTCR, is an international treaty. These concerns involve China's nuclear cooperation with Pakistan and Iran. China has maintained that it is cooperating in peaceful nuclear programs, which are allowed by the NPT. The U.S. government has argued that even if Chinese transfers are in compliance with the letter of the NPT, they contribute to Pakistan's and Iran's suspected nuclear weapons programs by transferring nuclear technology and expertise and by providing a civilian cover.

The BWC and CWC

The United States has been concerned about China's biological and chemical weapons as well as its exports of technology and components for suspected weapon programs, notably in Iran.

Despite these concerns, the Clinton administration judges that China is moving in the right direction as far as weapons proliferation is concerned. This is disputed by others, especially some in Congress. U.S. plans announced in January 1999 to develop and deploy a national ballistic missile defense and a theater missile defense system in East Asia prompted a harsh PRC reaction. Beijing officials were especially outspoken against reported U.S. interest in helping Taiwan develop missile defenses against the PRC. As a result, Beijing stalled its promised movement toward joining the MTCR. Analysts judged that China might take further steps to register displeasure if the United States went ahead with such missile defense plans.[64]

Notes

1. For background, see Lu Ning, *The Dynamics of Foreign Policy Decisionmaking in China*, Boulder, Colo.: Westview Press, 1997; Carol Lee Hamrin and Suisheng Zhao, eds., *Decision-Making in Deng's China*, Armonk, N.Y.: M. E. Sharpe, 1995.

2. Willy Wo-lap Lam, "Boost for Zhu's Foreign Policy Power," *South China Morning Post*, May 2, 1998, p. 1.

3. On Qian's accomplishments and popularity, see Lu, *Dynamics*.

4. This rumor was widespread among China watchers in Hong Kong during the lead up to the Fifteenth Party Congress in September 1997.

5. In the end, Tang was selected and the Hong Kong China watcher rumors were put to rest.

6. On the role of the State Council FAO, see Lu, *Dynamics*.

7. Chi and Xiong were very active in so-called "military diplomacy," discussed below.

8. Wang in 1998 feted U.S. dignitaries like former Defense Secretary William Percy and also feted his Taiwan counterpart in cross-strait relations, Kuo Chen-fu. Discussed in *Taiwan: Recent Developments and U.S. Policy Choices*, Washington, D.C.: Library of Congress (CRS), Issue Brief 98034 (updated regularly).

9. See, among others, Willy Wu-lap Lam, "Jiang Wants Foreign Role Immortalized," *South China Morning Post*, July 16, 1998, p. 7; and the same author's "Boost for Zhu's Foreign Policy Power," *South China Morning Post*, May 2, 1998, p. 1.

10. Based on discussions with twenty U.S. and Chinese foreign policy specialists, Washington, D.C., 1998.

11. *Xinhua* covered the meeting fully and promptly. See its coverage carried by Foreign Broadcast Information Service (FBIS), internet version.

12. "Russia, China Reject Use of Force against Iraq," *Reuters*, February 17, 1998 (internet version).

13. This stand was repeatedly stated by Chinese officials during private talks during 1998.

14. The Shanghai group was notably active in interaction with U.S. specialists in conferences and private discussions in the United States and China during 1998.

15. Liu Hong, "An Interview with Shen Guofang," *Zhongguo Xinwen She*, December 4, 1997, carried by FBIS (internet version).

16. See the excellent analysis by Steven Levine, "Perceptions and Ideology in Chinese Foreign Policy," in *Chinese Foreign Policy: Theory and Practice*, ed. Thomas Robinson and David Shambaugh, Oxford: Oxford University Press, 1994, pp. 30-46. The assessment presented here benefited from Levine and from other scholars whose names have been noted and was greatly assisted by the unpublished essay manuscript, "Ideology and Chinese Foreign Policy," by Alisa Ferguson, Georgetown University, October 22, 1997.

17. Levine, "Perceptions and Ideology," p. 35.

18. Edward Friedman, "Anti-Imperialism in Chinese Foreign Policy," in *China and the World*, ed. Samuel Kim, Boulder, Colo.: Westview Press, 1994, pp. 61-62.

19. John W. Garver, *Foreign Relations of the People's Republic of China*, Englewood Cliffs, N.J.: Prentice Hall, 1993, p. 157.

20. Levine, "Perceptions and Ideology," p. 31.

21. Ibid., p. 45.

22. Ibid., p. 31.

23. Heinz Timmermann, *The Decline of the World Communist Movement*, Boulder, Colo.: Westview Press, 1987, p. 99.

24. Levine, "Perceptions and Ideology," p. 34.

25. See, among others, Geremie R. Barme, "Spring Clamor and Autumnal Silence: Cultural Control in China," Current History 97, 620 (September 1998): 257-262.

26. Liu Hong, "An Interview with Shen Guofang," *Zhongguo Xinwen She*, December 4, 1997, carried by FBIS (internet version).

27. "China Says Actively Funding IMF Indonesia Plan," *Reuters*, March 17, 1998 (internet version); Wang Li, "Qian Qichen at Forum on Overseas Chinese Affairs," *Xinhua*, June 19, 1998, carried by FBIS (internet version); "Chinese Media Asked to Play down Indonesia Riots," *Ming Pao*, May 16, 1998, p. A15; "News Analysis Views ASEAN Challenges," *Xinhua*, July 21, 1998, carried by FBIS (internet version).

28. "New Year Report of Success," *Xinhua*, January 23, 1998, carried by FBIS (internet version).

29. She Zongxing and Luo Chunhua, "Wu Yi on China's Foreign Trade and Economic Relations," *Renmin Ribao*, December 16, 1997, p. 7.

30. "Ministry Reports More Overseas Contracts in '97," *Xinhua*, February 10, 1998, carried by FBIS (internet version).

31. "Foreign Aid Pacts Signed with 114 Countries," *Xinhua*, February 10, 1998, carried by FBIS (internet version).

32. See "PRC's Onshore Oil Production Up," *Xinhua*, December 29, 1997, carried by FBIS (internet version); Zhao Shaoqin, "New Goal Established for Oil, Gas Production," *China Daily*, December 27, 1997; "China's New Top Oil Supplier: Oman," unclassified cable, U.S. Embassy Beijing, December 19, 1997; "Active Overseas Oil Exportation," Jetro, China Newsletter 5 (1997): 1.

33. See the sources cited in note 32, especially "China's New Top Oil Supplier."

34. See, among others, Chen Fengying, "Environmental Protection? A Key to Sustainable Global Development," *Contemporary International Relations* (Beijing) 7, 11 (November 1997): 21-23.

35. Ibid. See also Huo Yan, "Environment Given Top Priority," *China Daily*, October 16, 1998; Zhao Shaoqin, "Clean Coal to Combat Pollution," *China Daily*, September 18, 1998.

36. Li's report was replayed by *Xinhua* and carried in FBIS (internet version).

37. Information gleaned from briefings provided by the Smithsonian Institution's Woodrow Wilson Center, China Environmental Series, 1997-1998.

38. Ibid.

39. These visits are reviewed earlier in this book.

40. "Eighth NPC Active in Diplomatic Exchanges," *Xinhua*, March 3, 1998, carried by FBIS (internet version).

41. "CPPCC Expands Foreign Exchanges," *China Daily*, March 2, 1998.

42. "CPC Records Fruitful Inter-Party Exchanges," *Beijing Review*, no. 52, December 29, 1997-January 4, 1998, pp. 7-9.

43. "CPC Willing to Forge Ties," *China Daily*, December 23, 1998.

44. Shi Xiaohui, "Step up Nongovernmental Contacts," *Renmin Ribao*, January 2, 1998, p. 7.

45. "Qian Qichen Addresses CAIFU Meeting," *Xinhua*, February 10, 1999 (internet version).

46. "Culture Ministry to Expand Cultural Exchanges," *Xinhua*, February 2, 1998, carried by FBIS (internet version).

47. "More Chinese Traveled Abroad in 1997," *Xinhua*, January 26, 1998, carried by FBIS (internet version); "Visitors Hit Record 57 Million in 1997," *South China Morning Post*, February 13, 1998, p. 4.

48. Chi Haotian, "A Year of Our Army's Active Foreign Contacts," *Renmin Ribao*, December 26, 1997, p. 7; "Expanding Military Contacts Part of Diplomatic Strategy," *Xinhua*, February 20, 1998, carried by FBIS (internet version); information gleaned from working group on PLA diplomacy, Stinson Center, Washington, D.C., July 16, 1998.

49. Chi, "A Year of Our Army's Active Foreign Contacts."

50. See, among others, Samuel Kim, "China's International Organizational Behavior," in *Chinese Foreign Policy*, ed. Robinson and Shambaugh, pp. 401-434. See also William Feeney, "China and the Multilateral Economic Institutions," in *China and the World*, ed. Kim, 1998, pp. 239-263.

51. Reviewed in Taiwan, CRS Issue Brief 98034.

52. *New York Times*, February 25, 1999.

53. Su Xiang Xin, "Diplomatic Achievements at the UN in 1997," *Zhongguo Xinwen She*, December 31, 1997, carried by FBIS (internet version).

54. Reviewed in sections of this book dealing with the Middle East and South Asia.

55. Su, "Diplomatic Achievements."

56. *New York Times*, March 2, 1999, p. 1.

57. *Xinhua*, November 11, 1997, carried by FBIS (internet version).

58. *Xinhua*, October 27, 1997, carried by FBIS (internet version).

59. See, among others, "Commentary on Sharing Proportions for UN Membership Fees," *Xinhua*, December 31, 1997, carried by FBIS (internet version); "Problems Plaguing the UN," *Xinhua*, December 7, 1997, carried by FBIS (internet version); Zhou Xisheng, "UN Faces More Challenges," *Xinhua*, December 19, 1997, carried by FBIS (internet version).

60. See sources cited in note 59; also Su, "Diplomatic Achievements."

61. These episodes are reviewed in sections above dealing with the United States, the Middle East, and South Asia.

62. This list is taken from Shirley Kan, "China's Compliance with International Arms Control Agreements," Washington, D.C.: Library of Congress, CRS Report 97-850, January 16, 1998.

63. This review is taken from Kan, "China's Compliance," pp. 2-11.

64. See, among others, China and U.S. Missile Defense Proposals, Washington, D.C.: Library of Congress, CRS Report RS 20031, January 28, 1999.

Chapter 11

Implications for the United States

The post-Deng Xiaoping leadership has established clear policy priorities for the next few years that have both specific and more broadly based implications for U.S. interests and U.S. government policy. The Chinese leaders' priorities will probably remain focused for at least several years on the ambitious agenda of economic and related government reforms set forth at the party and government congresses of 1997 and 1998. Success in the areas of reforming ailing state-owned enterprises, streamlining and making more efficient government operations, especially in regard to the economy, and reforming the weak financial system will be keys to determining the political success or failure of the central authorities. Without effective change, economic growth could slow markedly; Chinese people would see less material progress, and the regime's main source of political legitimacy —fostering a better material life for most people—could be called into question.

In this context, Chinese foreign policy, including relations with the United States, is less important. The Chinese leaders will seek out opportunities when foreign relations assist Chinese development, and they will seek to avoid entanglements and interactions abroad that would hamper effective growth. The Chinese authorities have other aspirations aside from economic development; they include protecting sovereignty and independence, and pursuing regional and global power and influence—but these have been tailored with a few exceptions (for example, Taiwan) to be generally consistent with Chinese development goals.

For U.S. interests and policy, this priority of Chinese policy concerns means that China has a strong interest in cooperating with the United States and little interest in confronting the United States, unless provoked. The United States is critically important in maintaining a stable balance of influence in East Asia and elsewhere around China's periphery conducive to Chinese goals of peace and development. United States-China trade and investment are of great importance for China. The United States-China relationship also indirectly but in significant ways influences China's relations with other Western powers, Japan, and the international financial institutions that collectively provide billions of dollars of investment and loans for China annually.

For some time after the end of the cold war, Chinese officials seemed to see their interests as well served by an emerging multipolar world. This implied that U.S. dominance would gradually decline, and that China and other power centers would enjoy more freedom of maneuver and other advantages as the United States encountered more and more difficulties at home and abroad. But in the latter part of the 1990s, especially in the context of improved U.S.-Chinese relations during the summit meetings of 1997 and 1998, Chinese officials began to adjust this view. In effect, they appeared to see U.S. dominance of world affairs in somewhat less sinister terms than in the recent past. They tended to judge that greater Chinese cooperation with the United States would enhance U.S. power, not wear it down as was implied by past Chinese emphasis on creating a multipolar world. Nonetheless, the Chinese officials judged that China's power would also rise as it cooperated with the United States, and for the time being at least, that was what was most important as far as they were concerned.[1]

Beijing continued to view U.S. policy toward China as one of "two hands"—a "soft" one of engagement and a "hard" one of containment.[2] The improvement in U.S.-China relations in 1997 and 1998 was still seen as basically tactical, as the United States and China continued to disagree on fundamental issues. Specifically, at least four perceived U.S. positions still worked against core interests of the Chinese government, and the Chinese government intended to resist them for the foreseeable future:

- The United States intended to remain the world's dominant power;
- The United States wanted to remain the dominant power in East Asia;
- The United States intended to continue support for Taiwan;
- The United States intended to continue working gradually for a "peaceful evolution" in China that would over time bring about the demise of the authoritarian communist regime.

Nevertheless, there was increasing evidence that these and other differences were being called into question as a result of the continued upswing in U.S.-China relations and the concurrent ferment in Chinese intellectual and policy circles broadly questioning previous assumptions, including those about the United States. Thus, for example, one foreign policy specialist said on April 27, 1998, that the "containment" view of the United States was continuing to lose ground in China as more Chinese officials and specialists came to see the continued U.S. dominance in the world in more lasting and also more benign terms. Specifically, some specialists were now arguing privately that U.S. world leadership was not a result of some sinister U.S. scheme to exert hegemony, which China must resist; it was said to reflect positive features of U.S. society and global systemic trends which have the support and encouragement of most countries in the world. A recent book, *China Doesn't Want to Be Mr. No*, also argued that peaceful evolution toward democracy both globally and in China, backed by the United States and others, was a natural and positive process that worked to the advantage of China's development.[3]

Meanwhile, the Chinese media in the period before and after the June 1998 summit in Beijing generally eschewed criticism in dealing with issues of U.S. power politics or possible intrusiveness into Chinese affairs. Their discretion surpassed the efforts made to create a positive atmosphere prior to and following the October 1997 Washington summit. Thus, though Beijing media and PRC-controlled Hong Kong media occasionally took issue with specific U.S. actions, they pulled their punches on U.S. policies that in the past were featured regularly for criticisms including:

- U.S. policy toward Iraq;
- NATO expansion;
- U.S.-Japan alliance relations;
- U.S.-Japan economic differences;
- U.S. policy in the Middle East peace process.

In addition, Chinese media played up positive statements by U.S. leaders, including President Clinton and National Security Adviser Berger, on the outlook for U.S.-China relations, while ignoring statements, such as that by Treasury Deputy Secretary Summers in late April 1998, that China's entry into the WTO would take a long time.[4]

Realpolitik analysis, not sentiment over U.S. visitors, lay behind Chinese leaders' calculus. Events in 1997 and 1998, notably the Asian economic crisis and the nuclear testing crisis in South Asia, had laid bare new realities of world power and their implications for China. As Chinese comment assessed the impact of the economic crisis on Asia and the world economy, it viewed the U.S. economy as supreme—"standing like a crane among chickens," as one Chinese commentator noted. Of all international factors important for China's successful coping with the crisis, close cooperation with the U.S. economic superpower was most important, according to this view.[5]

The rise of a new pole in the multipolar world—India, through its nuclear tests in May 1998—was viewed with alarm in China. Unable to deal with the situation on its own, China took on the role of the most active promoter of a strong U.S. policy in the region. Beijing cooperated in unprecedented ways with the United States, involving presidential and foreign minister-level phone consultations, and a joint (U.S.-PRC) conducted meeting of the Perm-Five foreign ministers on the issue in Geneva on June 4, 1998. Beijing judged that with U.S. leadership, the great powers might be able to muster enough diplomatic, economic, and other leverage on India and Pakistan to contain the crisis, avoid the creation of a threat to China's security, and avoid major entanglements and diversion of Chinese resources from the primary focus on nation building and development.[6]

Elsewhere around its periphery, Beijing also saw much to worry about and little ability to influence the situation, without a cooperative stance with the United States. Beijing had made little headway in dealing with ongoing high-priority problems involving Taiwan, the U.S.-Japan alliance, and the unsteady situation in North Korea. Despite strenuous PRC efforts, Taiwan remained openly determined to raise its political profile, especially among Southeast Asian nations seeking economic support from any quarter. Taiwanese voters seemed more inclined than ever to choose political leaders who would preserve Taiwan's separate status.

Beijing remained anxious over U.S.-Japanese efforts, announced in 1996, to "revitalize" the alliance relationship. Chinese criticism became more muted and focused on specific concerns regarding Taiwan, but Beijing continued to seek reassurances that the alliance did not target Chinese interests. The Chinese concerns escalated in early 1999, with U.S. announcements of a planned development of ballistic missile defenses with Japan and reported U.S. interest in providing ballistic missile defenses for Taiwan.

Even though China provided the bulk of international food and energy aid to North Korea, Chinese officials were nervous about stability and a potential flow of refugees. Beijing had yet to establish a high-level dialogue with the reclusive Kim Jong Il.

Other important foreign policy concerns along China's periphery involved the Asian economic crisis, Islamic fundamentalism, and others' suspicions of Chinese territorial ambitions in the South China Sea. Beijing had turned the financial crisis to its political benefit, garnering international kudos for its "responsible" stance in maintaining domestic economic growth and avoiding currency devaluation. But the fact remained that the crisis complicated internal Chinese economic reforms, had a negative impact on Chinese growth, and undermined previous Chinese expectations that a model of economically open Asian authoritarianism would prevail in the region. With respect to Islamic fundamentalism, Beijing had serious stability problems in Xinjiang and other parts of China caused, in part, by cross-border support of Islamic radicals and pan-Turkic separatists. Though Southeast Asian governments and China were distracted by their serious economic problems, they remained vigilant in defense of their various territorial claims to the disputed South China Sea. Reacting with extreme caution to fast-moving developments in Indonesia, Beijing at first had scrupulously eschewed initiatives or comment that would have exacerbated anti-Chinese violence or jeopardized fragile Chinese diplomatic relations with Jakarta. It became somewhat more vocal in response to outrage over anti-Chinese violence from Chinese communities worldwide. China's low posture also avoided highlighting the image of student demonstrations working to bring down an authoritarian regime to people in China who still remembered the Tiananmen incident.

At one level of analysis, this state of affairs, of considerable Chinese preoccupation and perceived vulnerability, should have argued for a strongly accommodating Chinese policy toward the United States in general and toward specific U.S. policy concerns in particular. It appeared that Chinese leaders very much needed to cultivate and promote good relations with the United States in order to help the Chinese leaders to deal with their many problems and concerns. In fact, the situation was quite different for a number of reasons.

Chinese leaders' concern over the economic consequences of state-owned enterprise (SOE) reform and the Asian economic crisis has made the Chinese leadership more cautious in prompting economic openness and change along the lines sought by the United States. Under these circumstances,

- U.S. efforts to open Chinese markets to U.S. products have continued to meet with frustration;
- China has followed its own course—allowing for continued administrative protection and intervention in the economy—toward meeting the conditions of entry into the World Trade Organization (WTO). These Chinese actions had difficulty meeting standards set by the U.S. trade representative;
- As China has continued to promote grain production in order to keep prices stable and consumer supplies high, the opportunities for U.S. grain exporters have been limited;

- Worried about declines in China's terms of trade with Asian countries, Beijing has focused all the more on exporting goods to the U.S. market, boosting the already very high U.S. trade deficit with China.

Meanwhile, recent political trends and priorities in China reinforced a tendency to go slow on significant change and to keep careful control of potentially disruptive situations. Pressures from disgruntled SOE workers, political dissidents, liberal reformers, ethnic separatists, and others were growing. This increased the possibility of serious incidents or crackdowns complicating U.S.-China relations.[7]

On specific PRC foreign policy issues of concern to the United States, Beijing's priorities posed mixed implications for U.S. interests and policy concerns.

1. Human Rights: Beijing's willingness to sign UN covenants and to engage in a flurry of diplomatic dialogues with Western and other countries was in one sense a step forward for U.S. policy interests. But the positive results of these actions for conditions in China appeared to be slow in coming. They seemed designed most immediately to benefit China by hindering the efforts of those in the United States and elsewhere who sought to bring the Chinese case before the UN Human Rights Commission (Beijing gave a very high priority to blocking this effort).

2. Weapons Proliferation: As part of the agreements leading to the implementation of the U.S.-China Nuclear Cooperation accord in 1997, Beijing agreed to not to engage in any new nuclear cooperation with Iran. It had already offered safeguards regarding reported nuclear cooperation with Pakistan seen as assisting Pakistani efforts to develop nuclear weapons. The Clinton administration hailed the change in Chinese behavior as a centerpiece of the October 1997 summit. China took further steps forward at the 1998 summit, notably agreeing to study membership in the Missile Technology Control Regime, and reaffirming a halt to ballistic missile cooperation with Pakistan.[8] Skeptics alleged that Beijing made the compromise in part because China had already seen Pakistan develop a sufficiently sophisticated nuclear weapons and missile delivery program, and had become disillusioned with Iran's unwillingness to pay for Chinese support. They charged that China continued actively to share missile and chemical weapons materials with Pakistan, Iran, and others in ways contrary to U.S. interests.[9]

3. Hong Kong: U.S. officials supported Hong Kong's continued autonomy while encouraging more political democracy. Beijing was very careful to avoid a perception of meddling in Hong Kong affairs after the July 1997 changeover. Hong Kong leader C. H. Tung and his administration were in the lead in managing several crises, notably the Asian economic situation, without anything but positive expressions of support from Beijing.

U.S. critics averred that Beijing could afford a low-key posture as Tung was following China's desired policies, including implementation of conditions, widely seen as nondemocratic, for the May 1998 election of the new Hong Kong legislature.[10]

4. East Asian Security: U.S. policy sought to avoid conflict and support the peaceful resolution of differences in East Asia. Beijing took several steps in line with U.S. goals, though China's longer-term aspirations appeared designed to reduce U.S. power and influence.[11]

Beijing worked smoothly with the United States, South Korea, and North Korea in the four-party peace talks on Korea that began in December 1997. So long as its territorial claims were not strongly challenged, China adopted a generally moderate position in handling territorial disputes with Japan and several Southeast Asian nations. China showed increased interest in and cooperation with the ASEAN Regional Forum—using such multilateral consultations in part as a means to reduce regional support for the revitalized U.S.-Japan alliance and thereby over time to isolate Tokyo and Washington.

To counter regional angst over China's rising defense spending and purchases of sophisticated Russian air and naval equipment that will substantially boost China's power projection abilities later on, Beijing sent top military officers on whirlwind tours and welcomed numerous foreign military delegations to China. Over two hundred such exchanges took place in 1997, including exchanges with heretofore excluded states like Japan and South Korea. The PLA high command, now among the most well traveled and internationally experienced in the world, focused on reducing international attention to arguments against a perceived "threat" from China, and discouraging some Asian powers, including Japan, from relying too heavily on the United States. Beijing also released its first comprehensive defense white paper in 1998.

5. Taiwan: Beijing had anticipated that giving high-level attention to isolating Taiwan diplomatically while promoting cross-strait economic exchanges would dampen separatist feelings on the island and open the way to political talks on Beijing's terms. This calculus was at its height immediately after the U.S.-China summit of 1997 but was later called into question by a variety of factors:

- The big victory by the pro-independence opposition party in island-wide local elections in late November 1997;
- The impact of the Asian economic crisis on Taiwan's investment in the mainland, with many in Taiwan holding back commitments until the situation in the region became more settled; and

• The ability of Taiwan to conduct high-level diplomacy with Southeast Asian and other officials who had shunned Taiwan contacts out of deference to Beijing but who now sought them out in order to obtain economic aid. Chinese frustration with Taiwan could have resulted in a softer approach to the island, but past practice suggested stepped-up pressure was more likely. Beijing weighed in strongly against any U.S. effort to support Taiwan's offers of several billion dollars of aid for the Asian bailout in return for international recognition of Taiwan's prominent supporting role.

6. South Asia: India's nuclear test and charges of a Chinese threat took Beijing by surprise. China condemned India's actions while expressing much milder regret over tests by Pakistan, China's long-standing ally in South Asia. Chinese leaders hoped that their strong support for the United States and the UN Security Council's five permanent members in pressing both sides in South Asia to halt further provocative action would lessen the dangers for Chinese security and international interests. Chinese leaders appeared reluctant to get entangled in a protracted foreign policy dispute at a time of urgent domestic reform priorities.

7. Russia, Central Asia, the Middle East: Beijing continued to support Russian efforts to counter the expansion of U.S. influence around Russia's periphery, notably through NATO enlargement. China backed Russia's role in the former Soviet republics of central Asia and built up its own relations in the area in part as a hedge against what Beijing saw as expanding U.S. influence in the area. Beijing acknowledged the U.S.'s leading role in the Middle East peace process and the strong U.S. military position in the Persian Gulf. It went along with the UN consensus on sanctions against Iraq but was outspoken in supporting Russia's lead in endeavoring to end the sanctions as soon as possible and to crimp U.S. efforts to increase pressure on Saddam Hussein. It also provided rhetorical support for France, Russia, and others whose economic contacts with Iran went against U.S. policy goals. Meanwhile, China sought a more active role in the Middle East peace process, notably sending its highest-level delegation ever to the frontline states in December 1997. China's pro-Arab stance complicated U.S.-led peace efforts, though Chinese officials averred they wished to cooperate with U.S. policy in the region.

Beyond these specific issues, the broad outlines of Chinese policy toward the United States were not as accommodating as one might have expected given the realities of international power and the policy priorities of Chinese leaders, which appeared to emphasize a need for working closely with the United States. In many cases, it appeared that it was the United States that was endeavoring to accommodate Chinese interests for the sake of establishing a closer U.S.-Chinese relationship, rather than the other way around. Beginning in 1996, for example, the Clinton administration embarked on a concerted series of high-level Sino-U.S. visits, accompanied by rhetoric designed to meet Chinese demands on sensitive issues, especially Taiwan. U.S. administration leaders also gave China pride of place among Asian powers, notably bypassing Japan as President Clinton made an exclusive nine-day trip to China in June-July 1998—the longest trip to China by any U.S. president. At the same time, they hailed China's apparent role as the main stabilizing economic power in the East Asian economic crisis, while they sharply criticized Japan's policies and institutions. Alarmed by the failure of world nonproliferation efforts and U.S. policy to halt the nuclear tests in South Asia, administration officials were also solicitous of Chinese interests and ambitions as they worked more closely with Beijing than with any other power in seeking to apply pressure on India and Pakistan, but especially India, in order to contain the nuclear arms race in South Asia.[12]

The keen solicitousness of the Clinton administration toward China after 1996 was well illustrated by President Clinton's rhetoric during much of his China trip in June-July 1998. He notably voiced understanding for the Chinese leadership's priorities of putting economic development ahead of political reform, and he lavished personal praise on President Jiang Zemin as a statesman of vision and imagination.[13]

Not surprisingly, Chinese officials calculated that such American solicitousness meant that China need not compromise its core interests in order to improve relations with the U.S. government. The Clinton administration's approach made it clear that China's need to sustain a good working relationship with the United States could be met largely by promoting areas of common ground and playing down areas of difference. Chinese leaders had no immediate need for a full resolution of the many issues dividing the United States and China, and particularly desired not to compromise China's interests regarding those issues. They could wait as long as the basic thrust of the relationship between the two powers remained positive and cooperative—something the Clinton administration was striving hard to do.

Of course, U.S. government policy had not always been so accommodating to Chinese concerns. In the wake of the cold war and the Tiananmen incident, U.S. policy had often pressed China hard on a variety of sensitive issues, and Chinese authorities at times had felt compelled to give ground in order to avoid serious worsening of U.S.-Chinese relations. But it quickly became evident to Chinese officials and others that U.S. policy toward China was not unified; and that through adroit maneuvering, Chinese officials would be able to use these divisions to effectively blunt whatever pressure the United States might seek to bring to bear on China in order to move Chinese policies and practices onto paths more consistent with U.S.-backed international norms. At first, Chinese officials were on the defensive against a broad range of U.S. critics who had influence in Congress, the media, and elsewhere and who strove to use economic and other sanctions to press for change in China. In general terms, Chinese officials relied on the Bush administration, backed by U.S. business interests and others concerned with sustaining workable economic relations with China, to offset the pressures of the critics.

With the election of Bill Clinton on an anti-China platform in 1992, Beijing had to shift tactics. It found strong allies in the U.S. business community who were increasingly interested in tapping the vibrantly growing China market. As a result, the threatened withdrawal of Chinese MFN trading status was repeatedly blocked and Chinese manufacturers continued to have ready access to the important U.S. export market. The U.S. business community, with a growing interest in China's market, was instrumental in persuading President Clinton to change his policy on MFN status in 1994. The president no longer linked the granting of the trading status with China's record on human rights.[14]

Beijing failed to thwart pro-Taiwan interests who lobbied hard and successfully in 1995 to get President Clinton to change U.S. policy and allow Taiwan's president to come to a function at Cornell University, his alma mater. But the subsequent Chinese-initiated military crisis in the Taiwan Strait alarmed U.S. administration policy makers, setting the stage for their continued efforts to engage Beijing in an accommodating way since then.

While experienced in using U.S. divisions over China policy to their advantage, Chinese officials also have come to realize that the divisions have a negative side for them as well. Thus, on the one hand, the divisions weaken any U.S. effort to press the Chinese government to change policies in areas where the Chinese government does not see any benefit for itself. On the other hand, the divisions also mean that any U.S. government effort to accommodate China in the process of moving relations forward will be slowed down.

Thus, Beijing seems aware that the mix of recent Chinese policy priorities and U.S. policy interests argues for continued U.S. debate over policy toward China, even when the U.S. government is led by a president who appears to have a strong personal interest in developing closer ties with Beijing. On the Chinese side, leaders headed by President Jiang Zemin do not appear to have sufficient will and/or power needed to reach major breakthroughs with the United States on the various human rights, trade, weapons proliferation, and other issues that divide the two governments. Clinton administration leaders are also viewed as constrained since their engagement policy faces a continuing barrage of opposition from important U.S. leaders in Congress, the media, and elsewhere. The administration also faced presidential impeachment and related domestic difficulties in 1998 and 1999.

Past patterns of behavior are not always good indicators of future behavior. Nonetheless, a careful review of developments in U.S.-China relations since the Tiananmen incident of 1989 appears to support the arguments of those who are more pessimistic than optimistic about substantial future progress in U.S.-China relations over the next two years, even if the Clinton administration continues a very positive posture toward the PRC.

1. Although Chinese officials hold different views of U.S. China policy, at bottom senior Chinese leaders remain deeply suspicious of U.S. policy. At times, at least some Chinese leaders suspect that the United States remains intent on "containing" China and "holding back" its rise in international power and influence. More uniformly, Chinese leaders view the United States as determined to maintain its status as the world's only superpower and a dominant strategic power in East Asia, and as determined to maintain strong ties with Taiwan and support the island against military pressure from the Chinese mainland.

They also are more uniform in suspicion of a long-term U.S. effort—publicly articulated by President Clinton in his first second-term press conference, and later during his China trip in 1998; and by President Bush before him—to seek to change China's political system along lines compatible with U.S. interests. Meanwhile, Chinese leaders in recent years have followed broad internal and international policies that enjoy support among various segments of the Chinese leadership, often as a result of protracted Chinese leadership negotiations. As a result, Beijing is not inclined to change its policy to accommodate the United States.

2. Beijing has made several adjustments in policy and practice in recent years in ways that favor U.S. interests and facilitate forward movement in Sino-U.S. relations. However, the review above shows that it has generally done so when the costs of not changing have outweighed the costs of change. Thus, when Chinese leaders feared China might lose U.S. MFN tariff treatment in 1990 and 1991, they made several last-minute but important concessions on sensitive human rights, proliferation, and other issues in order to buttress U.S. support for continued MFN for China. Later, when U.S. and world opinion pressed China on the issue of the Comprehensive Nuclear Test Ban, China changed its stance in order to avoid isolation and possible sanctions. China also agreed several times to accommodate the United States on market access, intellectual property rights, and other trade issues, when it was clear that the alternative was the loss of several billions of dollars of trade. When China realized that cutting off official ties with the United States after Taiwan President Lee Teng-hui's visit to the United

States in June 1995 was hurting Chinese interests without much likelihood of concessions from the United States, Beijing returned its ambassador and resumed normal relations. Similar cost-benefit analysis seemed to lie behind Beijing's decision in 1997 to curb nuclear exchanges with Iran and other states for the sake of winning U.S. agreement to revive the moribund U.S.-China nuclear cooperation agreement of 1985.

3. In the 1990s, Beijing's confidence in its own economic power and its growing standing in world affairs have grown. At the same time, as was noted earlier, Chinese leaders have become increasingly aware of, and able to use to their own advantage, the sharp divisions in the United States over policy toward China, in order to offset pressures for changes in China's policies and practices that are not favored by Chinese leaders themselves. For example, some U.S. business groups and some groups representing interests important to the United States in Hong Kong and other parts of Asia have seen their concerns as best served by aggressively countering the arguments of U.S. critics of China's policies and practices. The result has been particularly important in allowing Beijing to offset pressures from the United States pushing for changes in the Chinese government's policies and practices over human rights, proliferation, trade, and other sensitive issues.

On the U.S. side of the equation, China's inertia and reluctance or resistance to change in policy areas of concern to the United States add to the reasons why U.S. government officials in Congress and elsewhere, who are critical of Chinese policies and practices, are likely to continue to press hard for strong U.S. efforts to promote changes in China. These officials also appear likely to continue to receive strong support from U.S. media, interest groups, and others who strongly disapprove of China's behavior. Ironically, Chinese government inertia also gives assurances that those U.S. critics will probably face few immediate negative consequences from China for their attacks on it.

It is logical that U.S. officials and others concerned with human rights, weapons proliferation, trade, and other disputes will see China's continued reluctance to change as a reason for arguing for tougher U.S. policy toward China. It is also logical that since China follows its current policies for its own reasons, deeply rooted in protracted Chinese leadership deliberations over how to protect and enhance China's interests, Beijing is not likely to change them much for the sake of "punishing" China critics in the United States. Indeed, China continues to be solicitous of numerous congressional members who are sharply critical of China, urging them to visit and meet with high-level Chinese leaders.

Meanwhile, the Clinton administration thus far has given little sign that it is prepared to take concrete action against congressional and other critics of its policy of engagement toward China. Some U.S. specialists criticize the Clinton administration for not doing enough either to rally U.S. supporters of its engagement policy or to sanction those Americans who attack the policy.[15]

Trends in Chinese and U.S. decision-making since the Tiananmen incident add to the evidence that U.S. and Chinese leaders will have difficulty making substantial progress following their high-level meetings in 1997 and 1998. The trends depict Chinese leaders deeply suspicious of many of the changes advocated by the United States, more confident of their power and influence in world affairs and of their ability to use sharp divisions in the United States to China's advantage, and determined to adhere to long-standing Chinese policy approaches reached after often protracted efforts to achieve consensus among diverse Chinese leaders. They show that the many official and other U.S. critics of China's policies and practices have ample incentives and few immediate disincentives for continuing their harsh attacks against Chinese government behavior and the Clinton administration's engagement policy.

China-U.S. Relations: Post-Summit Stasis

Analysts and commentators differ on how to assess the current status and outlook of U.S.-China relations. Optimists see the two governments continuing to build on the positive momentum of the summit meetings to move U.S.-China relations into a period of unprecedented cooperation and goodwill. In this view, the differences between the two sides will be of diminishing importance as common ground grows on strategic, economic, political, and other issues.[16]

Skeptics tend to see more superficial than substantive improvement. Noting the many hard-to-resolve U.S.-Chinese differences over Taiwan, Tibet, human rights, trade, weapons proliferation, and other issues, U.S. skeptics have criticized the summit meetings as largely public-relations exercises.[17] Because of continued political controls in China, Chinese critics have voiced their views in private; they note in particular a perceived dualism in U.S. engagement policy toward China—alleging the United States seeks on the one hand cooperation with China but on the other hand containment of rising Chinese power and influence.[18]

A third view sees elements of truth in both camps.[19] It believes that the Clinton administration policy of engagement with China is premised on assumptions that the Chinese government policy is moving in the "right" direction from the American point of view. That means that China is moving to conform more to international norms on issues like human rights, weapons proliferation, trade practices, and the use of force that are important to the United States. But Americans are said to disagree on how to influence the Chinese government to conform more closely to such norms.[20]

Against the backdrop of the ups and downs in U.S.-China relations since the Tiananmen incident, as reviewed above, the mix of recent Chinese policy priorities and U.S. concerns argues in favor of general stasis and against extremes or abrupt changes in contemporary U.S.-China relations. Notably, the Clinton administration initially tried to apply strong pressure against China, only to pull back in the face of strong U.S. domestic opposition. More recently it has pushed for strong forward movement in relations with China, only to be brought up short by strong U.S. domestic opposition grounded in China's limited accommodation of international norms important to the United States.

Given the enduring U.S. domestic debate on China, which is widely seen as likely to last through the Clinton administration, the current balance in U.S.-China relations is more likely to be affected by events in China than in the United States. Examples include an economic collapse or decline in China similar to those elsewhere in Asia that presumably would have broad political and social repercussions and would warrant a major reassessment of U.S.-China relations. Chinese leaders under Jiang Zemin could also decide to go beyond the existing political consensus and call for a reevaluation of the Tiananmen incident. This decision would go far toward sharply changing U.S. attitudes toward China, though its likelihood under the current cautious and consensus-seeking Chinese leadership seems remote. Meanwhile, political changes in Taiwan could prompt initiatives that would result in Chinese military action against the island and a major crisis in U.S.-China relations. Of course, many other scenarios are possible.

Short of such major defining events, both sides appear prepared to pursue better relations amid the continued differences and debates that curb forward movement. The Chinese government is led by officials who think strategically. Their long-term goals may not be in line with U.S. objectives, but for the time being (the next few years) good relations with the United States are necessary and advantageous. U.S. government interests in China range widely and focus on a broad vision articulated by President Clinton of facilitating China's closer involvement as a constructive participant in the international order. The utility of this approach for specific U.S. interests is subject to debate. There is little U.S. support for costly opposition to or containment of China, although skeptics serve as a drag on forward movement in U.S.-China relations.

Notes

1. Based on interviews in Washington, D.C., with forty Chinese officials and opinion leaders, in the period after Jiang Zemin's visit to the United States during October-November 1997. On media coverage, see, among others, Wang Yizhou, "A Tentative Analysis of the U.S. Center of Gravity in the Field of International Politics," Beijing *Meiguo Yanjiu*, no. 1, March 5, 1998, pp. 57-78. Also see "Chinese Views of the United States," *Xinhua* (internet version), June 16, 1998.

2. Interviews in Beijing, China, and Washington, D.C., 1997-1998.

3. Interview with Chinese official, April 27, 1998, Washington, D.C.

4. This analysis is based mainly on a comparison of coverage of these two periods provided by Foreign Broadcast Information Service (FBIS), internet version.

5. Interviews, Washington, D.C., April-June 1998.

6. See Chinese media coverage of the Perm-Five meeting. See also the U.S.-China joint statement on South Asia released by the White House during the Clinton-Jiang summit, June 27, 1998.

7. See, among others, Li Peng, "NPC Has No Plans for Structural Reform," *China Daily*, December 2, 1998; "Democratic Reform Must Proceed in Steps," *China Daily*, December 15, 1998; "Beijing Toughens Crackdown," *New York Times*, December 22, 1998, A1.

8. White House, "Achievements of U.S.-China Summit—A Fact Sheet," June 27, 1998.

9. On debate over this issue, see *Chinese Proliferation of Weapons of Mass Destruction—Current Policy Issues*, Washington, D.C.: Library of Congress, Congressional Research Service (CRS) Issue Brief 92056 (updated regularly).

10. See "Slowly, Slowly in Hong Kong," *Washington Post*, March 16, 1998, p. A20; Center for Strategic and International Studies, Hong Kong update, July 1998, pp. 1-9.

11. See the contrast between the Chinese Defense White Paper, in *Xinhua* (internet version), July 27, 1998, and "The United States Security Strategy for the East Asia-Pacific Region," U.S. Department of Defense East Asia Strategy Report, 1998.

12. See South Asian declaration and other results of the June 1998 Beijing summit, White House, June 27, 1998.

13. See daily coverage of the president's trip in the *New York Times*.

14. For a review, see Nancy B. Tucker, "Clinton's Muddled China Policy," *Current History*, September 1998, pp. 243-249; Robert Sutter, *U.S. Policy toward China: An Introduction to the Role of Interest Groups*, Lanham, Md.: Rowman & Littlefield, 1998.

15. Sutter, *U.S. Policy toward China*, pp. 6-8.

16. See, among others, White House, "Fact Sheet on the Summit," June 27, 1998.

17. See, among others, commentary by Senator Trent Lott, *Washington Times*, June 24, 1998, July 7, 1998.

18. Interviews with Chinese military officers and Chinese government American-affairs specialists, Washington, D.C., July 2, 1998, July 8, 1998.

19. Based on consultations with eight U.S.-China specialists, Washington, D.C., late June-July 1998.

20. For background, see James Shinn, ed., *Weaving the Net*, New York: Council on Foreign Relations, 1996; and *China: Interest Groups and Recent U.S. Policy—An Introduction*, Washington, D.C.: Library of Congress, CRS Report 97-48F, December 30, 1996.

Index

About the Author

In his government service of over 30 years, Robert G. Sutter has held a variety of analytical and supervisory positions with the Central Intelligence Agency, the Department of State, the Senate Foreign Relations Committee, and the Congressional Research Service of the Library of Congress. Mr. Sutter specialized in Asian and Pacific Affairs and U.S. foreign policy with CRS from 1977 through May 1999.

He received a Ph.D. in History and East Asian Languages from Harvard University. He teaches regularly at Georgetown and George Washington Universities and at the University of Virginia. He has published eleven books and numerous articles dealing with contemporary East Asian countries and their relationships with the United States.

DATE DUE

DEC 0 6 2001			

HIGHSMITH #45230